Albert Bushnell Hart

Formation of the Union 1750-1829

Albert Bushnell Hart

Formation of the Union 1750-1829

1st Edition | ISBN: 978-3-75235-678-6

Place of Publication: Frankfurt am Main, Germany

Year of Publication: 2020

Outlook Verlag GmbH, Germany.

FORMATION OF THE UNION 1750-1829

BY ALBERT BUSHNELL HART

SUGGESTIONS FOR READERS AND TEACHERS.

Each of the volumes in the series is intended to be complete in itself, and to furnish an account of the period it covers sufficient for the general reader or student. Those who wish to supplement this book by additional reading or study will find useful the bibliographies at the heads of the chapters.

For the use of teachers the following method is recommended. A chapter at a time may be given out to the class for their preliminary reading, or the paragraph numbers may be used in assigning lessons. From the references at the head of the chapter a report may then be prepared by one or more members of the class on each of the numbered sections included in that chapter; these reports may be filed, or may be read in class when the topic is reached in the more detailed exercises. Pupils take a singular interest in such work, and the details thus obtained will add a local color to the necessarily brief statements of the text.

STUDENTS' REFERENCE LIBRARY.

The following brief works will be found useful for reference and comparison, or for the preparation of topics. The set should cost not more than twelve dollars. Of these books, Lodge's *Washington*, Morse's *Jefferson*, and Schurz's *Clay*, read in succession, make up a brief narrative history of the whole period.

1. EDWARD CHANNING: *The United States of America, 1765-1865*. New York: Macmillan Co., 1896.—Excellent survey of conditions and causes.

2. ALEXANDER JOHNSTON: *History of American Politics*. 2d ed. New York: Holt, 1890.—Lucid account of political events in brief space.

3, 4. HENRY CABOT LODGE: *George Washington* (*American Statesmen Series*). 2 vols. Boston: Houghton, Mifflin & Co., 1889.—Covers the period 1732-1799.

5. JOHN T. MORSE, JR.: *Thomas Jefferson* (*American Statesmen Series*). Boston: Houghton, Mifflin & Co., 1883.—Covers the period 1750-1809.

6. CARL SCHURZ: *Henry Clay, I.* (*American Statesmen Series*). Boston: Houghton, Mifflin & Co., 1887.—Covers the period 1777-1833.

7. EDWARD STANWOOD: *A History of Presidential Elections*. 3d ed. revised. Boston: Houghton, Mifflin & Co., 1892.—An account of the political events of each presidential campaign, with the platforms and a statement of the votes.

8. SIMON STERNE: *Constitutional History and Political Development of the United States*. 4th ed. revised. New York: Putnam's, 1888.—An excellent brief summary of the development of the Constitution.

9. HERMANN VON HOLST: *The Constitutional and Political History of the United States*. Vol. I. *1750-1833. State Sovereignty and Slavery*. Chicago: Callaghan & Co., 1877.—Not a consecutive history, but a philosophical analysis and discussion of the principal constitutional events.

SCHOOL REFERENCE LIBRARY.

The following works make up a convenient reference library of secondary works for study on the period of this volume. The books should cost not more than thirty-five dollars.

1-9. The brief works enumerated in the previous list.

10. EDWARD CHANNING and ALBERT BUSHNELL HART. *Guide to the Study of American History.* Boston: Ginn & Co., 1896.—A classified bibliography, with suggestions as to methods.

11. 12. GEORGE TICKNOR CURTIS: *Constitutional History of the United States from their Declaration of Independence to the Close of their Civil War.* 2 vols. New York: Harpers, 1889-1896.—Volume I. is a reprint of Curtis's earlier *History of the Constitution*, in two volumes, and covers the period 1774-1790. Chapters i.-vii. of Volume II. come down to about 1830.

13. RICHARD FROTHINGHAM: *The Rise of the Republic of the United States.* Boston: Little, Brown & Co., 1872.—A careful study of the progress of independence, from 1750 to 1783. Indispensable.

14. SYDNEY HOWARD GAY: *James Madison (American Statesmen Series).* Boston: Houghton, Mifflin & Co., 1884.

15. JUDSON S. LANDON: *The Constitutional History and Government of the United States.* A Series of Lectures. Boston: Houghton, Mifflin & Co., 1889.—The only recent brief constitutional history, except Sterne.

16. HENRY CABOT LODGE: *Alexander Hamilton (American Statesmen Series).* Boston and New York: Houghton, Mifflin & Co., 1882.

17. JOHN T. MORSE, JR.: *John Adams (American Statesmen Series).* Boston: Houghton, Mifflin & Co., 1885.

18. JOHN T. MORSE, JR.: *John Adams (American Statesmen Series).* Boston: Houghton, Mifflin & Co., 1882.

19-21. JAMES SCHOULER: *History of the United States of America under the Constitution.* New ed. 5 vols. New York: Dodd, Mead & Co., 1895.— This is the only recent and complete history which systematically covers the whole period from 1783 to 1861. The style is very inelegant, but it is an excellent repository of facts. Vols. I.-III. (sold separately) cover the period 1783-1830.

22. WILLIAM MILLIGAN SLOANE: *The French War and the Revolution (American History Series).* New York: Scribners, 1893.—Covers the period 1700-1783.

23. FRANCIS A. WALKER: *The Making of the Nation (American History Series).* New York: Scribners, 1894.—Covers the period 1783-1817.

LARGER REFERENCE LIBRARY.

For school use or for extended private reading, a larger collection of the standard works on the period 1750-1829 is necessary. The following books ought to cost about a hundred and fifty dollars. Many may be had at secondhand through dealers, or by advertising in the *Publishers' Weekly*.

Additional titles may be found in the bibliographies at the heads of the chapters, and through the formal bibliographies, such as Foster's *References to Presidential Administrations*, Winsor's *Narrative and Critical History*, Bowker and Iles's *Reader's Guide*, and Channing and Hart's *Guide*.

1-23. The books enumerated in the two lists above.

24-32. HENRY ADAMS: *History of the United States of America*. 9 vols. New York: Scribners, 1889-1891.—Period, 1801-1817. Divided into four sets, for the first and second administrations of Jefferson and of Madison; each set obtainable separately. The best history of the period.

33. HENRY ADAMS: *John Randolph (American Statesmen Series)*. Boston: Houghton, Mifflin & Co., 1882.

34-43. GEORGE BANCROFT: *History of the United States, from the Discovery of the American Continent*. 10 vols. Boston: Little, Brown & Co., 1834- 1874.—Vols. IV.-X. cover the period 1748-1782. Of the third edition, or "author's last revision," in six volumes (New York: Appleton, 1883-1885), Vols. III.-VI. cover the period 1763-1789. The work is rhetorical and lacks unity, but is valuable for facts.

44. WILLIAM CULLEN BRYANT and SYDNEY HOWARD GAY: *A Popular History of the United States*. 4 vols. New York: Scribners, 1876-1881.—Entirely the work of Mr. Gay. Well written and well illustrated.

45,46. JOHN FISKE: *The American Revolution*. 2 vols. Boston: Houghton, Mifflin & Co., 1891.

47. JOHN FISKE: *The Critical Period of American History*, 1783-1789. Boston: Houghton, Mifflin & Co., 1888.—Remarkable narrative style.

48. DANIEL C. GILMAN: *James Monroe (American Statesmen Series)*. Boston: Houghton, Mifflin & Co., 1883.

49-52. RICHARD HILDRETH: *The History of the United States of America*. Two series, each 3 vols. New York: Harpers, 1849-1856 (also later editions from the same plates).—Vols. II.-VI. cover the period 1750-1821. Very full and accurate, but without foot-notes. Federalist standpoint.

53. JAMES K. HOSMER: *Samuel Adams (American Statesmen Series)*. Boston: Houghton, Mifflin & Co., 1885.

54-57. JOHN BACH MCMASTER: *A History of the People of the United*

States, from the Revolution to the Civil War. 4 vols. New York: Appleton, 1883-1895.—The four volumes published cover the period 1784-1820. The point of view in the first volume is that of social history; in later volumes there is more political discussion.

58. JOHN T. MORSE, JR.: *Benjamin Franklin (American Statesmen Series).* Boston: Houghton, Mifflin & Co., 1889.

59, 60. FRANCIS PARKMAN: *Montcalm and Wolfe.* 2 vols. Boston: Little, Brown & Co., 1885.

61. GEORGE PELLEW: *John Jay (American Statesmen Series).* Boston: Houghton, Mifflin & Co., 1890.

62, 63. TIMOTHY PITKIN: *A Political and Civil History of the United States of America, from the Year 1763 to the Close of the Administration of President Washington, in March, 1797.* 2 vols. New Haven: Howe and Durrie & Peck, 1828.—An old book, but well written, and suggestive as to economic and social conditions.

64. THEODORE ROOSEVELT: *Gouverneur Morris (American Statesmen Series).* Boston: Houghton, Mifflin & Co., 1888.

65. JOHN AUSTIN STEVENS: *Albert Gallatin (American Statesmen Series).* Boston: Houghton, Mifflin & Co., 1884.

66-69. GEORGE TUCKER: *The History of the United States, from their Colonization to the End of the Twenty-Sixth Congress, in 1841.* 4 vols. Philadelphia: Lippincott, 1856-1857.—Practically begins in 1774. Written from a Southern standpoint.

70. MOSES COIT TYLER: *Patrick Henry (American Statesmen Series).* Boston: Houghton, Mifflin & Co., 1887.

71-78. JUSTIN WINSOR: *Narrative and Critical History of America.* 8 vols. Boston & New York: Houghton, Mifflin & Co., 1886-1889.—Vol. VI. And part of Vol. VII. cover the period 1750-1789. The rest of Vol. VII. covers the period 1789-1830. Remarkable for its learning and its bibliography, but not a consecutive history.

SOURCES.

In the above collections are not included the sources which are necessary for proper school and college work. References will be found in the bibliographies preceding each chapter below, and through the other bibliographies there cited.

CHAPTER I.

1. REFERENCES

BIBLIOGRAPHIES.—R. G. Thwaites, *Colonies*, §§ 39, 74, 90; notes to Joseph Story, *Commentaries*, §§ 1-197; notes to H. C. Lodge, *Colonies, passim*; notes to Justin Winsor, *Narrative and Critical History*, V. chs. ii.-vi., Channing and Hart, *Guide*, §§ 130-133.

HISTORICAL MAPS.—R. G. Thwaites, *Colonies*, Maps Nos. 1 and 4 (*Epoch Maps*, Nos. 1 and 4); G. P. Fisher *Colonial Era*, Maps Nos. 1 and 3; Labberton, *Atlas*, lxiii., B. A. Hinsdale, *Old Northwest* (republished from MacCoun's *Historical Geography*).

GENERAL ACCOUNTS.—Joseph Story *Commentaries*, §§ 146-190; W. E. H. Lecky, *England in the Eighteenth Century*, II. 1-21, III. 267-305; T. W. Higginson, *Larger History*, ch. ix.; Edward Channing, *The United States*, 1765-1865 ch. i.; H. E. Scudder, *Men and Manners in America*; Hannis Taylor, *English Constitution*, Introduction, I.; H. C. Lodge, *Colonies* (chapters on social life); T. Pitkin, *United States*, I. 85-138, Justin Winsor, *Narrative and Critical History*, V. chs. ii.-vi.; R. Frothingham, *Rise of the Republic*, chs. i., iv.; Grahame, *United States*, III. 145-176.

SPECIAL HISTORIES.—W. B. Weeden, *Economic and Social History of*

*New
England,* II. chs. xiv., xv.; G. E. Howard, *Local Constitutional
History,* I. chs. ii., iii., vii.-ix.; C. F. Adams, *History of Quincy,*
chs. iii.-xiv.; M. C. Tyler, *History of American Literature,* II.; Edward
Channing, *Town and County Government,* and *Navigation Acts;* F. B.
Dexter, *Estimates of Population;* C. F. Bishop, *Elections in the
Colonies;* Wm. Hill, *First Stages of the Tariff Policy;* W. E. DuBois,
Suppression of the Slave Trade; J. R. Brackett, *Negro in Maryland.*

CONTEMPORARY ACCOUNTS.—Benjamin Franklin, *Autobiography*
(1706-1771); John Woolman *Journal* (1720-1772); George Whitefield,
Journals (especially 1739); Kalm, *Travels* (1748-1749); Robert Rogers,
Concise Account of North America (1765); A. Burnaby, *Travels* (1759-1760);
Edmund Burke, *European Settlements in America;* William Douglass,
Summary; the various colonial archives and documents.—Reprints in II. W.
Preston, *Documents Illustrative of American History* (charters, etc.); *New
Jersey Archives,* XI., XII., XVIII. (extracts from newspapers); *American
History Leaflets,* No. 16; *Library of American Literature,* III.; *American
History told by Contemporaries,* II.

2. COLONIAL GEOGRAPHY.

[Sidenote: British America.]

By the end of the eighteenth century the term "Americans" was commonly
applied in England, and even the colonists themselves, to the English-
speaking subjects of Great Britain inhabiting the continent of North America
and the adjacent islands. The region thus occupied comprised the Bahamas,
the Bermudas, Jamaica, and some smaller West Indian islands,
Newfoundland, the outlying dependency of Belize, the territory of the great
trading corporation known as the Hudson's Bay Company, and—more
important than all the rest—the broad strip of territory running along the coast
from the Gulf of St. Lawrence to the Altamaha River.

[Sidenote: Boundaries.]

It is in this continental strip, lying between the sea and the main chain of the
Appalachian range of mountains, that the formation of the Union was
accomplished. The external boundaries of this important group of colonies
were undetermined; the region west of the mountains was drained by
tributaries of the St. Lawrence and the Mississippi rivers, and both these
rivers were held in their lower course by the French. Four successive colonial
wars had not yet settled the important question of the territorial rights of the

two powers, and a fifth war was impending.

So far as the individual colonies were concerned, their boundaries were established for them by English grants. The old charters of Massachusetts, Virginia, and the Carolinas had given title to strips of territory extending from the Atlantic westward to the Pacific. Those charters had lapsed, and the only colony in 1750 of which the jurisdiction exercised under the charter reached beyond the Appalachian mountains was Pennsylvania. The Connecticut grant had long since been ignored; the Pennsylvania limits included the strategic point where the Alleghany and Monongahela rivers unite to form the Ohio. Near this point began the final struggle between the English and the French colonies. The interior boundaries between colonies in 1750 were matters of frequent dispute and law-suits. Such questions were eventually brought to the decision of the English Privy Council, or remained to vex the new national government after the Revolution had begun.

[Sidenote: The frontiers.]

At this date, and indeed as late as the end of the Revolution, the continental colonies were all maritime. Each of them had sea-ports enjoying direct trade with Europe. The sea was the only national highway; the sea-front was easily defensible. Between contiguous colonies there was intercourse; but Nova Scotia, the last of the continental colonies to be established, was looked upon as a sort of outlyer, and its history has little connection with the history of the thirteen colonies farther south. The western frontier was a source of apprehension and of danger. In northern Maine, on the frontiers of New York, on the west and southwest, lived tribes of Indians, often disaffected, and sometimes hostile. Behind them lay the French, hereditary enemies of the colonists. The natural tendency of the English was to push their frontier westward into the Indian and French belt.

3. THE PEOPLE AND THEIR DISTRIBUTION.

[Sidenote: Population.]

This westward movement was not occasioned by the pressure of population. All the colonies, except, perhaps, Rhode Island, New Jersey, and Delaware, had abundance of vacant and tillable land. The population in 1750 was about 1,370,000. It ranged from less than 5,000 in Georgia to 240,000 in Virginia. Several strains of non-English white races were included in these numbers. There were Dutch in New York, a few Swedes in Pennsylvania and New Jersey, Germans in New York and Pennsylvania, Scotch Irish and Scotch Highlanders in the mountains of Pennsylvania and South Carolina, a few

9

Huguenots, especially in the South, and a few Irish and Jews. All the rest of the whites were English or the descendants of English. A slow stream of immigration poured into the colonies, chiefly from England. Convicts were no longer deported to be sold as private servants; but redemptioners—persons whose services were mortgaged for their passage— were still abundant. Many years later, Washington writes to an agent inquiring about "buying a ship-load of Germans," that is, of redemptioners. There was another important race-element,—the negroes, perhaps 220,000 in number; in South Carolina they far out-numbered the whites. A brisk trade was carried on in their importation, and probably ten thousand a year were brought into the country. This stream poured almost entirely into the Southern colonies. North of Maryland the number of blacks was not significant in proportion to the total population. A few Indians were scattered among the white settlements, but they were an alien community, and had no share in the development of the country.

[Sidenote: Settlements.]
[Sidenote: American character.]

The population of 1,370,000 people occupied a space which in 1890 furnished homes for more than 25,000,000. The settlements as yet rested upon, or radiated from, the sea-coast and the watercourses; eight-tenths of the American people lived within easy reach of streams navigable to the sea. Settlements had crept up the Mohawk and Susquehanna valleys, but they were still in the midst of the wilderness. Within each colony the people had a feeling of common interest and brotherhood. Distant, outlying, and rebellious counties were infrequent. The Americans of 1750 were in character very like the frontiersmen of to-day, they were accustomed to hard work, but equally accustomed to abundance of food and to a rude comfort; they were tenacious of their rights, as became offshoots of the Anglo-Saxon race. In dealing with their Indian neighbors and their slaves they were masterful and relentless. In their relations with each other they were accustomed to observe the limitations of the law. In deference to the representatives of authority, in respect for precedent and for the observances of unwritten custom, they went beyond their descendants on the frontier. Circumstances in America have greatly changed in a century and a half: the type of American character has changed less. The quieter, longer-settled communities of that day are still fairly represented by such islands of undisturbed American life as Cape Cod and Cape Charles. The industrious and thriving built good houses, raised good crops, sent their surplus abroad and bought English goods with it, went to church, and discussed politics. In education, in refinement, in literature and art, most of the colonists had made about the same advance as the present farmers of Utah. The rude, restless energy of modern America was not yet awakened.

4. INHERITED INSTITUTIONS.

[Sidenote: Sources of American government.]

In comparison with other men of their time, the Americans were distinguished by the possession of new political and social ideas, which were destined to be the foundation of the American commonwealth. One of the strongest and most persistent elements in national development has been that inheritance of political traditions and usages which the new settlers brought with them. Among the more rigid sects of New England the example of the Hebrew theocracy, as set forth in the Scriptures, had great influence on government; they were even more powerfully affected by the ideas of the Christian commonwealth held by the Protestant theologians, and particularly by John Calvin. The residence of the Plymouth settlers in the Netherlands, and the later conquest of the Dutch colonies, had brought the Americans into contact with the singularly wise and free institutions of the Dutch. To some degree the colonial conception of government had been affected by the English Commonwealth of 1649, and the English Revolution of 1688. The chief source of the political institutions of the colonies was everywhere the institutions with which they were familiar at the time of the emigration from England. It is not accurate to assert that American government is the offspring of English government. It is nearer the truth to say that in the middle of the seventeenth century the Anglo- Saxon race divided into two branches, each of which developed in its own way the institutions which it received from the parent stock. From the foundation of the colonies to 1789 the development of English government had little influence on colonial government. So long as the colonies were dependent they were subject to English regulation and English legal decisions, but their institutions developed in a very different direction.

[Sidenote: Political ideas.]

Certain fundamental political ideas were common to the older and the younger branches of the Anglo-Saxon race, and have remained common to this day. The first was the idea of the supremacy of law, the conception that a statute was binding on the subject, on the members of the legislative body, and even on the sovereign. The people on both sides of the water were accustomed to an orderly government, in which laws were made and administered with regularity and dignity. The next force was the conception of an unwritten law, of the binding power of custom. This idea, although by no means peculiar to the English race, had been developed into an elaborate "common law,"—a system of legal principles accepted as binding on subject and on prince, even without a positive statute. Out of these two underlying principles of law had gradually developed a third principle, destined to be of incalculable force in modern governments,— the conception of a superior law, higher even than the law-making body. In England there was no written constitution, but there was a succession of grants or charters, in which certain rights were assured to the individual. The long struggle with the Stuart dynasty in the seventeenth century was an assertion of these rights as against the Crown. In the colonies during the same time those rights were asserted against all comers,—against the colonial governors, against the sovereign, and against Parliament. The original colonies were almost all founded on charters, specific grants which gave them territory and directed in what manner they should carry on government therein. These charters were held by the colonists to be irrevocable except for cause shown to the satisfaction of a court of law; and it was a recognized right of the individual to plead that a colonial law was void because contrary to the charter. Most of the grants had lapsed or had been forcibly, and even illegally, annulled; but the principle still remained that a law was superior to the will of the ruler, and that the constitution was superior to the law. Thus the ground was prepared for a complicated federal government, with a national constitution recognized as the supreme law, and superior both to national enactments and to State constitutions or statutes.

[Sidenote: Principles of freedom.]

The growth of constitutional government, as we now understand it, was promoted by the establishment of two different sets of machinery for making laws and carrying on government. The older and the younger branches of the race were alike accustomed to administer local affairs in local assemblies, and more general affairs in a general assembly. The two systems in both countries worked side by side without friction; hence Americans and Englishmen were alike unused to the interference of officials in local matters, and accustomed through their representatives to take an educating share in larger affairs. The principle was firmly rooted on both sides of the water that taxes were not a matter of right, but were a gift of the people, voted directly or through their representatives. On both sides of the water it was a principle also that a subject was entitled to his freedom unless convicted of or charged with a crime, and that he should have a speedy, public, and fair trial to establish his guilt or innocence. Everywhere among the English-speaking race criminal justice was rude, and punishments were barbarous; but the tendency was to do away with special privileges and legal exemptions. Before the courts and before the tax-gatherers all Englishmen stood practically on the same basis.

5. COLONIAL DEVELOPMENT OF ENGLISH INSTITUTIONS.

Beginning at the time of colonization with substantially the same principles of liberty and government, the two regions developed under circumstances so different that, at the end of a century and a half, they were as different from each other as from their prototype.

[Sidenote: Separation of departments.]
[Sidenote: Aristocracy.]

The Stuart sovereigns of England steadily attempted to strengthen their power, and the resistance to that effort caused an immense growth of Parliamentary influence. The colonies had little occasion to feel or to resent direct royal prerogative. To them the Crown was represented by governors, with whom they could quarrel without being guilty of treason, and from whom in general they feared very little, but whom they could not depose. Governors shifted rapidly, and colonial assemblies eventually took over much of the executive business from the governors, or gave it to officers whom they elected. But while, in the eighteenth century, the system of a responsible ministry was growing up in England under the Hanoverian kings, the colonies were accustomed to a sharp division between the legislative and the executive departments. Situated as they were at a great distance from the mother-country, the assemblies were obliged to pass sweeping laws. The easiest way of checking them was to limit the power of the assemblies by strong clauses in the charters or in the governor's instructions; and to the very last the governors, and above the governors the king, retained the power of royal veto, which in England was never exercised after 1708. Thus the colonies were accustomed to see their laws quietly and legally reversed, while Parliament was growing into the belief that its will ought to prevail against the king or the judges. In a wild frontier country the people were obliged to depend upon their neighbors for defence or companionship. More emphasis was thus thrown upon the local governments than in England. The titles of rank, which continued to have great social and political force in England, were almost unknown in America. The patroons in New York were in 1750 little more than great land-owners; the fanciful system of landgraves, palsgraves, and caciques in Carolina never had any substance. No permanent colonial nobility was ever created, and but few titles were conferred on Americans. An American aristocracy did grow up, founded partly on the ownership of land, and partly on wealth acquired by trade. It existed side by side with a very open and accessible democracy of farmers.

[Sidenote: Powers of the colonies.]

The gentlemen of the colonies were leaders; but if they accepted too many of the governor's favors or voted for too many of that officer's measures, they found themselves left out of the assemblies by their independent constituents.

The power over territory, the right to grant wild lands, was also peculiar to the New World, and led to a special set of difficulties. In New England the legislatures insisted on sharing in this power. In Pennsylvania there was an unceasing quarrel over the proprietors' claim to quit-rents. Farther south the governors made vast grants unquestioned by the assemblies. In any event, colonization and the grant of lands were provincial matters. Each colony became accustomed to planting new settlements and to claiming new boundaries. The English common law was accepted in all the colonies, but it was modified everywhere by statutes, according to the need of each colony. Thus the tendency in colonial development was toward broad legislation on all subjects; but at the same time the limitations laid down by charters, by the governor's instructions, or by the home government, increased and were observed. Although the assemblies freely quarrelled with individual governors and sheared them of as much power as they could, the people recognized that the executive was in many respects beyond their reach. The division of the powers of government into departments was one of the most notable things in colonial government, and it made easier the formation of the later state and national governments.

6. LOCAL GOVERNMENT IN THE COLONIES.

[Sidenote: English local government.]

In each colony in 1750 were to be found two sets of governing organizations, —the local and the general. The local unit appears at different times and in different colonies under many names; there were towns, townships, manors, hundreds, ridings, liberties, parishes, plantations, shires, and counties. Leaving out of account minor variations, there were three types of local government,—town government, county government, and a combination of the two. Each of these forms was founded on a system with which the colonists were familiar at the time of settlement, but each was modified to meet the changed conditions of America. The English county in 1600 was a military and judicial subdivision of the kingdom; but for some local purposes county taxes were levied by the quarter sessions, a board of local government. The officers were the lord lieutenant, who was the military commander, and the justices of the peace, who were at the same time petty judges and members of the administrative board. The English "town" had long since disappeared except as a name, but its functions were in 1600 still carried out by two political bodies which much resembled it: the first was the parish,—an organization of persons responsible as tax-payers for the maintenance of the church building. In some places an assembly of these tax-payers met periodically, chose officers, and voted money for the church edifice, the poor, roads, and like local purposes. In other places a "select vestry," or corporation of persons filling its own vacancies, exercised the powers of parish government. In such cases the members were usually of the more important persons in the parish. The other wide-spread local organization was the manor; in origin this was a great estate, the tenants of which formed an assembly and passed votes for their common purposes.

[Sidenote: Towns.]

From these different forms of familiar local government the colonists chose those best suited to their own conditions. New Englanders were settled in compact little communities; they liked to live near the church, and where they could unite for protection from enemies. They preferred the open parish assembly, to which they gave the name of "town meeting." Since some of the towns were organized before the colonial legislatures began to pass comprehensive laws, the towns continued, by permission of the colonial governments, to exercise extended powers. The proceedings of a Boston town meeting in 1731 are thus reported:—

"After Prayer by the Revt. mr. John Webb,

"Habijah Savage Esqr. was chose to be Moderator for this meeting

"Proposed to Consider About Reparing mr. Nathaniell Williams His Kitchen &c.—

"In Answer to the Earnest Desire of the Honourable House of Representatives—

"Voted an Entire Satisfaction in the Town in the late Conduct of their Representatives in Endeavoring to preserve their Valuable Priviledges, And Pray their further Endeavors therein—

"Voted. That the Afair of Repairing of the Wharff leading to the North Battrey, be left with the Selectmen to do therein as they Judge best—"

[Sidenote: Counties.]

The county was also organized in New England, but took on chiefly judicial and military functions, and speedily abandoned local administration. In the South the people settled in separate plantations, usually strung out along the rivers. Popular assemblies were inconvenient, and for local purposes the people adopted the English select vestry system in what they called parishes. The county government was emphasized, and they adopted the English system of justices of the peace, who were appointed by the governor and endowed with large powers of county legislation. Hence in the South the local government fell into the hands of the principal men of each parish without election, while in New England it was in the hands of the voters.

[Sidenote: Mixed System.]

In some of the middle colonies the towns and counties were both active and had a relation with each other which was the forerunner of the present system of local government in the Western States. In New York each town chose a member of the county board of supervisors; in Pennsylvania the county officers as well as the town officers became elective. Whatever the variations, the effect of local government throughout the colonies was the same. The people carried on or neglected their town and county business under a system defined by colonial laws; but no colonial officer was charged with the supervision of local affairs. In all the changes of a century and a half since 1750 these principles of decentralization have been maintained.

7. COLONIAL GOVERNMENT.

[Sidenote: General form.]
[Sidenote: Suffrage.]

Earlier than local governments in their development, and always superior to them in powers, were the colonial governments. In 1750 there was a technical distinction between the charter governments of Connecticut, Massachusetts, and Rhode Island, the proprietary governments of Pennsylvania, Delaware, and Maryland, and the provincial governments of the eight other continental colonies. In the first group there were charters which were substantially written constitutions binding on both king and colonists, and unalterable except by mutual consent. In the second group some subject, acting under a royal charter, appointed the governors, granted the lands, and stood between the colonists and the Crown. In the third group, precedent and the governor's instructions were the only constitution. In essence, all the colonies of all three groups had the same form of government. In each there was an elective legislature; in each the suffrage was very limited; everywhere the ownership of land in freehold was a requisite, just as it was in England, for the county suffrage. In many cases there was an additional provision that the voter must have a specified large quantity of land or must pay specified taxes. In some colonies there was a religious requirement. The land qualification worked very differently from the same system in England. Any man of vigor and industry might acquire land; and thus, without altering the letter of the law to which they were accustomed, the colonial suffrage was practically enlarged, and the foundations of democracy were laid. Nevertheless, the number of voters at that time was not more than a fifth to an eighth as large in proportion to the population as at present. In Connecticut in 1775 among 200,000 people there were but 4,325 voters. In 1890, the fourth Connecticut district, having about the same population, cast a vote of 36,500.

[Sidenote: Legislature.]

The participation of the people in their own government was the more significant, because the colonies actually had what England only seemed to have,—three departments of government. The legislative branch was composed in almost all cases of two houses; the lower house was elective, and by its control over money bills it frequently forced the passage of measures unacceptable to the co-ordinate house. This latter, except in a few cases, was a small body appointed by the governor, and had the functions of the executive council as well as of an upper house. The governor was a third part of the legislature in so far as he chose to exercise his veto power. The only other limitation on the legislative power of the assemblies was the general proviso that no act "was to be contrary to the law of England, but agreeable thereto."

[Sidenote: Executive.]

The governor was the head of the executive department,—sometimes a native of the colony, as Hutchinson of Massachusetts, and Clinton of New York. But he was often sent from over seas, as Cornbury of New York, and Dunmore of Virginia. In Connecticut and Rhode Island the legislatures chose the governor; but they fell in with the prevailing practice by frequently re- electing men for a succession of years. The governor's chief power was that of appointment, although the assemblies strove to deprive him of it by electing treasurers and other executive officers. He had also the prestige of his little court, and was able to form at least a small party of adherents. As a representative of the home government he was the object of suspicion and defiance. As the receiver and dispenser of annoying fees, he was likely to be unpopular; and wherever it could do so, the assembly made him feel his dependence upon it for his salary.

[Sidenote: Judiciary.]

Colonial courts were nearly out of the reach of the assemblies, except that their salaries might be reduced or withheld. The judges were appointed by the governor, held during good behavior, and were reasonably independent both of royal interference and of popular clamor. The governor's council was commonly the highest court in the colony; hence the question of the constitutionality of an act was seldom raised: since the council could defeat the bill by voting against it, it was seldom necessary to quash it by judicial process. Legal fees were high, and the courts were the most unpopular part of the governments.

8. ENGLISH CONTROL OF THE COLONIES.

[Sidenote: English statutes.]
[Sidenote: The Crown.]
[Sidenote: Parliament.]

In Connecticut and Rhode Island, where the governor was not appointed by the Crown, the colonies closely approached the condition of republics; but even in these cases they acknowledged several powers in England to which they were all subject. First came English law. It was a generally accepted principle that all English statutes in effect at the time of the first colonization held good for the colonies so far as applicable; and the principles of the common law were everywhere accepted. Second came the Crown. When the colonies were founded, the feudal system was practically dead in England; but the conception that the Crown held the original title to all the lands was applied in the colonies, so that all titles went back to Indian or royal grants. Parliament made no protest when the king divided up and gave away the New World. Parliament acquiesced when by charter he created trading companies and bestowed upon them powers of government. Down to 1765 Parliament seldom legislated for individual colonies, and it was generally held that the colonies were not included in English statutes unless specially mentioned. The Crown created the colonies, gave them governors, permitted the local assemblies to grow up, and directed the course of the colonial executive by royal instructions.

[Sidenote: Means of control.]

The agent of the sovereign in these matters was from 1696 to 1760 the so-called Lords of the Board of Trade and Plantations. This commission, appointed by The Crown, corresponded with the governors, made recommendations, and examined colonial laws. Through them were exercised the two branches of English control. Governors were directed to carry out a specified policy or to veto specified classes of laws. If they were disobedient or weak, the law might still be voided by a royal rescript. The attorneys-general of the Crown were constantly called on to examine laws with a view to their veto, and their replies have been collected in Chalmers's "Opinions,"—a storehouse of material concerning the relations of the colonies with the home government. The process of disallowance was slow. Laws were therefore often passed in the colonies for successive brief periods, thus avoiding the effects of a veto; or "Resolves" were passed which had the force, though not the name, of statutes. In times of crisis the Crown showed energy in trying to draw out the military strength of the colonies; but if the assemblies hung back there was no means of forcing them to be active. During the Stuart period the troubles at home prevented strict attention to colonial matters. Under the Hanoverian kings the colonies were little disturbed by any active interference. In one respect only did the home government press hard upon the colonies. A succession of Navigation Acts, beginning about 1650, limited the English colonies to direct trade with the home country, in English or colonial vessels. Even between neighboring English colonies trade was hampered by restrictions or absolute prohibitions. Against the legal right of Parliament thus to control the trade of the colonies the Americans did not protest. Protest was unnecessary, since in 1750 the Acts were systematically disregarded: foreign vessels carried freights to and from American ports; American goods were shipped direct to foreign countries (§ 23; Colonies, §§ 44, 128).

9. SOCIAL AND ECONOMIC CONDITIONS.

[Sidenote: Social life.]
[Sidenote: Intellectual life.]
[Sidenote: Economic conditions.]

Thus, partly from circumstances, and partly by their own design, the colonies in 1750 were developing a political life of their own. Changes of dynasties and of sovereigns or of ministers in England little affected them. In like manner their social customs were slowly changing. The abundance of land favored the growth of a yeoman class accustomed to take part in the government. Savage neighbors made necessary a rough military discipline, and the community was armed. The distance from England and an independent spirit threw great responsibility on the assemblies. The general evenness of social conditions, except that some men held more land than others, helped on a democratic spirit. The conditions of the colonies were those of free and independent communities. On the other hand, colonial life was at best retired and narrow; roads were poor, inns indifferent, and travelling was unusual. The people had the boisterous tastes and dangerous amusements of frontiersmen. Outside of New England there were almost no schools, and in New England schools were very poor. In 1750 Harvard, Yale, William and Mary, and the College of New Jersey (now Princeton) were the only colleges, and the education which they gave was narrower than that now furnished by a good high school. Newspapers were few and dull. Except in theology, there was no special instruction for professional men. In most colonies lawyers were lightly esteemed, and physicians little known. City life did not exist; Philadelphia, Boston, New York, and Charleston were but provincial towns. The colonies had only three industries,—agriculture, the fisheries, and shipping. Tobacco had for more than a century been the staple export. Next in importance was the New England fishery, employing six hundred vessels, and the commerce with the West Indies, which arose out of that industry. Other staple exports were whale products, bread-stuffs, naval stores, masts, and pig-iron. The total value of exports in 1750 is estimated at Ł814,000. To carry these products a fleet of at least two hundred vessels was employed; they were built in the colonies north of Virginia, and most of them in New England. The vessels themselves were often sold abroad. With the proceeds of the exports the colonists bought the manufactured articles which they prized. Under the Navigation Acts these ought all to have come from England; but French silks, Holland gin, and Martinique sugar somehow found their way into the colonies. The colonists and the home government tried to establish new industries by granting bounties. Thus the indigo culture in South Carolina was begun, and many unsuccessful attempts were made to start silk manufactures and wine raising. The method of stimulating manufactures by laying protective duties was not unknown; but England could not permit the colonies to discriminate against home merchants, and had no desire to see them establish by protective duties competitors for English manufactures. Nevertheless, Pennsylvania did in a few cases lay low protective duties. Except for the sea-faring pursuits of the Northern colonies, the whole continental group was in the same dependent condition. The colonists raised their own food and made their own clothes; the surplus of their crops was sent abroad and converted into manufactured goods.

10. COLONIAL SLAVERY.

[Sidenote: Slave trade.]
[Sidenote: The sections.]

In appearance the labor system of all the colonies was the same. Besides paid white laborers, there was everywhere a class of white servants bound without wages for a term of years, and a more miserable class of negro slaves. From Nova Scotia to Georgia, in all the West Indies, in the neighboring French and Spanish colonies, negro slavery was in 1750 lawful, and appeared to flourish. Many attempts had been made by colonial legislatures to cut off or to tax the importation of slaves. Sometimes they feared the growing number of negroes, sometimes they desired more revenue. The legislators do not appear to have been moved by moral objections to slavery. Nevertheless, there was a striking difference between the sections with regard to slavery. In all the colonies north of Maryland the winters were so cold as to interfere with farming, and some different winter work had to be provided. For such variations of labor, slaves are not well fitted; hence there were but two regions in the North where slaves were profitably employed as field-hands,—on Narragansett Bay and on the Hudson: elsewhere the negroes were house or body servants, and slaves were rather an evidence of the master's consequence than of their value in agriculture. In the South, where land could be worked during a larger portion of the year, and where the conditions of life were easier, slavery was profitable, and the large plantations could not be kept up without fresh importations. Hence, if any force could be brought to bear against negro slavery it would easily affect the North, and would be resisted by the South; in the middle colonies the struggle might be long; but even there slavery was not of sufficient value to make it permanent.

[Sidenote: Anti-slavery agitation.]

Such a force was found in a moral agitation already under way in 1750. The Puritans and the Quakers both upheld principles which, if carried to their legitimate consequences, would do away with slavery. The share which all men had in Christ's saving grace was to render them brethren hereafter; and who should dare to subject one to another in this earthly life? The voice of Roger Williams was raised in 1637 to ask whether, after "a due time of trayning to labour and restraint, they ought not to be set free?" "How cursed a crime is it," exclaimed old Sewall in 1700, "to equal men to beasts! These Ethiopians, black as they are, are sons and daughters of the first Adam, brethren and sisters of the last Adam, and the offspring of God." On "2d mo. 18, 1688," the Germantown Friends presented the first petition against slavery recorded in American history. By 1750 professional anti-slavery agitators like John Woolman and Benezet were at work in Pennsylvania and New Jersey, and many wealthy Quakers had set free their slaves. The wedge which was eventually to divide the North from the South was already driven in 1750. In his great speech on the Writs of Assistance in 1761, James Otis so spoke that John Adams said: "Not a Quaker in Philadelphia, or Mr. Jefferson of Virginia, ever asserted the rights of negroes in stronger terms."

CHAPTER II.

11. REFERENCES.

BIBLIOGRAPHIES.—Justin Winsor, *Narrative and Critical History*, V. 560-622; Channing and Hart, *Guide*, §§ 131-132.

HISTORICAL MAPS.—No. 2, this volume (*Epoch Maps*, No. 5); Labberton, *Historical Atlas*, lxiii.; B. A. Hinsdale, *Old Northwest*, I. 38, 63 (republished from MacCoun, *Historical Geography*); S. R. Gardiner, *School Atlas*, No. 45; Francis Parkman, *Montcalm and Wolfe*, frontispiece; Oldmixen, *British Empire* (1741); *Mitchell's Map* (1755); *Evans's Map* (1755); school histories of Channing, Johnston, Scudder, Thomas.

GENERAL ACCOUNTS.—Geo. Bancroft, *United States*, III. chs. xxiii., xxiv., IV. (last revision, II. 419-565); R. Hildreth, *United States*, II. 433-513; W. E. H. Lecky, *England in the Eighteenth Century*, II. ch. viii., III. ch. x.; B. A. Hinsdale, *Old Northwest*, ch. v.; W. M. Sloane, *French War and Revolution*, ch. viii.; Bryant and Gay, *Popular History*, III. 254-328; J. R. Green, *English People*, IV. 166-218; Abiel Holmes, *Annals of America*, II. 41-123; Geo. Chalmers, *Revolt of the American Colonies*, II. book ix. ch. xx.; T. Pitkin, *Political and Civil History*, I. 138-154.

SPECIAL HISTORIES.—Francis Parkman, *Montcalm and Wolfe* (2 vols.), latest and best detailed account; G. Warburton, *Conquest of Canada*, (1849); T. Mante, *Late War* (1772); W. B. Weeden, *New England*, II. chs. xvi., xvii.; M. C. Tyler, *American Literature*, II. ch. xviii.; Theodore Roosevelt, *Winning of the West*, II.

CONTEMPORARY ACCOUNTS.—John Knox, *Historical Journal* (1757-1760); Pouchot, *Mémoires* (also in translation); Franklin, *Works* (especially on the Albany Congress); Washington, *Works*, especially his *Journal* (Sparks's edition, II. 432-447); Robert Rogers, *Journal; Documents relative to the Colonial History of New York*, X.—Reprints in *American History told by Contemporaries*, II.

12. RIVAL CLAIMS IN NORTH AMERICA (1690-1754).

[Sidenote: International rivalry.]

22

"The firing of a gun in the woods of North America brought on a conflict which drenched Europe in blood." In this rhetorical statement is suggested the result of a great change in American conditions after 1750. For the first time in the history of the colonies the settlements of England and France were brought so near together as to provoke collisions in time of peace. The attack on the French by the Virginia troops under Washington in 1754 was an evidence that France and England were ready to join in a struggle for the possession of the interior of the continent, even though it led to a general European war.

[Sidenote: Legal arguments.]

The peace of Aix-la-Chapelle of 1748 (Colonies, § 112) had not laid down a definite line between the French and the English possessions west of the mountains, According to the principles of international law observed at the time of colonization, each power was entitled to the territory drained by the rivers falling into that part of the sea-coast which it controlled. The French, therefore, asserted a *prima facie* title to the valleys of the St. Lawrence and of the Mississippi (§ 2); if there was a natural boundary between the two powers, it was the watershed north and west of the sources of the St. John, Penobscot, Connecticut, Hudson, Susquehanna, Potomac, and James. On neither side had permanent settlements been established far beyond this irregular ridge. This natural boundary had, however, been disregarded in the early English grants. Did not the charter of 1609 give to Virginia the territory "up into the land, from sea to sea, west and northwest"? (Colonies, § 29.) Did not the Massachusetts, Connecticut, and Carolina grants run westward to the "South Sea"? And although these grants had lapsed, the power of the king to make them was undiminished; the Pennsylvania charter, the latest of all, gave title far west of the mountains.

[Sidenote: Expediency.]

To these paper claims were added arguments of convenience: the Lake Champlain region, the southern tributaries of Lake Ontario, and the headwaters of the Ohio, were more easily reached from the Atlantic coast than by working up the rapids of the St Lawrence and its tributaries, or against two thousand miles of swift current on the Mississippi. To the Anglo-Saxon hunger for more land was added the fear of Indian attacks; the savages were alarmed by the advance of settlements, and no principles of international law could prevent frontiersmen from exploring the region claimed by France, or from occupying favorite spots. There was no opportunity for compromise between the two parties; agreement was impossible, a conflict was a mere matter of time, and the elaborate arguments which each side set forth as a basis for its claim were intended only to give the prestige of a legal title. In the struggle the English colonies had one significant moral advantage: they desired the land that they might occupy it; the French wished only to hold it vacant for some future and remote settlement, or to control the fur-trade.

13. COLLISIONS ON THE FRONTIER (1749-1754).

[Sidenote: The Iroquois]

For many years the final conflict had been postponed by the existence of a barrier state,—the Iroquois, or Six Nations of Indians. This fierce, brave, and statesmanlike race held a strip of the watershed from Lake Champlain to the Allegheny River. For many years they had been subject to English influence, exercised chiefly by William Johnson; but the undisturbed possession of their lands was the price of their friendship. They held back the current of immigration through the Mohawk. They aimed to be the intermediary for the fur-trade from the northwest. They remained throughout the conflict for the most part neutral, but forced the contestants to carry on their wars east or south of them.

[Sidenote: English claims.]

Southwest of the territory of the Iroquois lay the region of the upper Ohio and its tributaries, particularly the valleys of the Tennessee, the Muskingum, the Allegheny, the Monongahela and its mountain-descending tributary, the Youghioghany, of which the upper waters interlace with branches of the Potomac. In this rich country, heavily wooded and abounding in game, there were only a few Indians and no white inhabitants. In 1749 France began to send expeditions through the Ohio valley to raise the French flag and to bury leaden plates bearing the royal arms. A part of the disputed region was claimed by Pennsylvania as within her charter limits; Virginia claimed it, apparently on the convenient principle that any unoccupied land adjacent to her territory was hers; the English government claimed it as a vacant royal preserve; and in 1749 an Ohio company was formed with the purpose of erecting the disputed region into a "back colony." A royal grant of land was secured, and a young Virginian, named George Washington, was sent out as a surveyor. He took the opportunity to locate some land for himself, and frankly says that "it is not reasonable to suppose that those, who had the first choice, … were inattentive to … the advantages of situation."

[Sidenote: Attempts to occupy.]

Foreseeing the struggle, the French began to construct a chain of forts connecting the St. Lawrence settlements with the Mississippi. The chief strategic point was at the junction of the Allegheny and Monongahela rivers,

—the present site of Pittsburg. The Ohio company were first on the ground, and in 1753 took steps to occupy this spot. They were backed up by orders issued by the British government to the governors of Pennsylvania and Maryland "to repel force by force whenever the French are found within the undoubted limits of their province." Thus the French and English settlements were brought dangerously near together, and it was resolved by Virginia to send George Washington with a solemn warning to the French. In October, 1753, he set forth, and returned in December to announce that the French were determined to hold the country. They drove the few English out of their new post, fortified the spot, and called it Fort Duquesne. The crisis seemed to Benjamin Franklin so momentous that at the end of his printed account of the capture of the post he added a rude woodcut of a rattlesnake cut into thirteen pieces, with the motto, addressed to the colonies, "Join or die."

[Sidenote: No compromise.]

This was no ordinary intercolonial difficulty, to be patched up by agreements between the frontier commanders. Both French and English officers acted under orders from their courts. England and France were rivals, not only on the continent, but in the West Indies, in India, and in Europe. There was no disposition either to prevent or to heal the breach on the Pennsylvania frontier.

[Sidenote: Washington attacks.]

When Washington set out with a small force in April, 1754, it was with the deliberate intention of driving the French out of the region. As he advanced towards Fort Duquesne they came out to meet him. He was the quicker, and surprised the little expedition at Great Meadows, fired upon the French, and killed ten of them. A few days later Washington and his command were captured at Fort Necessity, and obliged to leave the country. As Half King, an Iroquois chief, said, "The French behaved like cowards, and the English like fools." The colonial war had begun. Troops were at once despatched to America by both belligerents. In 1755 hostilities also broke out between the two powers on the sea; but it was not until May 18, 1756, that England formally declared war on France, and the Seven Years' War began in Europe.

14. THE STRENGTH OF THE PARTIES (1754).

The first organized campaign in America was in 1755. Its effect was to show that the combatants were not far from equally matched. France claimed the position of the first European power: her army was large, her soldiers well trained; her comparative weakness at sea was not yet evident. The English navy had been reduced to 17,000 men; the whole English army counted 18,000 men, of whom there were in America but 1,000. Yet England was superior when it came to building ships, equipping troops, and furnishing money subsidies to keep her allies in the field. The advantage of prestige in Europe was thrown away when France allied herself with her hereditary enemy, Austria, and thus involved herself in wars which kept her from sending adequate reinforcements to America.

Until 1758 the war in the western world was fought on both sides chiefly by the colonists. Here the British Americans had a numerical advantage over the French. Against the 80,000 white Canadians and Louisianians they could oppose more than 1,100,000 whites. Had the English colonists, like the Canadians, been organized into one province, they might have been successful within a year; but the freedom and local independence of the fourteen colonies made them, in a military sense, weaker than their neighbors. In Canada there was neither local government nor public opinion; governors and intendants sent out from Paris ruled the people under regulations framed in Paris for the benefit of the court centred in Paris. While the colonies with difficulty raised volunteer troops, the French commander could make a *levée en masse* of the whole adult male population. During the four campaigns from 1755 to 1758 the Canadians lost little territory, and they were finally conquered only by a powerful expedition of British regular troops and ships.

One reason for this unexpected resistance was the aid of the Indians. The Latin races have always had more influence over savage dependents than the Anglo-Saxon. The French knew how to use the Indians as auxiliaries by letting them make war on their own account and in their own barbarous fashion. Nevertheless the Indians did not fight for the mere sake of obliging the French, and when the tide turned, in 1759, they were mostly detached. One other great advantage was enjoyed by the French: their territory was difficult of access. The exposed coast was protected by the strong fortresses of Louisbourg and Quebec, On the east, in the centre, and on the Ohio they were in occupation and stood on the defensive. Acting on the interior of their line, they could mass troops at any threatened point. In the end their line was rolled up like a scroll from both ends. Louisbourg and Fort Duquesne were both taken in 1758, but Montreal was able to hold out until 1760.

15. CONGRESS OF ALBANY (1754).

[Sidenote: Indian treaty.]
[Sidenote: Union proposed]

Foreseeing a general colonial war, the Lords of Trade, in September, 1753, directed the colonial governors to procure the sending of commissioners to Albany. The first purpose was to make a treaty with the Iroquois; but a suggestion was made in America that the commissioners also draw up a plan of colonial union. In June, 1754, a body of delegates assembled from the New England colonies, New York, Pennsylvania, and Maryland. The Indian treaty was duly framed, notwithstanding the ominous suggestion of one of the savages: "It is but one step from Canada hither, and the French may easily come and turn you out of your doors." On June 24 the Congress of Albany adopted unanimously the resolution that "a union of all the colonies is at present absolutely necessary for their security and defence;" and that "it would be necessary that the union be established by Act of Parliament."

[Sidenote: Franklin's scheme.]

Since the extinction of the New England Confederation in 1684 (Colonies, § 69) there had been no approach to any colonial union. The suggestions of William III., of the Lords of Trade, of ministers, of colonial governors, and of private individuals had remained without effect To Benjamin Franklin was committed the task of drawing up a scheme which should at the same time satisfy the colonial assemblies and the mother government. The advantages of such an union were obvious. Combined action meant speedy victory; separate defence meant that much of the border would be exposed to invasion. Franklin hoped to take advantage of the pressure of the war to induce the colonies to accept a permanent union. His draft, therefore, provided for a "President General," who should have toward the union the powers usually enjoyed by a governor towards his colony. This was not unlike a project in view when Andros was sent over in 1685. The startling innovation of the scheme was a "Grand Council," to be chosen by the colonial assemblies. The duty of this general government was to regulate Indian affairs, make frontier settlements, and protect and defend the colonists. The plan grew upon Franklin as he considered it, and he added a scheme for general taxes, the funds to be raised by requisitions for specific sums on the separate colonial treasurers.

The interest of the plan is that it resembles the later Articles of Confederation. At first it seemed likely to succeed; none of the twenty- five members of the congress seem to have opposed it, but not one colony accepted it. The charter and proprietary colonies feared that they might lose the guaranty afforded by their existing grants. The new union was to be established by Act of Parliament. Of government by that body they knew little, and they had no disposition to increase the power of the Crown. The town of Boston voted "to oppose any plan of union whereby they shall apprehend the Liberties and Priviledges of the People are endangered." The British government also feared a permanent union, lest it teach the colonies their own strength in organization. The movement for the union had but the faint approval of the Lords of Trade, and received no consideration in England. As Franklin said: "The assemblies all thought there was too much *prerogative*, and in England it was thought to have too much of the *democratic*."

16. MILITARY OPERATIONS (1755-1757).

[Sidenote: Character of the war]

Washington's defeat in 1754 was followed by active military preparations on both sides. So far as the number of campaigns and casualties goes, it was a war of little significance; but it was marked by romantic incidents and heroic deeds. Much of the fighting took place in the forest. The Indians showed their characteristic daring and their characteristic unwillingness to stand a long-continued, steady attack. Their scalping- knives and stakes added a fearful horror to many of the battles. On both sides the military policy seemed simple. The English must attack, the French must do their best to defend. The French were vulnerable in Nova Scotia and on the Ohio; their centre also was pierced by two highways leading from the Hudson,—one through Lake Champlain, the other through the Mohawk and Lake Ontario. These four regions must be the theatre of war, and in 1755 the British government, seconded by the colonists, planned an attack on the four points simultaneously.

[Sidenote: Braddock's expedition.]

The most difficult of the four tasks was the reduction of Fort Duquesne, and it was committed to a small force of British regulars, with colonial contingents, under the command of General Braddock. The character of this representative of British military authority is summed up in a phrase of his secretary's: "We have a general most judiciously chosen for being disqualified for the service

28

he is employed on in almost every respect." Before him lay three plain duties, —to co-operate with the provincial authorities in protecting the frontier, to impress upon the Indians the superior strength of the English, and to occupy the disputed territory. He did none of them. Among the provincials was George Washington, whose experience in this very region ought to have influenced the general; but the latter obstinately refused to learn that the rules of war must be modified in a rough and wooded country, among frontiersmen and savage enemies. July 9, 1755, the expedition reached a point eight miles from Fort Duquesne. As Braddock's little army marched forward, with careful protection against surprise, it was greeted with a volley from 250 French Canadians and 230 Indian allies. Though the Canadians fled, the Indians stood their ground from behind trees and logs. The Virginians and a few regulars took to trees also, but were beaten back by the oaths and blows of Braddock. "We would fight," they said, "if we could see anybody to fight with." After three hours' stand against an invisible foe, Braddock's men broke and abandoned the field. Out of 1,466 officers and men, but 482 came off safe. The remnant of the expedition fled, abandoned the country, left the frontier unprotected; and over the road which they had constructed came a stream of marauding Indians.

[Sidenote: Removal of the Acadians.]

In the centre the double campaign was equally unfruitful. On the borders of Nova Scotia the French forts were captured. The victors felt unable to hold the province, although it had been theirs since 1713, except by removing the French Acadian inhabitants. It was a strong measure, carried out with severity. Six thousand persons were distributed among the colonies farther south, where their religion and their language both caused them to be suspected and often kept them from a livelihood. The justification was that the Acadians were under French influence, and were likely to be added to the fighting force of the enemy; the judgment of Parkman is that the "government of France began with making the Acadians its tools, and ended with making them its victims."

[Sidenote: Campaigns of 1756, 1757.]

The campaigns of 1756 and 1757 were like that of 1755. After the retreat of Braddock's expedition the frontier of Virginia and Pennsylvania was left to the ravages of the Indians. The two colonies were slow to defend themselves, and had no help from England. Systematic warfare was still carried on in the centre and in the East. The French, under the guidance of their new commander, Montcalm, lost no ground, and gained Oswego and Fort William Henry. The English cause in Europe was declining. In the Far East alone had great successes been gained; and the battle of Plassey in 1757 gave to

England the paramount influence in India which she has ever since exercised.

17. THE CONQUEST OF CANADA (1756-1780).

[Sidenote: William Pitt.]
[Sidenote: Campaign of 1758.]

Few characters in history are indispensable. From William of Orange to William Pitt the younger there was but one man without whom English history must have taken a different turn, and that was William Pitt the elder. In 1757 he came forward as a representative of the English people, and forced his way into leadership by the sheer weight of his character. He secured a subsidy for Prussia, which was desperately making head against France, Austria, and Russia in coalition. He made a comprehensive plan for a combined attack on the French posts in America. He organized fleets and armies. He was able to break through the power of court influence, and to appoint efficient commanders. The first point of attack was Louisbourg, the North Atlantic naval station of the French. Since its capture by the New Englanders in 1745 (Colonies, § 127) it had been strongly fortified. An English force under Amherst and Wolfe reduced it after a brief siege in 1758. The attack through Lake George failed in consequence of the inefficiency of the English commander, Abercrombie, but the English penetrated across Lake Ontario and took Niagara. Nov. 25, 1758, Fort Duquesne was occupied by the English, and the spot was named Pittsburg, after the great minister. For the first time the tide of war set inward towards the St. Lawrence.

[Sidenote: Capture of Quebec.]

It is not evident that at the beginning the English expected more than to get control of Lake Champlain and of the country south of Lake Erie. The successes of 1758 led the way to the invasion, and eventually to the occupation, of the whole country. France sent thousands of troops into the European wars, but left the defence of its American empire to Montcalm with 5,000 regulars, 10,000 Canadian militia, and a few thousand savage allies. England, meanwhile, was able to send ships with 9,000 men to take Quebec. No exploit is more remarkable than the capture of that famous fortress. It was the key to the whole province; it was deemed impregnable; it was defended by superior numbers. The English, after vain attempts, were on the point of abandoning the siege. Wolfe's resolution and daring found a way over the cliffs; and on the morning of Sept. 13, 1759, the little English army was drawn up on the Plains of Abraham outside the landward fortifications of the city; the fate of Canada was decided in a battle in the open; the dying Wolfe defeated the dying Montcalm, and the town surrendered. The fall of the rest of

Canada was simply a matter of time. One desperate attempt to retake Quebec was made in 1760, but the force of Canada had spent itself. The 2,400 defenders of Montreal surrendered to 17,000 assailants. The colony of New France ceased to exist. For three years English military officers formed the only government of Canada.

18. GEOGRAPHICAL RESULTS OF THE WAR (1763).

[Sidenote: European war.]
[Sidenote: George III.]
[Sidenote: The war continued.]

The conflict in Europe continued for three years after the colonial war was at an end. During 1758, 1759, and 1760 Frederick the Second of Prussia had held his own, with English aid; he was now to lose his ally. The sudden death of George the Second had brought to the throne the first energetic sovereign since William the Third. An early public utterance of George the Third indicated that a new dynasty had arisen: "Born and bred in England, I glory in the name of Briton." With no brilliancy of speech and no attractiveness of person or manner, George the Third had a positive and forcible character. He resented the control of the great Whig families, to whom his grandfather and great-grandfather had owed their thrones. He represented a principle of authority and resistance to the unwritten power of Parliament and to the control of the cabinet. He had virtues not inherited and not common in his time; he was a good husband, a kind-hearted man, punctilious, upright, and truthful. He had, therefore, a certain popularity, notwithstanding his narrow-mindedness, obstinacy, and arrogance. Resolved to take a personal part in the government of his country, he began by building up a party of the "king's friends," which later supported him in the great struggle with the colonies. In a word, George the Third attempted to restore the Crown to the position which it had occupied under the last Stuart. Between such a king and the imperious Pitt there could not long be harmony. The king desired peace with all powers, and especially with France; Pitt insisted on continuing aggressive war. In 1761 Pitt was forced to resign, and Frederick the Second was abandoned. A change of sovereigns in Russia caused a change of policy, and Prussia was saved. Still peace was not made, and in 1762 Spain joined with France in the war on England; but the naval supremacy of England was indisputable. The French West India Islands and Havana, the fortress of the Spanish province of Cuba, were taken; and France was forced to make peace.

[Sidenote: Question of Annexations.]
[Sidenote: Canada ceded.]

In the negotiations the most important question was the disposition of the English conquests in America. Besides the Ohio country, the ostensible object of the war, Great Britain held both Canada and the French West Indies. The time seemed ripe to relieve the colonies from the dangers arising from the French settlements on the north, and the Spanish colonies in Florida and Cuba. The ministry wavered between keeping Guadeloupe and keeping Canada; but if they were unable to deal with 8,000 Acadians in 1755, what should they do with 80,000 Canadians in 1763? Was the inhospitable valley of the Lower St. Lawrence worth the occupation. And if the French were excluded from North America, could the loyalty of the colonies be guaranteed? France, however, humbled by the war, was forced to yield territory somewhere; Canada had long been a burden on the French treasury; since concession must be made, it seemed better to sacrifice the northern colonies rather than the profitable West Indies. Choiseul, the French Minister of Foreign Affairs, therefore ceded to England all the French possessions east of the Mississippi except the tract between the Amitic and the Mississippi, in which lay the town of New Orleans. The island of Cape Breton went with Canada, of which it was an outlyer. The wound to the prestige of France he passed over with a jaunty apothegm: "I ceded it," he said, "on purpose to destroy the English nation. They were fond of American dominion, and I resolved they should have enough of it."

[Sidenote: Louisiana ceded.]

Meanwhile, the Spaniards clamored for some compensation for their own losses. The English yielded up Havana, and kept the two provinces of Florida lying along the Gulf; and France transferred to Spain all the province of Louisiana not already given to England, that is, the western half of the Mississippi valley, and the Isle d'Orléans. The population was stretched along the river front of the Mississippi and its lower branches; it was devotedly French, and it was furious at the transfer. Of all her American possessions France retained only her West Indies and the insignificant islands of St. Pierre and Miquelon in the Gulf of St Lawrence. Thenceforward there were but two North American powers. Spain had all the continent from the Isthmus of Panama to the Mississippi, and northward to the upper watershed of the Missouri, and she controlled both sides of the Mississippi at its mouth. England had the eastern half of the continent from the Gulf to the Arctic Ocean, with an indefinite stretch west of Hudson's Bay.

[Sidenote: Interior boundaries.]

The interior boundaries of the English colonies were now defined by proclamations and instructions from Great Britain. A colony of Canada was established which included all the French settlements near the St. Lawrence.

Cape Breton was joined to Nova Scotia. On the south Georgia was extended to the St. Mary's River. Florida was divided into two provinces by the Appalachicola. The interior country from Lake Ontario to the Gulf was added to no colony, and a special instruction forbade the governors to exercise jurisdiction west of the mountains. In Georgia alone did the governor's command cover the region west to the Mississippi. The evident expectation was that the interior would be formed into separate colonies.

19. THE COLONIES DURING THE WAR (1754-1763).

[Sidenote: Internal quarrels.]

Seven years of war from 1754 to 1760, and two years more of military excitement, had brought about significant changes in the older colonies. It was a period of great expenditure of men and money. Thirty thousand lives had been lost. The more vigorous and more exposed colonies had laid heavy taxes and incurred burdensome debts. The constant pressure of the governors for money had aggravated the old quarrels with the assemblies. The important towns were all on tide water, and not one was taken or even threatened; hence the sufferings of the frontiersmen were not always appreciated by the colonial governments. In Pennsylvania the Indians were permitted to harry the frontier while the governor and the assembly were in a deadlock over the question of taxes on proprietary lands. Braddock's expedition in 1755 was intended to assert the claim of the English to territory in the limits of Pennsylvania; but it had no aid from the province thus concerned. Twice the peaceful Franklin stepped forward as the organizer of military resistance.

[Sidenote: English control.]

In the early part of the war Massachusetts took the lead, inasmuch as her governor, Shirley, was made commander-in-chief. Military and civil control over the colonies was, during the war, divided in an unaccustomed fashion. The English commanders, and even Governor Dinwiddie, showed their opinion of the Provincials by rating all their commissions lower than those of the lowest rank of regular British officers. The consequence was that George Washington for a time resigned from the service. In 1757 there was a serious dissension between Loudoun and the Massachusetts assembly, because he insisted on quartering his troops in Boston. At first the colonies were called on to furnish contingents at their own expense: Pitt's more liberal policy was to ask the colonies to furnish troops, who were paid from the British military chest. New England, as a populous region near the seat of hostilities, made great efforts; in the last three campaigns Massachusetts kept up every year five to seven thousand troops, and expended altogether Ł500,000. The other colonies, particularly Connecticut, made similar sacrifices, and the little colony of New York came out with a debt of $1,000,000.

[Sidenote: Colonial trade.]

As often happens during a war, some parts of the country prospered, notwithstanding the constant loss. New England fisheries and trade were little affected except when, in 1758, Loudoun shut up the ports by a brief embargo. As soon as Fort Duquesne was captured, settlers began to pass across the mountains into western Pennsylvania, and what is now Kentucky and eastern Tennessee. The Virginia troops received ample bounty lands; Washington was shrewd enough to buy up claims, and located about seventy thousand acres. The period of 1760 to 1763 was favorable to the colonies. Their trade with the West Indies was large. For their food products they got sugar and molasses; from the molasses they made rum; with the rum they bought slaves in Africa, and brought them to the West Indies and to the continent. The New Englanders fitted out and provisioned the British fleets. They supplied the British armies in America. They did not hesitate to trade with the enemy's colonies, or with the enemy direct, if the opportunity offered. The conclusion of peace checked this brisk trade and commercial activity. When the war was ended the agreeable irregularities stood more clearly revealed.

20. POLITICAL EFFECTS OF THE WAR (1763).

[Sidenote: Free from border wars.]
[Sidenote: Pontiac's conspiracy.]

In government as well as in trade a new era came to the colonies in 1763. Nine years had brought about many changes in the social and political conditions of the people. In the first place, they no longer had any civilized enemies. The Canadians, to be sure, were still mistrusted as papists; but though the colonists had no love for them, they had no fear of them; and twelve years later, at the outbreak of the Revolution, they tried to establish political brotherhood with them. The colonies were now free to expand westward, or would have been free, except for the resistance of the Western Indians gathered about the Upper Lakes. In 1763 Pontiac organized them in the most formidable Indian movement of American history. He had courage; he had statesmanship; he had large numbers. By this time the British had learned the border warfare, and Pontiac was with difficulty beaten. From that time until well into the Revolution Indian warfare meant only the resistance of scattered tribes to the steady westward advance of the English.

[Sidenote: Military experience.]

For the first time in their history the colonists had participated in large military operations. Abercrombie and Amherst each had commanded from twelve to fifteen thousand men. The colonists were expert in fortification. Many Provincials had seen fighting in line and in the woods. Israel Putnam had been captured, and the fires lighted to burn him; and Washington had learned in the hard school of frontier warfare both to fight, and to hold fast without fighting.

[Sidenote: United action.]

The war had further served to sharpen the political sense of the people. Year after year the assemblies had engaged in matters of serious moment They laid heavy taxes and collected them; they discussed foreign policy and their own defence; they protested against acts of the British government which affected them. Although no union had been formed at Albany in 1754, the colonies had frequently acted together and fought together. New York had been in great part a community of Dutch people under English rule during the war; now, as most exposed to French attack, it became the central colony. Military men and civilians from the different colonies learned to know each other at Fort William Henry and at Crown Point.

[Sidenote: Scheme of Britishcontrol.]
[Sidenote: Theory of co-operation.]
[Sidenote: Proposed taxes.]
[Sidenote: Navigation Acts.]

This unwonted sense of power and of common interest was increased by the pressure of the British government. Just before the war broke out, plans had been set on foot in England to curb the colonies; legislation was to be more carefully revised; governors were to be instructed to hold out against their assemblies; the Navigation Acts were to be enforced. The scheme was dropped when the war began, because the aid of the colonies in troops and supplies was essential. Then arose two rival theories as to the nature of the war. The British took the ground that they were sending troops to protect the colonies from French invasion, and that all their expeditions were benefactions to the colonies. The colonists felt that they were co-operating with England in breaking down a national enemy, and that all their grants were bounties. The natural corollary of the first theory was that the colonies ought at least to support the troops thus generously sent them; and various suggestions looking to this end were made by royal governors. Thus Shirley in 1756 devised a general system of taxation, including import duties, an excise, and a poll-tax; delinquents to be brought to terms by "warrants of distress and imprisonment of persons." When, in 1762, Governor Bernard of Massachusetts promised £400 in bounties on the faith of the colony, James

Otis protested that he had "involved their most darling privilege, the right of originating taxes." On the other hand, the colonies systematically broke the Navigation Acts, of which they had never denied the legality. To organize the control over the colonies more carefully, to provide a colonial revenue for general colonial purposes, to execute the Navigation Acts, and thus to confine the colonial trade to the mother-country,—these were the elements of the English colonial policy from 1763 to 1775. Before these ends were accomplished the colonies had revolted.

CHAPTER III.

21. REFERENCES.

BIBLIOGRAPHIES.—Justin Winsor, *Handbook of the Revolution*, 1-25, and *Narrative and Critical History*, VI. 62-112; W. E. Foster, *Monthly Reference Lists*, No. 79; Channing and Hart, *Guide*, §§ 134-136.

HISTORICAL MAPS.—No. 2, this volume (Epoch Maps, No. 5); Labberton, *Historical Atlas*, lxiv.; Gardiner, *School Atlas*, No. 46; Francis Parkman, *Pontiac*, frontispiece; Putzger, *Atlas*, No. 21; B. A. Hinsdale, *Old Northwest*, I. 68 (reprinted from MacCoun, *Historical Geography*).

GENERAL ACCOUNTS.—R. Frothingham, *Rise of the Republic*, 158-401; E. Channing, *United States*, 1765-1865, ch. ii.; Geo. Bancroft, *United States* (original ed.) V., VII, chs. i-xxvi. (last revision III., IV. chs. i-viii.); W. E. H. Lecky, *England in the Eighteenth Century*, III. ch. xii.; R. Hildreth, *United States*, II. 514-577; III. 25-56; G. T. Curtis, *Constitutional History*, I. i.; J. M. Ludlow, *War of Independence*, ch. iii.; Abiel Holmes, *Annals of America*, II. 124-198; Bryant and Gay, *United States*, III. 329-376; Justin Winsor, *Narrative and Critical History*, VI. ch. i.; T. Pitkin, *United States*, I. 155-281; H, C. Lodge, *Colonies*, ch. xxiii.; J. R. Green, *English People*, IV., 218-234; W. M. Sloane, *French War and Revolution*, chs. x.-xiv.; Adolphus,*England*, II. 134-332 *passim*; Grahame, *United States*, IV. book xi. Biographies of John Adams, Samuel Adams, Otis, Dickinson, Hutchinson, Franklin, and Washington.

SPECIAL HISTORIES.—W. B. Weeden, *Economic and Special History of New England*, II. chs. xviii., xix.; Wm. Tudor, *Life of James Otis*; J. K. Hosmer, *Samuel Adams*, 21-312; J. T. Morse, *Benjamin Franklin*, 99-201; M. C. Tyler, *Literature of the Revolution*, I., and *Patrick Henry*, 32-147; H. C. Lodge, *George Washington*, I. ch. iv.

CONTEMPORARY ACCOUNTS.—Works of Washington, Franklin, Patrick Henry, and John Adams; James Otis, *Rights of the British Colonies asserted and proved*: Examination of Franklin (Franklin, *Works*, IV. 161-195); W. B. Donne, *Correspondence of George III. with Lord North* [1768-1783]; John

Dickinson, *Farmer's Letters*; Jonathan Trumbull, McFingal (epic poem); Mercy Warren, *History of the American Revolution*; Thomas Hutchinson, *History of Massachusetts*, III., and *Diary and Letters*; Joseph Galloway, *Candid Examination*; Stephen Hopkins, *Rights of the Colonies Examined.*—Reprints in *Library of American Literature*, III.; *Old South Leaflets*; *American History told by Contemporaries*, II.

22. THE CONDITION OF THE BRITISH EMPIRE (1763).

[Sidenote: England's greatness.]

In 1763 the English were the most powerful nation in the world. The British islands, with a population of but 8,000,000 were the administrative centre of a vast colonial empire. Besides their American possessions, the English had a foothold in Africa through the possession of the former Dutch Cape Colony, and had laid the foundation of the present Indian Empire; small islands scattered through many seas furnished naval stations and points of defence. The situation of England bears a striking resemblance to the situation of Athens at the close of the Persian wars: a trading nation, a naval power, a governing race, a successful military people; the English completed the parallel by tightening the reins upon their colonies till they revolted. Of the other European powers, Portugal and Spain still preserved colonial empires in the West; but Spain was decaying. Great Britain had not only gained territory and prestige from the war, she had risen rich and prosperous, and a national debt of one hundred and forty million pounds was borne without serious difficulty.

[Sidenote: English government.]

It was a time of vigorous intellectual life, the period of Goldsmith, Edmund Burke, and Dr. Johnson. It was also a period of political development. The conditions seemed favorable for internal peace and for easy relations with the colonies. The long Jacobite movement had come to an end; George the Third was accepted by all classes and all parties as the legitimate sovereign. The system of government worked out in the preceding fifty years seemed well established; the ministers still governed through their control of Parliament; but the great Tory families, which for two generations had been excluded from the administration, were now coming forward. A new element in the government of England was the determination of George the Third to be an active political force. From his accession, in 1760, he had striven to build up a faction of personal adherents, popularly known as the "king's friends;" and he had broken down every combination of ministers which showed itself opposed to him. Although the nation was not yet conscious of it, the forces were at work which eventually were to create a party advocating the king's prerogative, and another party representing the right of the English people to govern themselves.

[Sidenote: Effect on the colonies.]

This change in political conditions could not but affect the English colonial policy. The king's imperious tone was reflected in all departments, and was especially positive when the colonies began to resist. It cannot be said that English parties divided on the question of governing the colonies, but when the struggle was once begun, the king's bitterest opponents fiercely criticised his policy, and made the cause of the colonists their own. The great struggle with the colonies thus became a part of the struggle between popular and autocratic principles of government in England.

23. NEW SCHEMES OF COLONIAL CONTROL (1763).

[Sidenote: Grenville's colonial policy.]

Allusion has already been made (§ 19) to vague schemes of colonial control suggested during the war. More serious measures were impending. When George Grenville became the head of the cabinet, in April, 1763, he took up and elaborated three distinctly new lines of policy, which grew to be the direct causes of the American Revolution. The first was the rigid execution of the Acts of Trade; the second was the taxation of the colonies for the partial support of British garrisons; the third was the permanent establishment of British troops in America. What was the purpose of each of these groups of measures?

[Sidenote: Navigation acts.]
[Sidenote: Effect of the system.]

The object of the first series was simply to secure obedience to the Navigation Acts (Colonies, Section 44, 128),—laws long on the statute book, and admitted by most Americans to be legal. The Acts were intended simply to secure to the mother-country the trade of the colonies; they were in accordance with the practice of other nations; they were far milder than the similar systems of France and Spain, because they gave to colonial vessels and to colonial merchants the same privileges as those enjoyed by English ship-owners and traders. The Acts dated from 1645, but had repeatedly been re-enacted and enlarged, and from time to time more efficient provision was made for their enforcement. In the first place, the Navigation Acts required that all the colonial trade should be carried on in ships built and owned in England or the colonies. In the second place, most of the colonial products were included in a list of "enumerated goods," which could be sent abroad, even in English or colonial vessels, only to English ports. The intention was to give to English home merchants a middleman's profit in the exchange of American for foreign goods. Among the enumerated goods were tobacco, sugar, indigo, copper, and furs, most of them produced by the tropical and sub-tropical colonies. Lumber, provisions, and fish were usually not enumerated; and naval stores, such as tar, hemp, and masts, even received an English bounty. In 1733 was passed the "Sugar Act," by which prohibitory duties were laid on sugar and molasses imported from foreign colonies to the English plantations, Many of these provisions little affected the continental colonies, and in some respects were favorable to them. Thus the restriction of trade to English and colonial vessels stimulated ship- building and the shipping interest in the colonies. From 1772 to 1775 more than two thousand vessels were built in America.

[Sidenote: Illegal trade.]
[Sidenote: Difficulty of enforcement.]

The chief difficulty with the system arose out of the obstinate determination of the colonies, especially in New England, to trade with their French and Spanish neighbors in the West Indies, with or without permission: they were able in those markets to sell qualities of fish and lumber for which there was no demand in England. Well might it have been said, as a governor of Virginia had said a century earlier: "Mighty and destructive have been the obstructions to our trade and navigation by that severe Act of Parliament,... for all are most obedient to the laws, while New England men break through them and trade to any place where their interests lead them to." The colonists were obliged to register their ships; it was a common practice to register them at much below their actual tonnage, or to omit the ceremony altogether. Colonial officials could not be depended upon to detect or to punish infractions of the Acts, and for that purpose the English Government had placed customs officers in the principal ports. Small duties were laid on imports, not to furnish revenue, but rather to furnish fees for those officers. The amount thus collected was not more than two thousand pounds a year; and the necessary salaries, aggregating between seven and eight thousand pounds, were paid by the British government.

24. WRITS OF ASSISTANCE (1761-1764).

[Sidenote: Smuggling.]
[Sidenote: Argument of James Otis.]

Under the English acts violation of the Navigation Laws was smuggling, and

40

was punishable in the usual courts. Two practical difficulties had always been found in prosecutions, and they were much increased as soon as a more vigorous execution was entered upon. It was hard to secure evidence, for smuggled goods, once landed, rapidly disappeared; and the lower colonial judges were both to deal severely with their brethren, engaged in a business which public sentiment did not condemn. In 1761 an attempt was made in Massachusetts to avoid both these difficulties through the use of the familiar Writs of Assistance. These were legal processes by which authority was given to custom-house officers to make search for smuggled goods; since they were general in their terms and authorized the search of any premises by day, they might have been made the means of vexatious visits and interference. In February, 1761, an application for such a writ was brought before the Superior Court of Massachusetts, which was not subject to popular influence. James Otis, advocate-general of the colony, resigned his office rather than plead the cause of the government, and became the leading counsel in opposition. The arguments in favor of the writ were that without some such process the laws could not be executed, and that similar writs were authorized by English statutes. Otis in his plea insisted that no English statute applied to the colonies unless they were specially mentioned, and that hence English precedents had no application. But he went far beyond the legal principles involved. He declared in plain terms that the Navigation Acts were "a taxation law made by a foreign legislature without our consent." He asserted that the Acts of Trade were "irreconcilable with the colonial charters, and hence were void." He declared that there were "rights derived only from nature and the Author of nature;" that they were "inherent, inalienable, and indefeasible by any laws, pacts, contracts, governments, or stipulations which man could devise." The court, after inquiring into the practice in England, issued the writs to the custom-house officers, although it does not appear that they made use of them.

[Sidenote: Effect of the discussion.]

The practical effect of Otis's speech has been much exaggerated. John Adams, who heard and took notes on the argument, declared, years later, that "American independence was then born," and that "Mr. Otis's oration against Writs of Assistance breathed into this nation the breath of life." The community was not conscious at the time that a new and startling doctrine had been put forth, or that loyalty to England was involved. The arguments drawn from the rights of man and the supremacy of the charters were of a kind familiar to the colonists. The real novelty was the bold application of these principles, the denial of the legality of a system more than a century old.

[Sidenote: Enforcement.]

So far was the home government from accepting these doctrines that in 1763 the offensive Sugar Act was renewed. New import duties were laid, and more stringent provisions made for enforcing the Acts of Trade; and the ground was prepared for a permanent and irritating controversy, by commissioning the naval officers stationed on the American coast as revenue officials, with power to make seizures.

25. THE STAMP ACT (1763-1765).

[Sidenote: Plan for a stamp duty.]
[Sidenote: Questions of troops.]

The next step in colonial control met an unexpected and violent resistance. In the winter of 1763-1764 Grenville, then English prime minister, called together the agents of the colonies and informed them that he proposed to lay a small tax upon the colonies, and that it would take the form of a stamp duty, unless they suggested some other method. Why should England tax the colonies? Because it had been determined to place a permanent force of about ten thousand men in America. A few more English garrisons would have been of great assistance in 1754; the Pontiac outbreak of 1763 had been suppressed only by regular troops who happened to be in the country; and in case of later wars the colonies were likely to be attacked by England's enemies. On the other hand, the colonies had asked for no troops, and desired none. They were satisfied with their own halting and inefficient means of defence; they no longer had French enemies in Canada, and they felt what seems an unreasonable fear that the troops would be used to take away their liberty. From the beginning to the end of the struggle it was never proposed that Americans should be taxed for the support of the home government, or even for the full support of the colonial army. It was supposed that a revenue of one hundred thousand pounds would be raised, which would meet one-third of the necessary expense.

[Sidenote: Stamp Act passed.]

Notwithstanding colonial objections to a standing army, garrisons would doubtless have been received but for the accompanying proposition to tax. On March 10, 1764, preliminary resolutions passed the House of Commons looking towards the Stamp Act. There was no suggestion that the proposition was illegal; the chief objection was summed up by Beckford, of London, in a phrase: "As we are stout, I hope we shall be merciful."

The news produced instant excitement in the colonies. First was urged the practical objection that the tax would draw from the country the little specie which it contained. The leading argument was that taxation without representation was illegal. The remonstrances, by an error of the agents who had them in charge, were not presented until too late. Franklin and others protested to the ministry, and declared the willingness of the colonies to pay taxes assessed in a lump sum on each colony. Grenville silenced them by asking in what way those lump sums should be apportioned. After a short debate in Parliament the Act was passed by a vote of 205 to 49. Barré, one of the members who spoke against it, alluded to the agitators in the colonies as "Sons of Liberty;" the phrase was taken up in the colonies, and made a party war-cry. George the Third was at that moment insane, and the Act was signed by a commission.

[Sidenote: Expectations of success.]

Resistance in the colonies was not expected. Franklin thought that the Act would go into effect; even Otis said that it ought to be obeyed. It laid a moderate stamp-duty on the papers necessary for legal and commercial transactions. At the request of the ministry, the colonial agents suggested as stamp collectors some of the most respected and eminent men in each colony. Almost at the same time was passed an act somewhat relaxing the Navigation Laws; but a Quartering Act was also passed, by which the colonists were obliged, even in time of peace, to furnish the troops who might be stationed among them with quarters and with certain provisions.

26. THE STAMP ACT CONGRESS (1765.)

[Sidenote: Internal and external taxes.]

Issue was now joined on the question which eventually separated the colonies from the mother-country. Parliament had asserted its right to lay taxes on the colonists for imperial purposes. The colonies had up to this time held governmental relations only with the Crown, from whom came their charters. They had escaped taxation because they were poor, and because hitherto they had not occasioned serious expense; but they had accepted the small import duties. They found it hard to reconcile obedience to one set of laws with resistance to the other; and they therefore insisted that there was a distinction between "external taxation" and "internal taxation," between duties levied at the ports and duties levied within the colonies.

[Sidenote: Remonstrances.]

The moment the news reached America, opposition sprang up in many different forms. The colonial legislatures preferred dignified remonstrance. The Virginia Assembly reached a farther point in a set of bold resolutions, passed May 29, 1765, under the influence of a speech by Patrick Henry. They asserted "that the General Assembly of this colony have the only and sole exclusive right and power to lay taxes and impositions upon the inhabitants of this colony;" and that the Stamp Act" has a manifest tendency to destroy British as well as American freedom." On June 8, 1765, Massachusetts suggested another means of remonstrance, by calling upon her sister colonies to send delegates to New York "to consider of a general and united, dutiful, loyal, and humble representation of their condition to his Majesty and to the Parliament."

[Sidenote: Riots.]
[Sidenote: Non-Importation.]

Meanwhile opposition had broken out in open violence. In August there were riots in Boston; the house of Oliver, appointed as collector of the stamp taxes, was attacked, and he next day resigned his office. Hutchinson was acting governor of the colony: his mansion was sacked; and the manuscript of his History of Massachusetts, still preserved, carries on its edges the mud of the Boston streets into which it was thrown. The town of Boston declared itself "particularly alarmed and astonished at the Act called the Stamp Act, by which we apprehend a very grievous tax is to be laid upon the colonies." In other colonies there were similar, though less violent, scenes. Still another form of resistance was suggested by the organizations called "Sons of Liberty," the members of which agreed to buy no more British goods. When the time came for putting the act into force, every person appointed as collector had resigned.

[Sidenote: Stamp Act Congress.]

These three means of resistance—protest, riots, and non-importation—were powerfully supplemented by the congress which assembled at New York, Oct. 1765. It included some of the ablest men from nine colonies. Such men as James Otis, Livingston of New York, Rutledge of South Carolina, and John Dickinson of Pennsylvania, met, exchanged views, and promised co-operation. It was the first unmistakable evidence that the colonies would make common cause. After a session of two weeks the congress adjourned, having drawn up petitions to the English government, and a "Declaration of Rights and Grievances of the Colonists in America." In this document they declared themselves entitled to the rights of other Englishmen. They asserted, on the one hand, that they could not be represented in the British House of Commons, and on the other that they could not be taxed by a body in which they had no representation. They complained of the Stamp Act, and no less of the amendments to the Acts of Trade, which, they said, would "render them unable to purchase the manufactures of Great Britain." In these memorials there is no threat of resistance, but the general attitude of the colonies showed that it was unsafe to push the matter farther.

[Sidenote: Repeal of the Stamp Act.]

Meanwhile the Grenville ministry had given place to another Whig ministry under Rockingham, who felt no responsibility for the Stamp Act. Pitt took the ground that "the government of Great Britain could not lay taxes on the colonies." Benjamin Franklin was called before a committee, and urged the withdrawal of the act. The king, who had now recovered his health, gave it to be understood that he was for repeal. The repeal bill was passed by a majority of more than two to one, and the crisis was avoided.

[Sidenote: Right of taxation asserted.]

To give up the whole principle seemed to the British government impossible; the repeal was therefore accompanied by the so-called Dependency Act. This set forth that the colonies are "subordinate unto and dependent upon the Imperial Crown and Parliament of Great Britain, and that Parliament hath, and of right ought to have, full power to make laws and statutes of sufficient force and validity to bind the colonies and people of America subjects to the Crown of Great Britain in all cases whatsoever." Apparently matters had returned to their former course. The gratitude of the colonies was loudly expressed; but they had learned the effect of a united protest, they had learned how to act together, and they were irritated by the continued assertion of the power of Parliament to tax and otherwise to govern the colonies.

27. REVENUE ACTS (1767).

[Sidenote: Townshend's plans.]
[Sidenote: Quarrel with New York.]

The repeal of the Stamp Act removed the difficulty without removing the cause. The year 1766 was marked in English politics by the virtual retirement of Pitt from the government. His powerful opposition to taxation of the colonies was thus removed, and Charles Townshend became the leading spirit in the ministry. Jan. 26, 1767, he said in the House of Commons: "I know a mode in which a revenue may be drawn from America without offence…. England is undone if this taxation of America is given up." And he pledged himself to find a revenue nearly sufficient to meet the military expenses in America. At the moment that the question of taxation was thus revived, the New York Assembly became involved in a dispute with the home government by declining to furnish the necessary supplies for the troops. An Act of Parliament was therefore passed declaring the action of the New York legislature null,—a startling assertion of a power of disallowance by Parliament.

[Sidenote: Enforcement.]

The three parts of the general scheme for controlling the colonies were now all taken up again. For their action against the troops the New York Assembly was suspended,—the first instance in which Parliament had undertaken to destroy an effective part of the colonial government. For the execution of the Navigation Acts a board of commissioners of customs was established, with large powers. In June, 1767, a new Taxation Act was introduced, and rapidly passed through Parliament. In order to avoid the objections to "internal taxes," it laid import duties on glass, and white lead, painters' colors, paper, and tea. The proceeds of the Act, estimated at, Ł40,000, were to pay governors and judges in America. Writs of Assistance were made legal. A few months afterwards,—December, 1767,—a colonial department was created, headed by a secretary of state. The whole machinery of an exasperating control was thus provided.

[Sidenote: Question of right of taxation.]

Issue was once more joined both in England and America on the constitutional power of taxation. The great principle of English law that taxation was not a right, but a gift of the persons taxed through their representatives, was claimed also by the colonies. Opinions had repeatedly been given by the law officers of the Crown that a colony could be taxed only by its own representatives. The actual amount of money called for was too small to burden them, but it was to be applied in such a way as to make the governors and judges independent of the assemblies. The principle of taxation, once admitted, might be carried farther. As an English official of the time remarked: "The Stamp Act attacked colonial ideas by sap; the Townshend scheme was attacking them by storm every day."

28. COLONIAL PROTESTS AND REPEAL (1767-1770).

[Sidenote: Colonial protest.]
[Sidenote: Massachusetts circular.]
[Sidenote: Coercive measures.]

This time the colonies avoided the error of disorderly or riotous opposition. The leading men resolved to act together through protests by the colonial legislatures and through non-importation agreements. Public feeling ran high. In Pennsylvania John Dickinson in his "Letters of a Farmer" pointed out that "English history affords examples of resistance by force." Another non-importation scheme was suggested by Virginia, but was on the whole unsuccessful. In February, 1768, Massachusetts sent out a circular letter to the other colonies, inviting concerted protests, and declaring that the new laws were unconstitutional. The protest was moderate, its purpose legal; but the ministry attempted to destroy its effect by three new repressive measures. The first of them, April, 1768, directed the governors, upon any attempt to pass protesting resolutions, to prorogue their assemblies. The second was the despatch of troops to Boston: they arrived at the end of September, and remained until the outbreak of the Revolution. The third coercive step was a proposition to send American agitators to England for trial, under an obsolete statute of Henry the Eighth.

[Sidenote: Effect of the tax.]

Meanwhile the duties had been levied. The result was the actual payment of about sixteen thousand pounds; this sum was offset by expenses of collection amounting to more than fifteen thousand pounds, and extraordinary military expenditures of one hundred and seventy thousand pounds. Once more the ministry found no financial advantage and great practical difficulties in the way of colonial taxation. Once more they determined to withdraw from an untenable position, and once more, under the active influence of the king and his "friends," they resolved to maintain the principle. In April, 1770, all the duties were repealed except that upon tea. Either the ministry should have applied the principle rigorously, so as to raise an adequate revenue, or they should have given up the revenue and the principle together.

29. SPIRIT OF VIOLENCE IN THE COLONIES (1770-1773).

[Sidenote: Troops in Boston.]
[Sidenote: Collision with the mob.]

Repeal could not destroy the feeling of injury in the minds of the colonists; and repeal did not withdraw the coercive acts nor the troops. The garrison in Boston, sustained at the expense of the British treasury, was almost as offensive to the colonists of Massachusetts as if they had been taxed for its support. From the beginning the troops were looked upon as an alien body, placed in the town to execute unpopular and even illegal acts. There was constant friction between the officers and the town and colonial governments, and between the populace and the troops. On the night of March 5, 1770, an affray occurred between a mob and a squad of soldiers. Both sides were abusive and threatening; finally the soldiers under great provocation fired, and killed five men. The riot had no political significance; it was caused by no invasion upon the rights of Americans: but, in the inflamed condition of the public mind, it was instantly taken up, and has gone down to history under the undeserved title of the Boston Massacre. Next morning a town meeting unanimously voted "that nothing can rationally be expected to restore the peace of the town and prevent blood and carnage but the immediate removal of the troops." The protest was effectual; the troops were sent to an island in the harbor; on the other hand, the prosecution of the soldiers concerned in the affray was allowed to slacken. For nearly two years the trouble seemed dying down in Massachusetts.

[Sidenote: Samuel Adams.]
[Sidenote: Committee of Correspondence.]

That friendly relations between the colonies and the mother-country were not re-established is due chiefly to Samuel Adams, a member of the Massachusetts General Court from Boston. His strength lay in his vehemence, his total inability to see more than one side of any question, and still more in his subtle influence upon the Boston town meeting, upon committees, and in private conclaves. He seems to have determined from the beginning that independence might come, ought to come, and must come. In November, 1772, he introduced into the Boston town meeting a modest proposition that "a committee of correspondence be appointed ... to state the Rights of the Colonists and of this Province in particular as Men, as Christians, and as Subjects;—and also request of each Town a free communication of their Sentiments on this subject." The committee blew the coals by an enumeration of rights and grievances; but its chief service was its unseen but efficient work of correspondence, from town to town. A few months later the colony entered into a similar scheme for communication with the sister colonies. These committees of correspondence made the Revolution possible. They disseminated arguments from province to province: they had lists of those ripe for resistance; they sounded legislatures; they prepared the organization which was necessary for the final rising of 1774 and 1775.

[Sidenote: "Gaspee" burned.]
[Sidenote: Tea.]
[Sidenote: Hutchinson letters.]
[Sidenote: Boston Tea-party.]

Shortly before the creation of this committee, an act of violence in Rhode Island showed the hostility to the enforcement of the Acts of Trade. The "Gaspee," a royal vessel of war, had interfered legally and illegally with the smuggling trade. On June 9, 1772, while in pursuit a vessel, she ran aground. That night the ship was attacked by armed men, who captured and burned her. The colonial authorities were indifferent: the perpetrators were not tried; they were not prosecuted; they were not even arrested. On Dec. 16, 1773, a similar act of violence marked the opposition of the colonies to the remnant of the Townshend taxation acts. The tea duty had been purposely reduced, till the price of tea was lower than in England. Soon after the appointment of the Committees of Correspondence public sentiment in Massachusetts was again aroused by the publication of letters written by Hutchinson, then governor of Massachusetts, to a private correspondent in England. The letters were such as any governor representing the royal authority might have written. "I wish," said Hutchinson, "the good of the colony when I wish to see some fresh restraint of liberty rather than the connection with the parent state should be broken." The assembly petitioned for the removal of Hutchinson, and this unfortunate quarrel was one of the causes of a decisive step, the Boston Tea-party. An effort was made to import a quantity of tea, not for the sake of the tax, but in order to relieve the East India Company from financial difficulties. On December 16, the three tea ships in the harbor were boarded by a body of men in Indian garb, and three hundred and forty- two chests of tea were emptied into the sea. Next morning the shoes of at least one reputable citizen of Massachusetts were found by his family unaccountably full of tea. In other parts of the country, as at Edenton in North Carolina, and at Charleston in South Carolina, there was similar violence.

30. COERCIVE ACTS OF 1774.

[Sidenote: Public feeling in England.]

The British government had taken a false step by its legislation of 1770, but the colonies had now put themselves in the wrong by these repeated acts of violence. There seemed left but two alternatives,—to withdraw the Tea Act, and thus to remove the plea that Parliament was taxing without representation; or to continue the execution of the Revenue Act firmly, but by the usual course of law. It was not in the temper of the English people, and still less like the king, to withdraw offensive acts in the face of such daring resistance. The failure to secure the prosecution of the destroyers of the "Gaspee" caused the British government to distrust American courts as well as American juries. One political writer, Dean Tucker, declared that the American colonies in their defiant state had ceased to be of advantage to England, and that they had better be allowed quietly to separate. Pitt denied the right to tax, but declared that if the colonies meant to separate, he would be the first to enforce the authority of the mother-country.

[Sidenote: Coercive statutes.]
[Sidenote: Quebec Act.]

Neither orderly enforcement, conciliation, nor peaceful separation was the policy selected. England committed the fatal and irremediable mistake of passing illegal statutes as a punishment for the illegal action of the colonists. Five bills were introduced and hastily pushed through Parliament. The first was meant as a punishment for the Tea-party. It enacted that no further commerce was to be permitted with the port of Boston till that town should make its submission. Burke objected to a bill "which punishes the innocent with the guilty, and condemns without the possibility of defence." The second act was intended to punish the whole commonwealth of Massachusetts, by declaring void certain provisions of the charter granted by William III. in 1692. Of all the grievances which led to the Revolution this was the most serious, for it set up the doctrine that charters proceeding from the Crown could be altered by statute. Thenceforward Parliament was to be omnipotent in colonial matters. The third act directed that "Persons questioned for any Acts in Execution of the Law" should be sent to England for trial. It was not intended to apply to persons guilty of acts of violence, but to officers or soldiers who, in resisting riots, might have made themselves amenable to the civil law. The fourth act was a new measure providing for the quartering of soldiers upon the inhabitants, and was intended to facilitate the establishment of a temporary military government in Massachusetts. The fifth act had no direct reference to Massachusetts, but was later seized upon as one of the grievances which justified the Revolution. This was the Quebec Act, providing for the government of the region ceded by France in 1763. It gave to the French settlers the right to have their disputes decided under the principles of the old French civil law; it guaranteed them the right of exercising their own religion; and it annexed to Quebec the whole territory between the Ohio and Mississippi Rivers and the Great Lakes. The purpose of this act was undoubtedly to remove the danger of disaffection or insurrection in Canada, and at the same time to extinguish all claims of Connecticut, Massachusetts, and Virginia to the region west of Pennsylvania.

31. THE FIRST CONTINENTAL CONGRESS (1774).

[Sidenote: Gage's quarrel with Massachusetts.]

The news of this series of coercive measures was hardly received in Massachusetts before General Gage appeared, bearing a commission to act as governor of the province; and in a few weeks the Port Bill and the modifications of the charter were put in force. If the governor supposed that Boston stood alone, he was quickly undeceived. From the other towns and from other colonies came supplies of food and sympathetic resolutions. On June 17th, under the adroit management of Samuel Adams, the General Court passed a resolution proposing a colonial congress, to begin September 1st at Philadelphia. While the resolutions were going through, the governor's messenger in vain knocked at the locked door, to communicate a proclamation dissolving the assembly. The place of that body was for a time taken by the Committee of Correspondence, in which Samuel Adams was the leading spirit, and by local meetings and conventions. In August, Gage came to an open breach with the people. In accordance with the Charter Act, he proceeded to appoint the so-called "mandamus" councillors. An irregularly elected Provincial Congress declared that it stood by the charter of 1692, under which the councillors were elected by the General Court. The first effect of the coercive acts was, therefore, to show that the people of Massachusetts stood together.

[Sidenote: Delegates chosen.]
[Sidenote: The Congress.]

Another effect was to enlist the sympathy of the other colonies. The movement for a congress plainly looked towards resistance and revolution. In vain did the governors dissolve the assemblies that seemed disposed to send delegates. Irregular congresses and conventions took their place, and all the colonies but Georgia somehow chose delegates. The first Continental Congress which assembled in Philadelphia on September 5, 1774, was, therefore, a body without any legal status. It included, however, some of the most influential men in America. From Massachusetts came Samuel Adams and John Adams; from New York, John Jay; from Virginia, Patrick Henry and George Washington. The general participation in this congress was an assurance that all America felt the danger of parliamentary control, and the outrage upon the rights of their New England brethren.

[Sidenote: Declaration of Rights.]

This feeling was voiced in the action of the Congress. Early resolutions set forth approval of the action of Massachusetts. Then came the preparation of a "Declaration of Rights" of the colonies, and of their grievances. They declared that they were entitled to life, liberty, and property, and to the rights and immunities of free and natural born subjects within the realm of England. They denied the right of the British Parliament to legislate in cases of "taxation and internal polity," but "cheerfully consent to the operation of such Acts of the British Parliament as are *bona fide* restrained to the regulation of our external commerce." They protested against "the keeping up a standing army in these colonies in times of peace." They enumerated a long list of illegal Acts, including the coercive statutes and the Quebec Act.

[Sidenote: The Association.]

The only action of the First Continental Congress which had in any degree the character of legislation was the "Association,"—the only effective non-importation agreement in the whole struggle. The delegates united in a pledge that they would import no goods from England or other English colonies, and particularly no slaves or tea; and they recommended to the colonies to pass efficient legislation for carrying it out. The Revolutionary "congresses" and "conventions," and sometimes the legislatures themselves, passed resolutions and laid penalties. A more effective measure was open violence against people who persisted in importing, selling, or using British goods or slaves.

[Sidenote: Action of the Congress.]

The First Continental Congress was simply the mouthpiece of the colonies. It expressed in unmistakable terms a determination to resist what they considered aggressions; and it suggested as a legal and effective means of resistance that they should refuse to trade with the of mother-country. Its action, however, received the approval of an assembly or other representative body in each of the twelve colonies. Before it adjourned, the congress prepared a series of addresses and remonstrances, and voted that if no redress of grievances should have been obtained, a second congress should assemble in May, 1775.

32. OUTBREAK OF HOSTILITIES (1775).

[Sidenote: Attitude of the Whigs.]
[Sidenote: Coercion]

When Parliament assembled in January, 1775, it was little disposed to make concessions; but the greatest living Englishman now came forward as the defender of the colonies. Pitt declared that the matter could only be adjusted on the basis "that taxation is theirs, and commercial regulation ours." Although he was seconded by other leading Whigs, the reply of the Tory ministry to the remonstrance of the colonies was a new series of acts. Massachusetts was declared in a state of rebellion; and the recalcitrant colonies were forbidden to trade with Great Britain, Ireland, or the West Indies, or to take part in the Newfoundland fisheries.

[Sidenote: Affairs inMassachusetts.]
[Sidenote: Lexington and Concord.]

Before these acts could be known in America, matters had already drifted to a point where neither coercion nor conciliation could effect anything. Through the winter 1774-1775 Gage lay for the most part in Boston, unable to execute his commission outside of his military lines, and unwilling to summon a legislature which was certain to oppose him. The courts were broken up, jurors could not be obtained, the whole machinery of government was stopped. Meanwhile, in February, 1775, the people had a second time elected a provincial congress, which acted for the time being as their government. This body prepared to raise a military force, and asked aid of other New England colonies. April 19, 1775, a British expedition was sent from Boston to Lexington and Concord to seize military stores there assembled for the use of the provincial forces. The British were confronted on the village green of Lexington by about one hundred militiamen, who refused to disperse, and were fired upon by the British. At Concord the British found and destroyed the stores, but were attacked and obliged to retire, and finally returned to Boston with a loss of three hundred men. The war had begun. Its issue depended upon the moral and military support which Massachusetts might receive from the other colonies.

33. JUSTIFICATION OF THE REVOLUTION.

[Sidenote: Malcontents put down.]

The cause of Massachusetts was unhesitatingly taken up by all the colonies, from New Hampshire to Georgia. America was united. This unanimity proceeded, however, not from the people, but from suddenly constituted revolutionary governments. No view of the Revolution could be just which does not recognize the fact that in no colony was there a large majority in favor of resistance, and in some the patriots were undoubtedly in a minority. The movement, started by a few seceders, carried with it a large body of men who were sincerely convinced that the British government was tyrannical. The majorities thus formed, silenced the minority, sometimes by mere intimidation, sometimes by ostracism, often by flagrant violence. One kind of pressure was felt by old George Watson of Plymouth, bending his bald head over his cane, as his neighbors one by one left the church in which he sat, because they would not associate with a "mandamus councillor." A different argument was employed on Judge James Smith of New York, in his coat of tar and feathers, the central figure of a shameful procession.

[Sidenote: Early organization.]

Another reason for the sudden strength shown by the Revolutionary movement was that the patriots were organized and the friends of the established government did not know their own strength. The agent of British influence in almost every colony was the governor. In 1775 the governors were all driven out. There was no centre of resistance about which the loyalists could gather. The patriots had seized the reins of government before their opponents fairly understood that they had been dropped.

[Sidenote: Feeling of common interest.]

Another influence which hastened the Revolution was a desire to supplant the men highest in official life. There was no place in the colonial government for a Samuel Adams or a John Adams while the Hutchinsons and the Olivers were preferred. But no personal ambitions can account for the agreement of thirteen colonies having so many points of dissimilarity. The merchants of Boston and New Haven, the townsmen of Concord and Pomfret, the farmers of the Hudson and Delaware valleys, and the aristocratic planters of Virginia and South Carolina, deliberately went to war rather than submit. The causes of the Revolution were general, were wide-spread, and were keenly felt by Americans of every class.

[Sidenote: Resistance of taxation.]

The grievance most strenuously put forward was that of "taxation without representation." On this point the colonists were supported by the powerful authority of Pitt and other English statesmen, and by an unbroken line of precedent. They accepted "external taxation;" at the beginning of the struggle they professed a willingness to pay requisitions apportioned in lump sums on the colonies; they were accustomed to heavy taxation for local purposes; in the years immediately preceding the Revolution the people of Massachusetts annually raised about ten shillings per head. They sincerely objected to taxation of a new kind, for a purpose which did not interest them, by a power which they could not control. The cry of "Taxation without representation" had great popular effect. It was simple, it was universal, it sounded like tyranny.

[Sidenote: Resistance of garrisons.]

A greater and more keenly felt grievance was the establishment of garrisons. The colonies were willing to run their own risk of enemies. They asserted that the real purpose of the troops was to overawe their governments. The despatch of the regiments to Boston in 1768 was plainly intended to subdue a turbulent population. The British government made a serious mistake in insisting upon this point, whether with or without taxes.

[Sidenote: Resistance to Acts of Trade.]

By far the most effective cause of the Revolution was the English commercial system. One reason why a tax was felt to be so great a hardship was, that the colonies were already paying a heavy indirect tribute to the British nation, by the limitations on their trade. The fact that French and Spanish colonists suffered more than they did, was no argument to Englishmen accustomed in most ways to regulate themselves. The commercial system might have been enforced; perhaps a tax might have been laid: the two together made a grievance which the colonies would not endure.

[Sidenote: Stand for the charters.]

The coercive acts of 1774 gave a definite object for the general indignation. In altering the government of Massachusetts they destroyed the security of all the colonies. The Crown was held unable to withdraw a privilege once granted; Parliament might, however, undo to-morrow what it had done to-day. The instinct of the Americans was for a rigid constitution, unalterable by the ordinary forms of law. They were right in calling the coercive acts unconstitutional. They were contrary to the charters, they were contrary to precedent, and in the minds of the colonists the charters and precedent, taken together, formed an irrepealable body of law.

[Sidenote: Oppression not grievous.]
[Sidenote: Restraints on trade.]
[Sidenote: Resistance to one-man power.]

In looking back over this crisis, it is difficult to see that the colonists had suffered grievous oppression. The taxes had not taken four hundred thousand pounds out of their pockets in ten years. The armies had cost them nothing, and except in Boston had not interfered with the governments. The Acts of Trade were still systematically evaded, and the battle of Lexington came just in time to relieve John Hancock from the necessity of appearing before the court to answer to a charge of smuggling. The real justification of the Revolution is not to be found in the catalogue of grievances drawn up by the colonies. The Revolution was right because it represented two great principles of human progress. In the first place, as the Americans grew in importance, in numbers, and in wealth, they felt more and more indignant that their trade should be hampered for the benefit of men over seas. They represented the principle of the right of an individual to the products of his own industry; and their success has opened to profitable trade a thousand ports the world over. In the second place the Revolution was a resistance to arbitrary power. That arbitrary power was exercised by the Parliament of Great Britain; but, at that moment, by a combination which threatened the existence of popular government in England, the king was the ruling spirit over Parliament. The colonists represented the same general principles as the minority in England. As Sir Edward Thornton said, when minister of Great Britain to the United States, in 1879: "Englishmen now understand that in the American Revolution you were fighting our battles."

CHAPTER IV.

34. REFERENCES.

BIBLIOGRAPHIES.—Justin Winsor, *Narrative and Critical History*, VI. *passim*, VII. 1-214, VIII. App.; and *Readers' Handbook of the Revolution*; W. F. Allen, *History Topics*, 107, 108; W. E. Foster, *References to the Constitution of the United States*, 11-14; Channing and Hart, *Guide*, §§ 136-141.

HISTORICAL MAPS.—Nos. 2 and 3 this volume (*Epoch Maps*, Nos. 4 and 5); H. C Lodge, *Colonies*, frontispiece; Scribner, *Statistical Atlas*, Pl. 12; Rhode, *Atlas*, No. xxviii.; Geo. Bancroft, *United States* (original edition), V. 241; Labberton, *Atlas*, lxiv.; B. A. Hinsdale, *Old Northwest*, I. 176, 180 (republished from T. MacCoun, *Historical Geography*); List of contemporary maps in Winsor, *Handbook*, 302, school histories of Channing, Johnston, Scudder, Thomas.

GENERAL ACCOUNTS.—G T. Curtis, *Constitutional History*, I. chs. i.- iv. (History of the Constitution, I 28-123); W. E. H. Lecky, *England in the Eighteenth Century*, IV. ch iv.; Geo. Bancroft, *United States*, VII. chap. xxvii. (last revision, IV. Chs. ix.-xxvii, V.); R. Hildreth, *United States*, IV. 57-373, 411-425, 440-444; Edward Channing, *United States*, 1765-1865, ch iii.; W. M. Sloane, *French War and Revolution* chs. xviii.- xxiv.; H. C. Lodge, *George Washington*, I. chs. v.-xi.; Abiel Holmes, *Annals of America*, II. 199-353; Bryant and Gay, *United States*, III. 377-623, IV. 1-74; Justin Winsor, *Narrative and Critical History*, VI chs ii.-ix., VII. chs. i., ii.; J. R. Green, *English People*, IV. 254-271; Adolphus, *England*, II. 333-433, *passim*; Story, *Commentaries*, §§ 198-217; T. Pitkin, United States, I. 282-422, II. 37-153.

SPECIAL HISTORIES.—G. W. Greene, *Historical View*; R. Frothingham, *Rise of the Republic*, 403-568; John Fiske, *American Revolution*; J. M. Ludlow, *War of American Independence*, chs. v.-viii.; Geo. Pellew, *John Jay*, 59-228; E. J. Lowell, *Hessians*; Charles Borgeaud, *Rise of Modern Democracy*; M. C. Tyler, *Literature of the Revolution*, II.; L. Sabine, *American Loyalists*; H. B. Carrington, *Battles of the Revolution*; W. B. Weeden, *New England*, II. chs. xx, xxi.; W. G. Sumner, *Financier and Finances of the American Revolution*.

CONTEMPORARY ACCOUNTS.—*Journals of Congress, Secret Journals of*

Congress, works and full biographies of the Revolutionary Statesmen; Peter Force, *American Archives*; Jared Sparks, *Correspondence of the Revolution*; F. Wharton, *Diplomatic Correspondence*; John Adams and Abigail Adams, *Familiar Letters*; Tom Paine, *Common Sense*; Crevecoeur, *Letters from an American Farmer* [1770-1781]; J. Anbury, *Travels* [1776-1781]; Chastellux, *Voyage de Newport* [also in translation, 1780-1781]; W. B. Donne, *Correspondence of George III. with Lord North* [1768-1783]; Francis Hopkins, *Essays and Writings*; Philip Freneau, *Poems*; Baroness Riedesel, *Letters and Memoirs.*—Reprints in Niles, *Principles and Acts of the Revolution*; D. R. Goodloe, *Birth of the Republic*, 205-353; Mathew Carey, *Remembrancer*; Frank Moore, *Diary of the American Revolution, Old South Leaflets, American History told by Contemporaries*, II.

35. THE STRENGTH OF THE COMBATANTS (1775).

[Sidenote: Power of Great Britain.]

When we compare the population and resources of the two countries, the defiance of the colonists seems almost foolhardy. In 1775 England, Ireland, and Scotland together had from eight to ten million souls; while the colonies numbered but three millions. Great Britain had a considerable system of manufactures, and the greatest foreign commerce in the world, and rich colonies in every quarter of the globe poured wealth into her lap. What she lacked she could buy. In the year 1775 the home government raised ten million pounds in taxes, and when the time came she was able to borrow hundreds of millions in all the colonies together, two million pounds in money was the utmost that could be raised in a single year by any system of taxes or loans. In 1776 one hundred and thirty cruisers and transports brought the British army to New York: the whole American navy had not more than seventeen vessels. In moral resources Great Britain was decidedly stronger than America. Parliament was divided, but the king was determined. On Oct 15, 1775, he wrote: "Every means of distressing America must meet with my concurrence." Down to 1778 the war was popular in England, and interfered little with her prosperity.

[Sidenote: Weakness of America.]

How was it in America? Canada, the Floridas, the West Indies, and Nova Scotia held off. Of the three millions of population, five hundred thousand were negro slaves, carried no muskets, and caused constant fear of revolt. John Adams has said that more than a third part of the principal men in America were throughout opposed to the Revolution; and of those who agreed with the principles of the Revolution, thousands thought them not worth fighting for. There were rivalries and jealousies between American public men and between the sections. The troops of one New England State refused to serve under officers from another State. The whole power of England could be concentrated upon the struggle, and the Revolution would have been crushed in a single year if the eyes of the English had not been so blinded to the real seriousness of the crisis that they sent small forces and inefficient commanders. England was at peace with all the world, and might naturally expect to prevent the active assistance of the colonies by any other power.

[Sidenote: The two armies.]
[Sidenote: Hessians.]
[Sidenote: Indians.]
[Sidenote: Discipline.]

When the armies are compared, the number and enthusiasm of the Americans by no means made up for the difference of population. On the average, 33,000 men were under the American colors each year; but the army sometimes fell, as at the battle of Princeton, Jan. 2, 1777, to but 5,000. The English had an average of 40,000 troops in the colonies, of whom from 20,000 to 25,000 might have been utilized in a single military operation; and in the crisis of the general European war, about 1780, Great Britain placed 314,000 troops under arms in different parts of the world. The efficiency of the American army was very much diminished by the fact that two kinds of troops were in service,— the Continentals, enlisted by Congress; and the militia, raised by each colony separately. Of these militia, New England, with one fourth of the population of the country, furnished as many as the other colonies put together. The British were able to draw garrisons from other parts of the world, and to fill up gaps with Germans hired like horses; yet, although sold by their sovereign at the contract price of thirty-six dollars per head, and often abused in service, these Hessians made good soldiers, and sometimes saved British armies in critical moments. Another sort of aliens were brought into the contest, first by the Americans, later by the English. These were the Indians. They were intractable in the service of both sides, and determined no important contest; but since the British were the invaders, their use of the Indians combined with that of the Hessians to exasperate the Americans, although they had the same kind of savage allies, and eventually called in foreigners also. In discipline the Americans were far inferior to the English. General Montgomery wrote: "The privates are all generals, but not soldiers;" and Baron Steuben wrote to a Prussian officer a little later: "You say to your soldier, 'Do this,' and he doeth it; but I am obliged to say to mine, 'This is the reason why you ought to do that,' and then he does it." The British officers were often incapable, but they had a military training, and were accustomed to require and to observe discipline. The American officers came in most cases from civil life, had no social superiority over their men, and were so unruly that John Adams wrote in 1777: "They quarrel like cats and dogs. They worry one another like mastiffs, scrambling for rank and pay like apes for nuts."

[Sidenote: Commanders.]

The success of the Revolution was, nevertheless, due to the personal qualities of these officers and their troops, when directed by able commanders. In the early stages of the war the British generals were slow, timid, unready, and inefficient. Putnam, Wayne, Greene, and other American generals were natural soldiers; and in Washington we have the one man who never made a serious blunder, who was never frightened, who never despaired, and whose unflinching confidence was the rallying point of the military forces of the nation.

[Sidenote: Plans of campaign.]

The theatre of the war was more favorable to the British than to the Americans. There were no fortresses, and the coast was everywhere open to the landing of expeditions. The simplest military principle demanded the isolation of New England, the source and centre of the Revolution, from the rest of the colonies. From 1776 the British occupied the town of New York, and they held Canada. A combined military operation from both South and North would give them the valley of the Hudson. The failure of Burgoyne's expedition in 1777 prevented the success of this manoeuvre. The war was then transferred to the Southern colonies, with the intention to roll up the line of defence, as the French line had been rolled up in 1758; but whenever the British attempted to penetrate far into the country from the sea-coast, they were eventually worsted and driven back.

36. THE SECOND CONTINENTAL CONGRESS (1775).

[Sidenote: Conception of a "Congress."]

Before the war could be fought, some kind of civil organization had to be formed. On May 10, 1775, three weeks after the battle of Lexington, the second Continental Congress assembled in Philadelphia, and continued, with occasional adjournments, till May 1, 1781. To the minds of the men of that day a congress was not a legislature, but a diplomatic assembly, a meeting of delegates for conference, and for suggestions to their principals. To be sure, this Congress represented the people, acting through popular conventions, and not the old colonial assemblies; yet those conventions assumed to exercise the powers of government in the colonies, and expected the delegates to report back to them, and to ask for instructions. Nevertheless, the delegates at once began to pass resolutions which were to have effect without any ratification by the legislatures. Of the nine colonies which gave formal instructions to their representatives, all but one directed them to "order" something, or to "determine" something, or to pass "binding" Acts.

[Sidenote: Advisory action.]

Thus Congress began rather as the adviser than as the director of the colonies; but it advised strong measures. On May 30, 1775, a plan of conciliation suggested by Lord North was pronounced "unreasonable and insidious." On the request of the provincial congress of Massachusetts Bay, it recommended that body to "form a temporary colonial government until a governor of his Majesty's appointment will consent to govern the colony according to its charter." June 12, Congress issued a proclamation recommending "a day of public humiliation, fasting, and prayer." Like the First Continental Congress, it framed several petitions and addresses to the British people and to the king of Great Britain. During the first six weeks of its existence, therefore, the Second Continental Congress acted chiefly as the centre for common consultation, and as the agent for joint expostulation.

37. THE NATIONAL GOVERNMENT FORMED (1775).

[Sidenote: War in Massachusetts.]
[Sidenote: National military measures.]

The situation rapidly passed beyond the stage of advice. The people of Massachusetts and the neighboring colonies, on their own motion, had shut up the governor of the colony and his troops in the town of Boston, and were formally besieging him. On June 17 the British made their last sortie, and attacked and defeated the besieging forces at Bunker Hill. Neither the country nor Congress could long stand still. Precisely a week after assembling, Congress voted that certain commerce "must immediately cease." A week later, May 26, they "Resolved, unanimously, that the militia of New York be armed and trained ... to prevent any attempt that may be made to gain possession of the town;" and on June 14 the momentous resolution was reached that "an American continental army should be raised." On the following day George Washington, Esq., of Virginia, "was unanimously selected to command all the continental forces raised or to be raised for the defence of American liberty." In October the fitting out of a little navy and the commissioning of privateers were authorized.

These acts were acts of war such as up to this time had been undertaken only by individual colonies or by the home government. They were, further, acts of united resistance, and in form they pledged the whole country to the establishment of a military force, and the maintenance of hostilities until some accommodation could be reached.

[Sidenote: National diplomacy.]
[Sidenote: Other national powers.]

In other directions the Continental Congress showed similar energy. November 29, 1775, "a Committee of Correspondence with our friends abroad" was ordered, and thus began, the foreign relations of the United States of America. National ambassadors were eventually sent out; no colony presumed to send its own representative across the sea; foreign affairs from this time on were considered solely a matter for the Continental Congress. In like manner, Congress quietly took up most of the other matters which had been acknowledged up to this time to belong to the home government. Congress assumed the control of the frontier Indians, till this time the wards of England. The post-national office had been directed by English authority; Congress took it over. The boundaries and other relations of the colonies had been strictly regulated by the home government; Congress undertook to mediate in boundary disputes. Parliament had controlled trade; Congress threw open American ports to all foreign nations, and prohibited the slave-trade. In financial matters Congress went far beyond any powers ever exercised by England. June 22 it ordered an issue of two million dollars in continental paper currency, and subscriptions to national loans were opened both at home and abroad.

[Sidenote: Basis of national authority.]

This assumption of powers is the more remarkable since their exercise by England had caused the Revolution. The right to raise money by national authority, the right to maintain troops without the consent of the colonies, and the right to enforce regulations on trade,—these were the three disputed points in the English policy of control. They were all exercised by the Continental Congress, and accepted by the colonies. In a word, the Continental Congress constituted a government exercising great sovereign powers. It began with no such authority; it never received such authority until 1781. The war must be fought, the forces of the people must be organized; there was no other source of united power and authority; without formally agreeing to its supremacy, the colonies and the people at large acquiesced, and accepted it as a government.

[Sidenote: Organization of the government.]

For the carrying out of great purposes Congress was singularly inefficient.

The whole national government was composed of a shifting body of representatives elected from time to time by the colonial or State legislatures. It early adopted the system of forming executive committees out of its own number: of these the most important was the Board of War, of which John Adams was the most active member. Later on, it appointed executive boards, of which some or all the members were not in Congress: the most notable example was the Treasury Office of Accounts. Difficult questions of prize and maritime law arose; and Congress established a court, which was only a committee of its own members. In all cases the committees, boards, or officials were created, and could be removed, by Congress. The final authority on all questions of national government in all its forms was simply a majority of colonies or States in the Continental Congress.

38. INDEPENDENCE DECLARED (1776).

[Sidenote: Tendency towards independence.]

Under the direction of Congress and the command of General Washington the siege of Boston was successfully pushed forward during the winter of 1775-76. From the beginning of the struggle to this time two political currents had been running side by side,—the one towards a union of the colonies, the other towards independence. Of these the current of union had run a little faster. Notwithstanding the authority which they had set over themselves, the colonies still professed to be loyal members of the British empire. To be sure, there is a strong smack of insincerity in the protestations poured forth by the assemblies and the second Continental Congress. But John Adams says: "That there existed a general desire of independence of the Crown in any part of America before the Revolution, is as far from the truth as the zenith is from the nadir." Yet Patrick Henry declared as early as September, 1774. that "Government is dissolved. Fleets and armies and the present state of things show that government is dissolved. We are in a state of nature, sir.... All America is thrown into one mass."

[Sidenote: Hesitation.]
[Sidenote: Suggestion of independence.]

From the moment that the Second Continental Congress had ordered the colonies to be put in a state of defence, either independence must come, or thee colonies must submit. No far-seeing man could expect that England would make the concessions which the colonies declared indispensable. Yet for more than a year Congress hesitated to declare publicly that the Americans would not return to obedience. As forgiving and loyal subjects of a king misled by wicked advisers, they still seemed supported by precedent and acting on the rights of Englishmen. Suggestions were made throughout 1775 looking towards independence Thus the New Hampshire Revolutionary Convention declared that "the voice of God and of nature demand of the colonies to look to their own political affairs." In May, 1775, came the resolutions of a committee of Mecklenburg County, North Carolina. In declaring that the government of the colonies had ceased to exist, they were probably not different in spirit from many other resolutions passed by like bodies. On July 8, 1775, Congress sent its last formal petition to the Crown. In it "Your Majesty's faithful subjects" set forth "the impossibility of reconciling the usual appearance of respect with a just Attention to our own preservation against those artful and cruel Enemies who abuse your royal Confidence and Authority for the Purpose of effecting our destruction." Congress was determined to wait until the petition had been received. On the day when it was to have been handed to the king, appeared a royal proclamation announcing that open and armed rebellion was going on in America.

[Sidenote: Congress determined.]

The news of the fate of the petition reached Philadelphia on October 31. The hesitation of Congress was at an end. Three days later it resolved to recommend the people of New Hampshire to establish their own government. The next day similar advice was given to South Carolina, with the promise of continental troops to defend the colony. Here for the first time was an official recognition of the fact that the colonies stood no longer under English control. It was an assertion that independence existed, and the steps towards a formal declaration were rapid.

[Sidenote: Independence decided on.]
[Sidenote: Declaration of Independence.]
[Sidenote: Rights of man.]

In this as in other similar crises Congress waited to find out the wish of the colonial legislatures. By May 15, 1776, the opinion of so many colonies had been received in favor of a declaration of independence that Congress voted, "That it is necessary that the exercise of every kind of authority under the Crown of Great Britain should be totally suppressed." Congress was now committed; and during the next few weeks the form of the declaration was the important question for discussion. Throughout the country, resolutions in favor of independence were passed by legislatures, conventions, and public meetings. On July 4, 1776, Congress adopted a solemn Declaration of Independence. Like the statement of grievances of 1765 and the declaration of 1774, this great state paper, drawn by the nervous pen of Thomas Jefferson, set forth the causes of ill-feeling toward Great Britain. First comes a statement of certain self-evident truths, a reiteration of those rights of man upon which Otis had dwelt in his speech of 1761. Then follows an enumeration of grievances put forward in this crisis as their justification in the face of the world; yet of the twenty-nine specifications of oppressive acts, not more than five were manifestly illegal according to the prevailing system of English law. So far as the Declaration of Independence shows, liberality and concession on the part of England might even then have caused the Revolution to halt.

[Sidenote: Assertion of independence.]

Another part of the Declaration is a statement that "These United Colonies are free and independent states, dissolved from all allegiance to Great Britain, and have the powers of sovereign states." In form and spirit this clause does not create independent states, but declares that they are already independent. Independence in no wise changed the status or character of the Continental Congress: it continued to direct military operations and foreign negotiations, to deal with the Indians, and to regulate national finances. The immediate effect of the Declaration of Independence was that it obliged every American to take sides for or against the Revolution. No one could any longer entertain the delusion that he could remain loyal to Great Britain while making war upon her. It was, therefore, a great encouragement to the patriots, who speedily succeeded, in most colonies, in driving out or silencing the loyalists. There is a tradition that another member of Congress said to Franklin at this time, "We must all hang together." "Yes," replied Franklin, "we must all hang together, or we shall all hang separately."

39. NEW STATE GOVERNMENTS FORMED (1775-1777).

[Sidenote: Is the Union older than the States?]
[Sidenote: Revolutionary governments.]

A practical result of the Declaration of Independence was that from that day each colony assumed the name of State; and the union changed its name of "The United Colonies" to the proud title of "The United States of America." Were the new States essentially different from the colonies? This is one of the insoluble questions connected with the formation of the Union. Calhoun later declared that the Declaration of Independence changed the colonies from provinces subject to Great Britain to States subject to nobody. Lincoln in his message of July 4, 1861, said that "The Union gave each of them whatever of independence and liberty it has. The Union is older than any of the States, and in fact it created them as States." That the States did not regard independence as freeing them from their relation to Congress may be seen from the fact that their new governments were formed under the direction or with the permission of Congress. The outbreak of the Revolution in 1775 had suddenly destroyed the constitutional governments with which the colonies were familiar. Everywhere courts were prevented from sitting, and governors were impeded or driven out. In order to organize resistance and also to carry out the ordinary purposes of government, in each colony there arose a revolutionary and unauthorized body, known as the Provincial Convention, or Provincial Congress, which took upon itself all the powers of government. The new arrangement was unsatisfactory to a people accustomed to orderly government and to stable administrations. They turned to Congress for advice. At first Congress suggested only temporary arrangements. In November, 1775, it encouraged the colonies to form permanent organizations, and on May 10, 1776, it advised them all to "adopt such governments as shall … best conduce to the happiness and safety of their constituents in particular, and America in general."

[Sidenote: State constitutions.]

Acting under these suggestions, the colonies had already begun before July 4, 1776, to draw up written instruments of government. In two States, Connecticut and Rhode Island, the old charters were so democratic that with a few slight changes of phraseology they were sufficient for the new conditions. In all other colonies the opportunity was taken to alter the familiar machinery. The Provincial Conventions, or, in one case, a special Constitutional Convention, drew up a constitution and put it into force. Since the governor had been unpopular, in several cases his place was supplied by an executive council. The courts were reorganized on the old basis, and the judges were left appointive. The first constitution to be formed was that of New Hampshire. January 5, 1776, the Provincial Congress voted "to take up civil government as follows." By 1777, nine other new constitutions had thus been provided. They mark an epoch in the constitutional history of the world. The great English charters and the Act of Settlement were constitutional documents; but they covered only a small part of the field of government. Almost for the first time in history, representatives of the people were assembled to draw up systematic and complete constitutions, based on the consent of the governed.

[Sidenote: Constitution of Massachusetts.]

Singularly enough, the last State to form a definite constitution was Massachusetts. Till 1776, that colony claimed to be acting under a charter which England was ignoring. The General Court then chose councillors of its own to act as an executive. Dissensions broke out, and a considerable body of the people of Berkshire County repudiated this government and demanded a new constitution. In 1780 a constitution was drafted by a convention assembled solely for that purpose, and, for the first time in the history of America, the work of a convention was submitted for ratification by a popular vote.

40. THE FIRST PERIOD OF THE WAR (1775-1778).

[Sidenote: British military policy.]

Two policies presented themselves to the British government at the beginning of the war. They might have used their great naval strength alone, blockading the coast and sealing every harbor; thus the colonies would be cut off from the rest of the world, and allowed to enjoy their independence until they were ready to return to their allegiance. The alternative of invasion was chosen; but it was useless, with the forces available, to occupy any considerable part of the interior. By threatening various parts of the coast, the Americans could be obliged to make many detachments of their few troops. By occupying the principal towns, such as Newport, New York, Philadelphia, Charleston, and Savannah, the centres of resistance could be broken up, the loyalists encouraged, and bases established, from which the main American armies were to be reached and destroyed. On the sea the navy was to be used to ruin American commerce and to prevent the importation of supplies.

[Sidenote: American military policy.]

The policy of the Americans was, not to attempt to defend the whole coast, but to keep as large a number of troops as they could raise together in one body, as a substantial army; to defend their land communication from New England to the South; and by standing ready for operations in the field, to prevent the British from making any large detachments. They must hold as much of their territory as possible, in order to prevent defections; and they must take every advantage of their defensive position, in order at length to hem in and capture the opposing armies on the coast, as they did finally at Yorktown. The open gate through the Hudson they strove to close early in the war by invasion of Canada. On the sea all they could do was to capture supplies and destroy commerce, and by the ravages of their privateers to inspire the enemy with respect.

[Sidenote: Plans frustrated.]

Neither party was able to carry out its plans. The British took all the principal seaports, but were able to hold none, except New York, to the end of the war. First Burgoyne and later Cornwallis made a determined attempt to penetrate far into the interior, and both were captured. On the other hand, the Americans could not shake off the main central army, and there was danger to

66

the very last that the British would beat them in one pitched battle which would decide the war.

[Sidenote: Campaign of 1776.]
[Sidenote: Princeton and Trenton.]

Military operations began with several surprises to the advantage of the colonists. They took Ticonderoga and invested Boston before the British government believed that a fight was impending. An expedition to Canada failed in 1775-76, but Boston fell. Down to the day of the Declaration of Independence the advantage was clearly with the colonists. The hard, stern struggle of the war began in August, 1776, with the arrival of the British in the harbor of New York. The Americans were attacked on Long Island, and obliged to retreat across the river; when the militia were attacked on that side Washington says: "They ran away in the greatest confusion, without firing a shot." Eye-witnesses relate that "His Excellency was left on the ground within eighty yards of the enemy, so vexed with the infamous conduct of the troops that he sought death rather than life." The American army with difficulty escaped northward, and Washington was obliged to abandon the important line of the Hudson, and to retreat before the British towards Philadelphia. The campaign of 1776 had gone against the Americans. Suddenly out of the gloom and despair came two brilliant little victories. Crossing the Delaware on Christmas night, 1776, Washington struck and beat parts of the British forces at Trenton and Princeton. They retired, and the patriots held Philadelphia during the winter.

[Sidenote: Campaign of 1777.]
[Sidenote: Steadfastness of the American army.]

In the spring of 1777 Howe transferred his troops by sea to the Chesapeake, beat the Americans, occupied Philadelphia, and lay in that city till the next year. It was a dear success. While the main British force was thus withdrawn from New York, an attempt was made to pierce the colonies from the northward. Burgoyne slowly descended during the summer of 1777; but, unsupported by Howe, on October 17 he was obliged to surrender his whole army at Saratoga. This victory roused the spirit and courage of the new nation, and strengthened the hands of the envoys who were begging for French alliance. It enabled Washington to maintain a small army in winter quarters at Valley Forge, twenty miles from Philadelphia. Whatever the early faults of American troops and officers, they had learned to obey and to suffer as soldiers, patriots, and heroes. At one time barely five thousand men were fit for duty. "Naked and starving as they are." wrote Washington, "we cannot sufficiently admire the incomparable patience and fidelity of the soldiers." With the first days of the year 1778 came the darkest hour of the Revolution.

The little army, the indispensable hope, was beginning to thin out; the finances of the country were desperate; nine hundred American vessels had been captured; an apathy had fallen upon the country. Yet light was beginning to dawn: Steuben, the German, had begun to introduce the discipline which was to make the American army a new and powerful instrument; Lafayette had brought the sympathy of France and his own substantial services; more than all, during these dark days the American envoys were concluding the treaty with France which was to save the Union.

41. FOREIGN RELATIONS (1776-1780).

[Sidenote: Interest of France.]
[Sidenote: English plan of reconciliation.]

From the beginning of the American struggle the French government had looked on with interest and pleasure. The arrogance of England during the previous war and during the negotiations of 1763 had excited a general dislike throughout Europe. When, in June, 1776, Silas Deane appeared at Paris as the American envoy, he found, not recognition, but at least sympathy and assistance. Beaumarchais, a play-writer and adventurer, was made an unofficial agent of France; and through him arms and supplies from royal arsenals came into the hands of the Americans. More to the purpose, money was placed at the disposal of the envoys. In 1776 a million francs were thus secured; in 1777 two millions. The arrival of Franklin in Paris in December, 1776, increased the American influence, and negotiations were entered upon for a treaty. The English cabinet, understanding the danger of a double war, made a last effort at reconciliation with the colonies. In 1778 Lord North brought forward an act declaring that Parliament "will not impose any duty, taxes, or assessment whatever ... in North America or the West Indies, except only such duties as it may be expedient to impose for the regulation of commerce, the net produce of such duties to be always paid and applied to and for the use of the colony in which the same shall be levied." The principle which had been so strenuously asserted by the home government from 1765 to 1774 was now abandoned; it might reasonably be expected that the violent acts of Massachusetts directed against taxation would be forgiven. Commissioners were sent to America with almost unlimited powers to remove the grievances of the colonies, and to restore peace and concord.

[Sidenote: Alliance with France.]

Before they were appointed, a treaty of alliance had been made, Feb. 6, 1778, between the United States and France. With it went a treaty of commerce, insuring reciprocal trade with France. The colonies, which in 1758 had been fiercely fighting the French as their hereditary enemies, were now delighted at the prospect of their support. The peace commission remained in America from June to October; but though they offered every concession short of absolute independence, the Americans remained firm, and entered with confidence on the campaign of 1778.

42. THE WAR ENDED (1778-1782).

[Sidenote: Stubbornness of George III.]
[Sidenote: Campaign of 1778.]

The European crisis was favorable to the Americans; the British government had hitherto been unable to reduce them; the Germans would furnish no more mercenaries; a strong minority in Parliament opposed the American war; France had declared war in March, 1778, and Spain was about to follow. Proper reinforcements could not be sent to America. The country cried out for Pitt, who had declared himself positively against American independence. The king resolutely refused. "No advantage to this country, no personal danger to myself," said he, "can ever make me address myself to Lord Chatham or to any other branch of the opposition." Pitt died on May 11, and the chance of a statesmanlike policy disappeared. When the French fleet, with four thousand troops, appeared in American waters in July, 1778, Washington formed the hopeful plan of driving the British out of the country. Philadelphia had been abandoned by Clinton, acting under orders of the British government. Only two places were left in the possession of the British,—New York city and Newport, Rhode Island. The combined American and French expedition against Newport was a failure, although, as Washington said, "it would have given the finishing blow to British pretensions of sovereignty over this country."

[Sidenote: The war continued.]

Meanwhile, in England the king was imposing his relentless will upon a ministry tired of the war, and upon the English people. It was the climax of George the Third's effort to escape from the principle of Parliamentary responsibility. "This country," he said, "will never regain a proper tone unless ministers, as in the reign of King William, will not mind now and then being in a minority." In April, 1779, Spain allied herself with France, and the combined fleets of those two powers obtained the mastery of the seas. Paul Jones, with a little fleet under an American commission, captured two British men-of-war, almost in sight of the English coast.

[Sidenote: Southern campaign.]

A new plan was formed for an American campaign in 1779. Forces were directed against Georgia and South Carolina,—States in which there were many loyalists. Savannah was taken, Charleston was assailed, and the expedition under Cornwallis penetrated far into North Carolina. Yet at the end of 1780 the British held, besides New York, only the provinces of South Carolina and Georgia. In September, 1780, Benedict Arnold all but delivered to the hands of the enemy the important fortress of West Point. He was weary of the struggle, and anxious to secure his own safety.

[Sidenote: Surrender of Yorktown.]

With renewed spirit the Americans in 1781 took the offensive in the Carolinas under Greene. Cornwallis moved northward to the peninsula of Yorktown. The moment had come. By a rapid movement of Washington's army and the effective cooperation of the French fleet, Cornwallis was trapped at Yorktown; and on Oct. 19, 1781, he surrendered, with eight thousand men. It was the first decided victory which Washington had himself gained. It made evident to England the hopelessness of continuing the contest; and in November, 1782, peace was made.

[Sidenote: Reasons for American success.]

The Revolutionary war was successful because the English underestimated the strength of the movement at the beginning, because the English commanders were incapable, and because in the later period, when the British were aroused, their strength was diverted by the dangerous European war. It was gained finally by the firmness and resolution of the people, and that resolution is typified in Washington. His patience and endurance, his ability to hold in check large forces with small armies imperfectly equipped, his power to keep the country up to the support of the war, mark him as one of the world's great military commanders.

43. FINANCES OF THE REVOLUTION (1775-1783).

[Sidenote: Resources.]

The successful termination of the war is the more remarkable because it was fought by a government almost without means, and finally without credit. The saddest part of the suffering at Valley Forge is that it was unnecessary. There was always food and clothing in the country, but Congress had no money to buy it. Congress had no power to lay taxes, and the colonies, most of which were spending large sums on their own militia, were not disposed to supply the general treasury. The pay of the Continental troops and of the general officers, the furnishing of equipments and stores, the support of foreign embassies, were burdens that must be borne, and Congress must find the means.

[Sidenote: Continental currency.]

The most successful and the most disastrous resource was the issue of paper-money. When, in June, 1775, it was proposed to meet the general expenses by putting forth two millions in Continental notes, there was but feeble objection. It was the only way of raising money which seemed to cost nobody anything. In the course of a year four millions more followed. Congress, with commendable foresight, called upon each colony to pay in a sum sufficient to retire its proportion of the issue. Nothing was paid, and the printing-press was again put in motion, until in January, 1779, fifty millions were issued at a time. In November, 1779, the limit of two hundred millions was reached. In order to float these notes the States passed acts making them a legal tender; but at the same time they were themselves issuing large sums in a similar currency. Counterfeits abounded, but it soon became a matter of little difference whether a bill was good or bad, since the best was worth so little. From the time of the capture of New York by the British in 1776 the notes began to fall. In 1778 the news of the French alliance caused a little rise; but in 1781 the bills fell to a point where a thousand dollars exchanged for one dollar in specie, and a Philadelphia wag made out of the notes a blanket for his dog. The Continental currency was never redeemed, and was consequently a forced tax on those who were least able to pay, since every holder lost by its depreciation while in his hands.

[Sidenote: Loans.]

The absolutely necessary expenditures, without which no army could make head against the British, were from twenty to twenty-five million specie dollars each year. Of this the Continental bills furnished on an average some eight or ten millions. Another method of raising money was that of borrowing on funded loans. Great schemes were put forth. The United States were to borrow at four per cent; they were to borrow two millions; they were to borrow ten millions; they were to borrow twenty millions. The result was that in three years $181,000 was thus loaned, and up to the end of the war but $1,600,000,—hardly a hundredth part of the necessary means. Failing to raise money directly, recourse was bad to the so-called loan-office certificates. These were issued to creditors of the government, and bore interest. The greater part of the military supplies were paid for in this extravagant and demoralizing fashion, and in 1789 they had to be settled, with accumulated interest amounting to nearly fifty per cent. Better success was had in Europe. No private banker would lend money to a set of rebels not recognized by any government as independent, but the French and Spanish governments were willing to advance both money and stores. In this way the United States received about three million dollars.

[Sidenote: Requisitions.]

When it was evident that the domestic loan had failed, Congress called upon the States to furnish five millions of dollars, apportioned among them according to their importance. These requisitions were repeated at intervals during the Revolution, but always with the same effect. Not a fourth part of the sums asked for was paid by the States. A system of "specific supplies" was adopted in 1778, by which the States were allowed to pay their quotas in kind. It added a new source of confusion, and brought no more revenue.

[Sidenote: Miscellaneous resources.]

Every device that the government could put into operation for raising money was eventually tried. A lottery brought considerable sums into the treasury, the supplies for the army were seized at Valley Forge and elsewhere, and paid for in certificates. Bills were drawn on foreign ministers for funds which it was hoped they might have in hand by the time the bills reached them, and the government bought, and sent abroad to meet its indebtedness, cargoes of tobacco and other products.

[Sidenote: Speculation.]

The financial burdens of the government were increased by a spirit of extravagance, speculation, and even of corruption. Washington wrote, "Unless extortion, forestalling, and other practices which have ... become exceedingly prevalent can meet with proper checks, we must inevitably sink under such a load of accumulated oppressions." The whole cost of the war is estimated at one hundred and thirty-five millions. Of this about one hundred millions had been raised through the Continental bills and other devices. About thirty-five millions remained as a national debt.

44. INTERNAL DIFFICULTIES (1775-1782).

[Sidenote: Weakness of Congress.]

That Congress was able to make no better provision for the finances was due to a decline in its prestige rather than to a lack of interest in the war. Some of the ablest members were drawn into military service, or sent on foreign missions. The committee system made it inefficient, and it was difficult to bring it to a decision upon the most important matters. In vain did Washington storm, and implore it to act quickly and intelligently on military matters of great moment. Its relations with the States changed as the war advanced. Dec.

7, 1776; Congress made Washington for a time almost a dictator. In 1779 the Virginia legislature formally denied that it was "answerable to Congress for not agreeing with any of its recommendations."

[Sidenote: The loyalists.]

To the frequent unfriendly relations with the States was added the constant conflict with the loyalists. Throughout the colonies the adherents to England or the sympathizers with the English government were under grave suspicion. Many of them left the country; some enlisted with the British, and returned to fight against their own land. A body of loyalists led the hostile Indians into the Wyoming valley to torture and to murder. The loyalists who remained at home were often the medium of communication with the British lines. Some of them, like Dr. Mather Byles of Boston, and George Watson of Plymouth, were allowed to remain on condition that they held their tongues. Washington was so exasperated with them that he termed them "execrable parricides." In every State the loyalists were feared and hated. When the British invaded the country, the loyalists joined them; when the British were repulsed, thousands of them were obliged to abandon their homes.

[Sidenote: Dissensions in States.]

The finances of the States were as much disturbed as those of the Union. Their paper-money issues shared the same fate. Their debts, funded and unfunded, increased. They were harassed by internal divisions, even among the patriots. In Massachusetts, Berkshire County remained until 1780 practically independent, and the county convention did not scruple to declare to the General Court that there were "other States which will, we doubt not, as bad as we are, gladly receive us."

45. FORMATION OF A CONSTITUTION (1776-1781).

[Sidenote: Preliminaries of a constitution.]
[Sidenote: Articles submitted.]

One cause of the weakness of Congress and the disorders in the States was the want of a settled national government. The Continental Congress understood that it was but a makeshift, and on the day when a committee was formed to frame a Declaration of Independence, another committee was appointed to draw up Articles of Confederation. It reported July 12, 1776; but the moment discussion began, it was seen that there were almost insuperable difficulties. The first was the question whether each State should have one vote, as in the existing government, or whether each should cast a number of votes in proportion to its population; the second question was how revenue should be raised and assessed; the third was how the western country should be held; the fourth was what powers should be given to the general government, and what retained by the States; the fifth, how disputes within the Union should be settled. When, on Nov. 15, 1777, Congress had finally adopted a draft of Articles of Confederation, the decline of its power and influence was reflected in the proposed instrument of government. On the question of representation, the rule of vote by States was continued. The only taxation was a formal system of requisitions on the States. Here the question of slavery was unexpectedly brought in: the Northern States desired to apportion the taxes according to total population, including slaves. "Our slaves are our property" said Lynch, of South Carolina; "If that is debated, there is an end of the Confederation. Being our property, why should they be taxed more than sheep?" A compromise was reached, by which requisitions were to be assessed in proportion to the value of lands in the several States. The question of control of territory was not distinctly settled by the articles. The powers to be conferred upon the Confederation were practically limited to war, peace, and foreign affairs. A cumbrous system of arbitration courts was established for disputes between States, but there was no machinery for settling quarrels between States and the national government.

[Sidenote: The Western lands.]
[Sidenote: Maryland will not ratify.]
[Sidenote: Articles in force.]

Congress had spent a year and a half in forming the Articles of Confederation. The States took three and a half years in ratifying them. Ten States early signified their willingness to adopt them. Three others stood out because the Western lands were left in dispute. In 1776 when the British authority had been declared no longer existent in the colonies, each of the new States considered itself possessed of all the British lands which at any time had been included within its boundary; and in 1778 Virginia had captured the few British posts northwest of the Ohio, and had shortly after created that immense region, now the seat of five powerful States, into the "County of Illinois." On the other hand, it was strongly urged that the Western territory had been secured through a war undertaken by all the colonies for the whole country, and that the lands ought to be reserved to reward the continental soldiers, and to secure the debt of the United States. For the sake of union, two of the three dissatisfied commonwealths agreed to the Articles of Confederation. One State alone stood firm: Maryland, whose boundaries could not be so construed as to include any part of the lands, refused to ratify unless the claims of Virginia were disallowed; Virginia and Connecticut proposed to close the Union without Maryland; Virginia even opened a land office for the sale of a part of the territory in dispute; but threats had no effect.

New York, which had less to gain from the Western territory than the other claimants, now came forward with the cession of her claims to the United States; and Virginia, on Jan. 2, 1781, agreed to do the like. On March 1, 1781, it was announced that Maryland had ratified the Articles of Confederation, and they were duly put into force. From that date the Congress, though little changed in personnel or in powers, was acting under a written constitution, and the States had bound themselves to abide by it.

46. PEACE NEGOTIATED (1779-1782).

[Sidenote: Instructions of 1779.]
[Sidenote: Instructions of 1781.]

Thus the settlement of the final terms of peace fell to the new government, but rather as a heritage than as a new task. Instructions issued by Congress in 1779 had insisted, as a first essential, on an acknowledgment by Great Britain of the independence of the United States. Next, adequate boundaries were to be provided; the United States must extend as far west as the Mississippi, as far south as the thirty-first parallel, and as far north as Lake Nipissing. The third desideratum was undisturbed fishery rights on the banks of Newfoundland. Finally, it was expected that a treaty of commerce would be yielded by Great Britain after the peace was made. In 1781 Virginia, alarmed by Cornwallis's invasion, succeeded in carrying a very different set of instructions. The only essential was to be the substantial admission that America was independent; in all else the treaty was to be made in a manner satisfactory to the French minister of foreign affairs.

[Sidenote: The king consents to peace.]
[Sidenote: Independence.]
[Sidenote: Boundary.]
[Sidenote: Instructions ignored.]

Before peace could be reached it was necessary to break down the iron opposition of the king. On Feb. 28, 1781 Conway's motion, looking to the cessation of the war, was adopted by Parliament. "The fatal day has come," said the king. It was not merely his American policy which had failed; the party of the "King's Friends" was beaten; North resigned; and after twelve years of strenuous opposition, the king was obliged to accept a Whig ministry, which he detested, and to let it negotiate for peace. A part of the ministry still cherished the delusion that the Americans would accept terms which did not leave them independent. The firmness of the American envoys was effectual; a royal commission was at last addressed to Oswald, authorizing him to treat with "the commissioners of the United States of America" in Paris. Then came the important question of boundary. Without the thirteen colonies the possession of the Floridas was of little value to England, and they had been reduced by a Spanish expedition in 1781; they were therefore returned to Spain. For a long time the English insisted that a neutral belt of Indian territory should be created west of the mountains. That point was finally waived; the Americans withdrew their pretensions to the territory north of Lake Erie; and the St. Lawrence River system, from the western end of Lake Superior to the forty-fifth parallel, was made the boundary. From the forty-fifth parallel to the sea, the boundary was described as following the "highlands which divide those rivers that empty themselves into the St. Lawrence from those which fall into the Atlantic Ocean." The country was little known; the commissioners were probably confused; and the ground was thus prepared for a dispute which lasted fifty-nine years. In the course of the negotiations the American ambassadors, Jay, Adams, Franklin, and Laurens, became suspicious of the French court. There is now some reason for believing that Vergennes, the French minister, had dealt honorably with the American interests, and could have secured excellent terms. "Would you break your instructions?" asked one of the fellow-commissioners of Jay. "I would," he replied, "as I would break this pipe." Thenceforward the Americans dealt directly and solely with the English envoys.

[Sidenote: The Mississippi.]
[Sidenote: The fisheries.]

The next question to be settled was the claim of the English to the navigation of the Mississippi, which was supposed to reach northward into British territory. It was yielded; the Americans, however, received no corresponding right of navigation through Spanish territory to the sea. Next came the fisheries. As colonists the New Englanders had always enjoyed the right to fish upon the Newfoundland banks, and to land at convenient spots to cure their fish. Adams, representing New England, insisted that "the right of fishing" should be distinctly stated; he carried his point.

[Sidenote: Loyalists.]
[Sidenote: Debts.]
[Sidenote: Slaves.]
[Sidenote: Treaty signed.]

The main difficulties disposed of, three troublesome minor points had to be adjusted. The first was the question of loyalists. They had suffered from their attachment to the British government; they had been exiled; their estates had been confiscated, their names made a by-word. The British government first insisted, and then pleaded, that the treaty should protect these persons if they chose to return to their former homes. The Americans would agree only that

76

Congress should "earnestly recommend" to the thirteen legislatures to pass Relief Acts. Then came the question of private debts due to the British merchants at the outbreak of the Revolution, and still unpaid. Some of the American envoys objected to reviving these obligations; but Adams, when he arrived, set the matter at rest by declaring that he had "no notion of cheating anybody." Finally came the question of the treatment of the slaves who had taken refuge with the British armies; and the English commissioners agreed that the British troops should withdraw "without causing any destruction or the carrying away any negroes or other property of the American inhabitants." On Nov. 30, 1782, a provisional treaty was signed; but it was not until Sept. 3, 1783 after the peace between France and England had been adjusted, that the definitive treaty was signed, in precisely the same terms.

With great difficulty a quorum was assembled, and on Jan. 14, 1784, it was duly ratified by Congress. The treaty was a triumph for American diplomacy. "It is impossible," says Lecky, the ablest historian of this period, "not to be struck with the skill, hardihood, and good fortune that marked the American negotiations. Everything the United States could with any show of plausibility demand from England, they obtained."

47. POLITICAL EFFECTS OF THE WAR.

[Sidenote: American union.]

Thus in seven years America had advanced from the condition of a body of subordinate colonies to that of a nation. Furthermore, the people, who at the beginning of the struggle were scattered and separated, and who scarcely knew each other, were now united under a government; the Confederation, however weak, was the strongest federation then in existence. The people had learned the lesson of acting together in a great national crisis, and of accepting the limitations upon their governments made necessary by the central power.

[Sidenote: Union not perfected.]

The spirit of the new nation was now to be subjected to a test more severe than that of the Revolution. Danger banded the colonies together during the war. Would they remain together during peace? Sectional jealousies had broken out in Congress and in camp; and in the crisis of 1777 an effort had been made to displace Washington. There had been repeated instances of treachery among military officers and among foreign envoys. The States were undoubtedly much nearer together than the colonies had been; they had accepted a degree of control from the general government which they had refused from England; but they were not used to accept the resolutions of Congress as self-operative. Their conception of national government was still that national legislation filtrated from Congress to the State legislatures, and through that medium to the people.

[Sidenote: Frontier difficulties.]

The interior of the country was in a confused and alarming state. The territorial settlement with the States had only begun, and was to be the work of years. The Indians were a stumbling-block which must be removed from the path of the settlers. Within the States there were poverty, taxation, and disorder, and a serious discontent.

[Sidenote: Common institutions.]

Nevertheless, the system of the colonies was a system of union. The State governments all rested on the same basis of revolution and defiance of former established law; but when they separated from England they preserved those notions of English private and public law which had distinguished the colonies. The laws and the governments of the States were everywhere similar. The States were one in language, in religion, in traditions, in the memories of a common struggle, and in political and economic interests.

[Sidenote: Trade hampered.]

Commercially, however, the situation of the country was worse than it had been in three quarters of a century. Though the fisheries had been saved by the efforts of Adams, the market for the surplus fish was taken away. As colonies they had enjoyed the right to trade with other British colonies; as an independent nation they had only those rights which England chose to give. For a time the ministry seemed disposed to make a favorable commercial treaty; but in 1783 an Order in Council was issued cutting off the Americans from the West Indian trade; and it was not until 1818 that they recovered it.

[Sidenote: Republican government encouraged.] A great political principle had been strengthened by the success of the Revolution: republican government had been revived in a fashion unknown since ancient times. The territory claimed by Virginia was larger than the island of Great Britain. The federal republic included an area nearly four times as large as that of France. In 1782 Frederick of Prussia told the English ambassador that the United States could not endure, "since a republican government had never been known to exist for any length of time where the territory was not limited and concentred." The problem was a new one; but in communities without a titled aristocracy, which had set themselves against the power of a monarch, and which had long been accustomed to self-government, the problem was successfully worked out. The suffrage was still limited to the holders of land;

but the spirit of the Revolution looked towards abolishing all legal distinctions between man and man; and the foundation of later democracy, with its universal suffrage, was thus already laid.

[Sidenote: Influence of rights of man.]

The influence of the republican spirit upon the rest of the world was not yet discerned; but the United States had established for themselves two principles which seriously affected other nations. If English colonies could by revolution relieve themselves from the colonial system of England, the French and Spanish colonies might follow that example; and forty years later not one of the Spanish continental colonies acknowledged the authority of the home government. The other principle was that of the rights of man. The Declaration of Independence contained a list of rights such as were familiar to the colonists of England, but were only theories elsewhere. The success of the Revolution was, therefore, a shock to the system of privilege and of class exemptions from the common burdens, which had lasted since feudal times. The French Revolution of 1789 was an attempt to apply upon alien ground the principles of the American Revolution.

CHAPTER V.

48. REFERENCES

BIBLIOGRAPHIES.—Justin Winsor, *Narrative and Critical History*, VI. 745, VII. 199-236, 527-543, VIII. 491;, notes to Curtis, Bancroft, McMaster, and Pitkin; W. F. Foster, *References to the Constitution*, 12-14; J. J. Lalor, *Cyclopedia*, I. 577; Channing and Hart, *Guide*, §§ 142, 149-153.

HISTORICAL MAPS.—Nos. 1, 3, this volume (*Epoch Maps*, Nos. 6, 7); Labberton, *Atlas*, lxvi.; Rhode, *Atlas*, No. xxviii.; Johnston, *History of the United States for Schools*, 133; Gordon *American Revolution*, I. frontispiece; B. A. Hinsdale, *Old Northwest*, I. 188, 201 (reprinted from MacCoun's *Historical Geography*), also I. frontispiece, and II. 393; Justin Winsor, *Narrative and Critical History*, VII. 140; school histories of Channing, Johnston, Scudder Thomas.

GENERAL ACCOUNTS.—Joseph Story, *Commentaries*, §§ 218-271; R. Hildreth, *United States*, III, 374-481; T. Pitkin, II. 9-36, 154-218; H. Von Hoist, *United States*, I. 1-46; Geo. Tucker, *United States*, I. 291-347; Justin Winsor, *Narrative and Critical History*, VII. ch. iii.; J. T. Morse, *Franklin*, 216-420; Abiel Holmes, *Annals of America*, II. 353-371; J. Schouler, *United States*, I. 1-30; Bryant and Gay, *Popular History*, IV. 79-99; F. A. Walker *Making of a Nation*, ch. 1; Edward Channing, *United States 1761-1865*. ch. iv.

SPECIAL HISTORIES.—G. T. Curtis *Constitutional History*, chs. v.-xiv. (*History of the Constitution* I. 214-347); George Bancroft, *United States* (last revision), VI. 5-194, *History of the Constitution*, I. 1- 266; John Fiske, *Critical Period*, 1-186; J. B. McMaster, *United States*, I. 103-416; J. F. Jameson *Essays on the Constitution*; T. Pitkin, *United States*, I. 283-422, II. 223; William B. Weeden, *New England*, II. chs. xxii., xxiii.; W. G. Sumner, *Financier and Finances*, II. chs. xvi.-xxvii.; B. A. Hinsdale, *Old Northwest*, chs. ix.-xvi.; H. B. Adams, *Maryland's Influence*; W. Hill, *First Stages of the Tariff Policy*; S. Sato, *Public Land Question*; Theodore Roosevelt. *Winning of the West*, III.

CONTEMPORARY ACCOUNTS.—*Journals of Congress*; *Secret Journals*; Madison's notes in H. D. Gilpin, *Papers of James Madison*, and in *Elliot's Debates*, V.; letters of Washington, Madison, John Jay, Hamilton, and

Franklin, in their works; Thomas Paine, *Public Good*; Noah Webster, *Sketches of American Policy*; Pelatiah Webster, *Dissertation on the Political Union*; Brissot de Warville's *Examen Critique* [1784], and *Nouveau Voyage* [1788], (also in translation); Thomas Jefferson, *Notes on Virginia.*—Reprints in *American History told by Contemporaries*, II., American History Leaflets, Nos. 20, 22, 28.

49. THE UNITED STATES IN 1781.

[Sidenote: Army.]
[Sidenote: Territory.]

The task thrown upon Congress in 1781 would have tried the strongest government in existence. An army of more than ten thousand men was under arms, and must be kept up until peace was formally declared, and then must be paid off. The territorial claims of the States and of the Union were still in confusion. Virginia roused the suspicion of the small States by making the promised cession in terms which Congress could not accept, and the other States had made no motion towards yielding their claims. Relations with the Indians were still confused. Superintendents of Indian affairs had been appointed, and in 1778 a treaty was negotiated with the Creeks; but the States, particularly Pennsylvania and Georgia, continued to make their own arrangements with Indian tribes.

[Sidenote: Finances.]
[Sidenote: Commerce.]
[Sidenote: General weakness.]

The finances of the country seemed to have reached their lowest ebb. An attempt was made to float a new issue of continental money at one dollar for forty of the old bills The new obligations speedily sank to the level of the old, and the country was practically bankrupt. The aid of the French was all that kept the government afloat (§ 43). The return of peace was expected to restore American commerce to its old prosperity; but having gone to war principally because colonial commerce with other countries was restricted, the Americans found themselves deprived of their old freedom of trade with England. They were subject to discriminating duties in English ports, and were excluded from the direct trade with the English West Indies, which had been the chief resource the colonial ship- owners. The State governments were in debt, embarrassed, and beset with the social difficulties which come in the train of war. The disbanded troops were not accustomed to regular employment or to a quiet life; taxes were heavy and odious; the far Western settlements clamored to be set free from the States to which they belonged.

Above all, the national government was weak, inefficient, and little respected by the army or the people at large.

60. FORM OF THE GOVERNMENT (1781-1788.)

[Sidenote: Congress.]

The first and fundamental defect of the government was in the organization of Congress. The Continental Congress had been a head without a body; under the Articles of Confederation, Congress was a body without a head. A single assembly continued to be the source of all national legislative, executive, and judicial power (§ 37). As though to prevent the country from getting the benefit of experience, no man could remain a member of Congress for more than three years in succession. The delegates of each State continued to cast jointly one vote; if only one member were present, the vote of a State was not counted; if but two were present, they might produce a tie. On important questions the approval of nine States was necessary, and often less than that number had voting representatives on the floor. Amendment was impossible, except by consent of all the State legislatures. Although Congress had to deal with difficult questions of peace, its principal power was that of carrying on war. Congress might make treaties, but it could pass no act in defence of American commerce.

[Sidenote: Executive departments.]

A great effort was made to improve the executive system. By resolutions passed early in 1781, secretaries were appointed for the three departments of Foreign Affairs, War, and Finance; the board system, championed by Samuel Adams and others, was to be abandoned. The importance of the War Department diminished after 1782. "The Secretary of the United States for the Department of Foreign Affairs" was quartered in two little rooms, and furnished with two clerks. The post was filled first by Robert R. Livingston, and from 1784 by John Jay. The office of Superintendent of Finance was bestowed upon Robert Morris of Pennsylvania.

[Sidenote: Courts.]

The Articles of Confederation provided for a special tribunal to settle territorial disputes between the States. The system was invoked in 1782, and a verdict was rendered in favor of Pennsylvania and against Connecticut in their rival claims to the Wyoming region. A second set of federal courts was constituted by designating certain State courts to try piracies and felonies committed on the high seas. A third and the only important federal tribunal was the Court of Appeals in prize cases, which began to sit in January, 1780, and before which were sued sixty-five cases. All the courts, like all the executive departments, were created by Congress, alterable by Congress, and subject to the control of Congress. In 1784 the Court of Appeals was allowed to lapse, by the refusal of Congress to pay the salaries of the judges.

51. DISBANDMENT OF THE ARMY (1783.)

To follow the history of the Confederation from year to year would be unprofitable. It was a confused period, with no recognized national leaders, no parties, no great crises. We shall therefore take up one after another the important questions which arose, and follow each to the end of the Confederation.

[Sidenote: Half-pay question.]
[Sidenote: Protests.]

The first duty of Congress after peace was declared was to cut off the military expenditures (§ 42). The food, clothing, and pay of the army amounted to about $400,000 a month. Provision had been made for bounty lands for the soldiers; the officers expected some more definite reward. On April 26, 1778, Congress, by a majority of one State, had voted half pay for life to the officers, as an essential measure for keeping the army together. In the four years following, five different votes had been passed, each annulling the previous one. Another proposition, in November, 1782, was to remit the whole matter to the States. On March 10, 1783, appeared the so-called "Newburgh addresses,"—an anonymous plea to the army, urging the officers not to separate until Congress had done justice in this respect. A crisis was threatened. Washington himself attended the meeting of the officers, and counselled moderation. He used his utmost influence with Congress, and on the 22d of March secured a vote of full pay for five years. As the treasury was empty, the only payment to the officers was in certificates of indebtedness, upon which interest accumulated during the next seven years. Massachusetts protested, declaring the grant to be "more than an adequate reward for their services, and inconsistent with that equality which ought to subsist among citizens of free and republican states." In June, 1783, three hundred mutineers surrounded the place of meeting of Congress, and demanded a settlement of their back pay; and the executive council of Pennsylvania declined to interfere. The result was that Congress changed its place of meeting, and ever after retained a lively resentment against the city of Philadelphia.

52. TERRITORIAL SETTLEMENT WITH THE STATES (1781-1802).

Although Congress had no power, under the Articles of Confederation, to regulate territory, it earnestly urged the States to cede their claims. The Ohio River divided the Western country into two regions, each having a separate territorial history. The northern part was claimed by Virginia, Massachusetts, and Connecticut, on the ground that their old charters, extending to the Pacific, were revived (§ 45). The United States, as representing the landless States, claimed the whole region as territory won by the common effort and sacrifice of the Revolutionary War. On March 1, 1784, Virginia ceded all her claims north of the Ohio River, except a reservation for bounty lands. Massachusetts followed in 1785; the commonwealth had large tracts of unoccupied land in Maine and in New York. Connecticut had no such resources, and in 1786 ceded only the western part of her claim, retaining till 1800, as a "Western Reserve," a strip, extending along Lake Erie, one hundred and twenty miles west from Pennsylvania.

[Sidenote: Territorial organization.]

The claims to the region north of the Ohio having thus been extinguished, the government began to make plans for the administration of its domain. On Oct. 10, 1780, the Continental Congress had promised that the lands ceded by the States should be "disposed of for the common benefit of the United States," and "be settled and formed into distinct republican States which shall become members of the federal union." These two principles are the foundation both of the territorial and the public land systems of the United States.

On April 23, 1784, an ordinance reported by Jefferson was passed, providing for representative legislatures as fast as the West grew sufficiently populous to maintain them. It is hardly a misfortune that the map was not encumbered with the names suggested by Jefferson for the new States,—Cherronesus, Metropotamia, Assenisippia, Polypotamia, and Pelisipia; but another clause was voted down which would have prohibited slavery in the Territories after 1800.

[Sidenote: Northwest Ordinance.]

June 13, 1787, a second ordinance passed Congress, which was inferior in importance only to the Federal Constitution. It provided minutely for a preliminary territorial government, in which laws were to be made by appointive judges, and for a later representative government. The conception was that the Territories were to occupy the position formerly claimed by the colonies; they were to be subject to no general taxation, but placed under a governor appointed by the general government; their laws were to be subject to his veto, and to later revision by the central authority. A new principle was the preparation of the Territories for statehood: the ordinance laid down a series of "Articles of Compact" to govern them after they were admitted into the Union. Religious liberty and personal rights were to be secured; general morality and education to be encouraged; and finally it was provided that "there shall be neither slavery nor involuntary servitude in the said Territory, otherwise than in the punishment of crimes whereof the party shall have been duly convicted." The introduction of this clause is due to New England men, who were anxious to form a colony on the Ohio, and who desired to secure the freedom with which they were familiar. The clause had no effect upon slaves held in the Territory at the time of the passage of the ordinance, but it distinctly expresses the dissatisfaction of the country with the system of human slavery. As soon as the Northwest Territory was organized, the sale of lands began; but nothing was received in cash till long after the Confederation had expired.

[Sidenote: Southern cessions.]

In the southern block of States the territorial settlement proceeded more slowly, and was in every way less satisfactory. Virginia retained both jurisdiction and land in Kentucky. North Carolina in 1790 granted the jurisdiction in what is now Tennessee, but every acre of the land had already been granted by the State. South Carolina had almost nothing to cede, and yielded it in 1787. Georgia stood out on the claim to the whole territory between her present boundary and the Mississippi, and would not yield until 1802. Slavery was not prohibited.

53. FINANCES (1781-1788).

[Sidenote: Financial status.]
[Sidenote: Requisitions.]

The financial condition of the Confederation was throughout deplorable (§ 43). The Revolution imposed upon the country a heavy debt. The accounts of the government were so badly kept that to this day it is impossible to state the amount; but it was probably about thirty millions, with an annual interest charge of about two millions. The necessary expenditure for the support of Congress, of the army on a peace-footing, and of the executive and judicial boards and departments, called for about half a million more. The continental currency had practically been repudiated, and no more could be floated; Congress had no power to lay either direct or indirect taxes; the post-office had an income of about $25,000 a year, all of which was expended upon the service. Hence Congress fell back on requisitions apportioned on the States:

one of its principal functions was each year to calculate the amount necessary for the public service, and to call upon the State legislatures for their quota. The total sum required from 1781 to 1788 was about $16,000,000. Of this there had actually been paid during the seven years $3,500,000 in specie, and $2,500,000 in certificates of national indebtedness. The annual cash income of the government was therefore about half a million, which was entirely absorbed by the necessary running expenses of the government, leaving nothing for the payment of interest.

[Sidenote: Morris's administration.]

This condition of virtual bankruptcy might have been avoided had Robert Morris been able to carry out the reforms which he proposed when he became superintendent of finance in 1781. He found the financial administration complicated and corrupt. He attempted to substitute business methods and punctuality of payment. While the war lasted, however, the only financial system possible was to squeeze every source of revenue, and to pay only what could not be avoided. When peace returned, the States would provide no better system. To keep up the credit of the government the first necessity was the prompt payment of interest: the payment of interest required money; money must come from taxes, and the State declined to levy the taxes. In 1784 Morris resigned in despair, and thenceforward a Treasury Board mismanaged the finances of the nation.

[Sidenote: Bank of North America.]

May 26, 1781, Congress had taken the important step of chartering the Bank of North America. The United States was to furnish part of the capital, and to make the bank its financial agent. Its notes were to be receivable in the duties and taxes of every State in the Union. Morris asked Jay to get specie from Spain to start the bank. "I am determined," said he, "that the bank shall be well supported until it can support itself, and then it will support us." Its connection with the government practically ceased after the retirement of Morris in 1784, although it remained under a State charter a prosperous and useful institution, and is still in existence, a sound and healthy bank.

[Sidenote: The currency.]

Another financial measure was the attempt to correct the currency. After the end of the war there was found in circulation an extraordinary mixture of gold and silver coins of all nations, especially the Spanish milled dollar, which had been accepted by the Continental Congress as the unit of its issues. All the currency was badly counterfeited, defaced, and clipped. In 1782 the quartermaster-general, Timothy Pickering, who was about to pay out a part of the French subsidy in coin, wrote as follows: "I must trouble you for the necessary apparatus for clipping. 'Tis a shameful business and an unreasonable hardship on a public officer.... A pair of good shears, a couple of punches, and a leaden anvil of two or three pounds weight. Will you inquire how the goldsmiths put in their plugs?" The Confederation, upon Jefferson's report, July 6, 1785, adopted the dollar as its unit, and provided for a decimal ratio; but a few tons of copper cents made up the only national currency put into circulation.

[Sidenote: Foreign loans.]

Towards the end of its existence the Confederation found itself on the brink of a default of interest on debts due to foreign governments and bankers. France in 1783 made a final loan of six hundred thousand francs; and from 1783 to 1788 Dutch bankers were found who had sufficient confidence in the government to advance it $1,600,000 on favorable terms. With the proceeds of these loans the government was able to pay the accumulated interest on the foreign loans, and thus to keep its credit above water in Europe.

54. DISORDERS IN THE STATES (1781-1788).

[Sidenote: State financial legislation.]

The finances of the States were little better than those of the Union. The States controlled all the resources of the country; they could and did raise taxes, but they appropriated the proceeds to their own pressing necessities; and the meagre sums paid to Congress represented a genuine sacrifice on the part of many States, particularly Pennsylvania and Massachusetts. Unfortunately the States exercised unlimited powers over their own currency and commercial relations. Times were hard, debts had accumulated, property had been destroyed by the war. State after State passed stay laws delaying the collection of debts; or "tender laws" were enacted, by which property at an appraised value was made a legal tender, Cattle, merchandise, and unimproved real estate were the usual currency thus forced upon creditors. After peace was declared, a second era of State paper-money issues came on, and but four of the thirteen States escaped the craze.

[Sidenote: Weakness of the States.]
[Sidenote: Proposed new states.]
[Sidenote: Insurrections.]

These remedies bore hard on the creditors in other States, created a feeling of insecurity among business men, and gave no permanent relief. The discontented, therefore, sought a remedy for themselves. The Revolutionary War had left behind it an eddy of lawlessness and disregard of human life.

The support of the government was a heavy load upon the people. The States were physically weak, and the State legislatures habitually timid. In several States there were organized attempts to set off outlying portions as independent governments. Vermont had set the example by withdrawing from New York in 1777, and throughout the Confederation remained without representation either in the New York legislature or in Congress. In 1782 the western counties of Pennsylvania and Virginia threatened to break off and form a new State. From 1785 to 1786 the so-called State of "Franklin," within the territory of what is now eastern Tennessee, had a constitution and legislature and governor, and carried on a mild border warfare with the government of North Carolina, to which its people owed allegiance. The people of Kentucky and of Maine held conventions looking toward separation. The year 1786 was marked by great uneasiness in what had been supposed to be the steadiest States in the union. In New Hampshire the opposition was directed against the legislature; but General Sullivan, by his courage, succeeded in quelling the threatened insurrection without bloodshed. In Massachusetts in the fall of 1786 concerted violence prevented the courts from sitting; and an organized force of insurgents under Captain Shays threatened to destroy the State government. As a speaker in the Massachusetts convention of 1788 said, "People took up arms; and then if you went to speak to them you had the musket of death presented to your breast. They would rob you of your property, threaten to burn your houses; obliged you to be on your guard night and day…. How terrible, how distressing was this!… Had any one that was able to protect us come and set up his standard, we should all have flocked to it, even though it had been a monarch." The arsenal at Springfield was attacked. The State forces were met in the open field by armed insurgents. Had they been successful, the Union was not worth one of its own repudiated notes. The Massachusetts authorities were barely able to restore order, and Congress went beyond its constitutional powers in an effort to assist.

55. SLAVERY (1777-1788).

[Sidenote: Anti-slavery spirit.]
[Sidenote: Emancipation acts.]
[Sidenote: Southern sentiment.]

One evidence that the States were still sound and healthful was the passage of Emancipation acts. The Revolutionary principles of the rights of man, the consent of the governed, and political equality, had been meant for white men; but it was hard to deny their logical application to the blacks. New anti-slavery societies were formed, particularly in Pennsylvania; but the first community to act was Vermont. In the Declaration of Rights prefixed to the Constitution of 1777 it was declared that since every man is entitled to life, liberty, and happiness, therefore "no ... person born in this country, or brought here over sea, ought to be holden by law to serve any person as a servant, slave, or apprentice" after he arrives at the age of maturity. A few years later this was supplemented by an act abolishing the institution of slavery outright. The number of slaves in Vermont was inconsiderable, but in 1780 two States, Massachusetts and Pennsylvania, took similar action, affecting several thousand persons. The Massachusetts constitution of 1780 declared that "all men are born free and equal." This clause was a few years later interpreted by the courts to mean that after 1780 no person could legally be held as a slave. In Pennsylvania in the same year a gradual Emancipation Act was passed, under which persons then in bondage were to serve as slaves during their lives; their children, born after 1780, were eventually to become free; and no person was to be brought into the State and sold as a slave. Within four years New Hampshire and Connecticut passed similar Emancipation Acts. In Rhode Island the number of slaves, 3,500, was considerable in proportion to the population, and that State therefore made a distinct sacrifice for its principles by its act of 1785. Thus at the expiration of the Confederation in 1788, all the States north of Maryland, except New York and New Jersey, had put slavery in process of extinction; those two States followed in 1799 and 1804. Many Southern statesmen hoped that the institution was dying out even in the South. Jefferson in 1787 wrote: "Indeed, I tremble for my country when I reflect that God is just, and that His justice cannot sleep forever." Some steps were taken, particularly in Virginia and Kentucky, for the amelioration of the condition of the blacks; and the slave-trade was forbidden in most of the States of the Union during this period.

56. FOREIGN RELATIONS AND COMMERCE (1781-1788).

[Sidenote: Relations with England.]

In no respect, not even in finance, was the weakness of the Confederation so evident as in the powerlessness of Congress to pass commercial laws, and its consequent inability to secure commercial treaties. In 1785 John Adams was sent as minister to Great Britain, and was received with civility by the sovereign from whom he had done so much to tear the brightest jewel of his crown; but when he endeavored to come to some commercial arrangement, he could make no progress. It is easy now to see that the best policy for Great Britain would have been in every way to encourage American commerce; the

Americans were accustomed to trade with England; their credits and business connections were established with English merchants; the English manufactured the goods most desired by America. When the Whigs were driven out of power in 1783, the last opportunity for such an agreement was lost. July 2, 1783, an Order in Council was issued, restraining the West India trade to British ships, British built; and on March 26, 1785, the Duke of Dorset replied to the American commissioners who asked for a treaty: "The apparent determination of the respective States to regulate their own separate interests renders it absolutely necessary, towards forming a permanent system of commerce, that my court should be informed how far the commissioners can be duly authorized to enter into any engagement with Great Britain which it may not be in the power of any one of the States to render totally useless and inefficient."

[Sidenote: Loyalists.]
[Sidenote: British debts.]
[Sidenote: Posts.]

There were other reasons why the British continued to subject American ships in English ports to discriminations and duties from which the vessels of most other powers were exempt. The treaty of 1783 had provided that Congress would recommend to the States just treatment of the loyalists; the recommendation was made. Most of the States declined to comply; men who had been eminent before the Revolution returned to find themselves distrusted, and sometimes were mobbed; their estates, which in most cases had been confiscated, were withheld, and they could obtain no consideration. This was unfriendly, but not a violation of any promise. The action of the States in placing obstacles in the way of collecting debts due to British merchants before the Revolution was a vexatious infraction of the treaty. Five States had passed laws for the partial or complete confiscation of such debts, and even after the treaty Pennsylvania and Massachusetts passed similar Acts. As an offset, the British minister in 1786 declared that the frontier posts would not be surrendered so long as the obstacles to the collection of British debts were left standing.

[Sidenote: The Spanish treaty.]

The only other power with which the United States desired commercial relations without possessing them was Spain. The Eastern States were very anxious to obtain privileges of trade. The Spanish were willing to grant them, but made it a condition that the Americans should not have the right of free navigation of the lower Mississippi. Jay, acting under the instruction of Congress, in 1786 negotiated a treaty in which he agreed to the Spanish conditions. Instantly the West was aroused, and violent threats were made by the people of Kentucky and the adjacent region that if that treaty went into effect they would withdraw from the Union. "The tendency of the States," said Madison, a few months later, "to violations of the laws of nations and treaties ... has been manifest.... The files of Congress contain complaints already from almost every nation with which treaties have been formed."

57. DISINTEGRATION OF THE UNION (1786, 1787).

[Sidenote: The Confederation violated.]
[Sidenote: Danger of anarchy.]

The year 1786 marks a crisis in the development of the Union. The inefficiency of Congress was reflected in the neglect of constitutional duties by the States: Rhode Island recalled her delegates, and refused to appoint new members; New Jersey felt so much injured by a New York tariff that an act was passed taxing the lighthouse established by New York on Sandy Hook; Massachusetts, Pennsylvania, North Carolina, and Georgia already had raised troops on their own account and for their own purposes, in violation of the Articles of Confederation. Davie, of North Carolina, a little later declared that the "encroachments of some States on the rights of others, and of all on those of the Confederation, are incontestable proofs of the weakness and imperfections of that system." Of the requisition of that year for $2,000,000 in specie, only about $400,000 was paid. Some States offered their own depreciated notes, and New Jersey refused to make any contribution until the offensive New York Acts were withdrawn. In May, 1786, Charles Pinckney on the floor of Congress declared that "Congress must be invested with more powers, or the federal government must fall."

58. REORGANIZATION ATTEMPTED (1781-1787).

[Sidenote: Five percent scheme.]
[Sidenote: Revenue scheme.]

Before the Articles of Confederation had gone into effect, Congress had already proposed a radical amendment; and within three years it suggested two others. The first proposition, made February 3, 1781, was that the States allow Congress to levy an import duty of five per cent, the proceeds to be applied "to the discharge of the principal and interest of the debts already contracted ... on the faith of the United States for supporting the present war." In the course of about a year twelve States had complied with this reasonable request. Rhode Island alone stood out, and the plan failed. Forthwith

Congress presented another financial scheme, which was called a "general revenue plan." April 12, 1783, it asked the States to allow Congress to lay low specific import duties for twenty-five years, to be collected by officers appointed by the States. The States were further recommended to lay some effective taxes, the proceeds to be set aside for government requisitions. The effect was precisely the same as before. Twelve States agreed; but the opposition of New York prevented the first part of the plan from being carried out. Not a single State had condescended to pay attention to the second request.

[Sidenote: Commerce amendment.]

Apparently abandoning any hope of an adequate revenue, Congress, on April 30, 1784, proposed a third amendment, that the States should permit it to pass commercial laws discriminating against foreign powers which refused to make commercial treaties. This was aimed at Great Britain. Washington urged the measure in vigorous language. "We are," said he, "either a united people, or we are not so. If the former, let us in all matters of national concern act as a nation which has a national character to support." Yet he could not bring even Virginia to agree to the plan, and it quickly failed.

[Sidenote: Schemes of revision.]

A poor constitution, which could be amended only by unanimous vote, was likely to stifle the nation. A few feeble suggestions were heard that the experiment of republican government be given over; others urged that the Americans be brought within one centralized government. Alexander Hamilton would have established a government "controlling the internal police of the States, and having a federal judiciary." Upon the last of his three schemes, dated 1783, is written: "Intended to be submitted to Congress, but abandoned for want of support." Even Washington's vastly greater influence had no effect. In a circular letter to the governors, dated June, 1783, he says: "It is indispensable to the happiness of the individual States that there should be lodged somewhere a supreme power to regulate and govern the general concerns of the confederated republic." Yet not a State would take the initiative in reforming the constitution.

From 1784 to 1786 pamphlets began to appear in which more definite suggestions were made for a new government. Pelatiah Webster proposed a government with enlarged powers, and a legislature of two houses. "If they disagree," said he, "let them sit still until they recover their good humor." The method in which the new government was to enforce its powers was put in a quaint and incisive form. "My principle is," said Webster, "the soul that sinneth, it shall die. Every person ... who shall disobey the supreme authority shall be answerable to Congress." The idea that the constitution needed radical amendment had at last found a lodgment in the public mind.

CHAPTER VI.

THE FEDERAL CONSTITUTION (1787-1789).

59. REFERENCES.

BIBLIOGRAPHIES.—P. L. Ford, *Bibliography and Reference List of the Constitution*; Justin Winsor, *Narrative and Critical History*, VII. 256-266; W. E. Foster, *References to the Constitution*, 15, 21; Channing and Hart, *Guide*, §§ 154-156; A. B. Hart, *Federal Government*, §§ 38, 469.

HISTORICAL MAPS.—As in § 48 above, § 69 below.

GENERAL ACCOUNTS.—J. B. McMaster, *People of the United States*, I. 416-524; R. Hildreth, *United States*, III. 482-546; T. Pitkin, *United States*, II. 218-316; H. C. Lodge, *Washington*, II. ch. I.; J. Story, *Commentaries*, §§ 272-372; J. Schouler, *United States*, I. 31-70; Geo. Tucker, *United States*, I. 347-383; Justin Winsor, *Narrative and Critical History*, VII. ch. iv.; H. Von Hoist, *Constitutional History*, I. 47-63; J. S. Landon, *Constitutional History*, 59-96; F. A. Walker, *Making of the Nation*, chs. ii., iii.

SPECIAL HISTORIES.—G. T. Curtis, _Constitutional History, I. chs. xv.-xxxvi. (*History of the Constitution*, III. 232-604); Geo. Bancroft, *United States*, last revision, VI. 195-462 (*History of the Constitution*, I. 267-278, II. 1-47, 144, 350); William C. Rives, *James Madison*, II. 313-633; H. L. Carson, *One Hundredth Anniversary of the Constitution*; J. B. McMaster, *Pennsylvania and the Federal Constitution*; John Fiske, *Critical Period*, 183-350; S. H. Gay, *Madison*, 88-127; J. C. Hamilton, *Republic*, III. 236-569; J. H. Robinson, *Sources of the Constitution*; S. B. Harding, *Federal Constitution in Massachusetts*; C. E. Stevens, *Sources of the Constitution*; C. Borgeaud, *Adoption and Amendment of Constitutions*; the various State histories.

CONTEMPORARY ACCOUNTS.—Journal of the Convention, Madison's notes, Yates's notes, Luther Martin's letter, proceedings of State conventions,—all in *Elliot's Debates* (5 vols.); H. D. Gilpin, *Papers of James Madison*, vols. II., III.; brief references in the works of Washington, Madison, Hamilton, and Jefferson; letters in the biographies of Madison, Hamilton, Rufus King, Gerry; *The Federalist*.—Reprints in P. L. Ford, *Pamphlets on the Constitution of the United States*, and *Essays on the Constitution; American History told by Contemporaries*, III.; *Library of*

60. THE FEDERAL CONVENTION ASSEMBLED (1787).

[Sidenote: A convention suggested.]
[Sidenote: Annapolis Convention.]
[Sidenote: Action of Congress.]

That Congress did not possess the confidence of the country was evident from the failure of all its amendments. It had, therefore, been suggested first by Hamilton in 1780, later by Tom Paine in his widespread pamphlet "Public Good," that a convention be specially summoned to revise the Articles of Confederation. The initiative in the movement was finally taken by the States. In 1786 the intolerable condition of internal commerce caused Virginia to suggest to the sister States that a conference be held at Annapolis. The few delegates who appeared separated, after recommending that there be held "a convention of delegates from the different States ... to devise such further provisions as shall appear to them necessary to render the constitution of the federal government adequate." Congress was no longer able to resist the movement: on Feb. 1, 1787, it resolved that a convention be held "for the sole and express purpose of revising the Articles of Confederation, and reporting to Congress and the several legislatures such alterations and provisions therein as shall, when agreed to by Congress and confirmed by the States, render the federal government adequate to the exigencies of government and the preservation of the union."

[Sidenote: Convention assembled.]

By May, 1787, delegates to the proposed convention had been chosen in all the States except New Hampshire and Rhode Island. Many of the ablest and most experienced public men were included. Among them were Francis Dana and Elbridge Gerry of Massachusetts, Alexander Hamilton of New York, Benjamin Franklin of Pennsylvania, and James Madison and George Washington of Virginia. The convention was the most distinguished body which had ever assembled in America; if its work could not command public confidence, there was no hope for the Union.

61. DIFFICULTIES OF THE CONVENTION (1787).

[Sidenote: Task of the convention.]

When on May 25, 1787, the convention assembled at Philadelphia, its task, under the call of Congress, was limited to the preparation of amendments to the old Confederation. The first formal resolution to which it came after organization reads as follows: "That a national government ought to be established, consisting of a supreme legislature, executive, and judiciary." The convention from the beginning was evidently resolved to recommend a new, elaborate, and powerful form of government. The key to this action is found in the history of the twelve years from 1775 to 1787. The country had tried a revolutionary, irresponsible, form of government, and it had not worked well. It had tried a union of sovereign States; neither the Union nor the States had prospered. The time had come to change the government in form, in powers, and in the means of carrying out its powers. The States must be held to their duties; Congress must be restrained; local quarrels must cease; revenue must be secured, commerce protected, and treaties guaranteed; the West must be saved, and insurrections put down. The first duty of the convention was to repair the errors of the Confederation.

[Sidenote: Want of authority.]

Americans have become accustomed to look upon the Constitution as a kind of political revelation; the members of the convention themselves felt no sense of strength or inspiration. They had no authority of their own. Their work must be submitted for the ratification of States which had been unable to agree upon a single modification of the articles. They must encounter the jealousy of Congress and the prejudices of the people. While the convention sat, a rumor went abroad that they would report in favor of a monarchy.

In order to bring the discussion to a focus, the Virginia delegates had agreed upon a plan drawn by Madison, who had been in communication with Washington; it was presented by Edmund Randolph. This plan in the end formed the basis of the constitution as adopted.

[Sidenote: Divisions.]

No sooner had debate actually begun than the convention proved to be divided into many factions. Some members, like Patterson, were on principle opposed to a strong government; others, like Hamilton, desired to break down the State boundaries, and to create a centralized republic. Still more distinct was the opposition between the large States and the small: the former inclined to a representation based on population; the latter insisted that the States should be equal units. Again, the trading States—New England, New York, and Maryland—were inclined to grant large powers over commerce; the agricultural States, particularly Virginia, wished to see commerce regulated still by the States in part. Another line of division was between the slaveholding and the non-slaveholding States; here the champions were Massachusetts on one side, and South Carolina on the other. Throughout the convention these various elements combined and recombined as their interests seemed affected. Although there were no permanent parties, the members of which regularly voted together, there was disagreement and disappointment from the beginning to the end.

62. SOURCES OF THE CONSTITUTION.

[Sidenote: American experience.]

Another popular delusion with regard to the Constitution is that it was created out of nothing; or, as Mr. Gladstone puts it, that "It is the greatest work ever struck off at any one time by the mind and purpose of man." The radical view on the other side is expressed by Sir Henry Maine, who informs us that the "Constitution of the United States is a modified version of the British Constitution … which was in existence between 1760 and 1787." The real source of the Constitution is the experience of Americans. They had established and developed admirable little commonwealths in the colonies; since the beginning of the Revolution they had had experience of State governments organized on a different basis from the colonial; and, finally, they had carried on two successive national governments, with which they had been profoundly discontented. The general outline of the new Constitution seems to be English; it was really colonial. The President's powers of military command, of appointment, and of veto were similar to those of the colonial governor. National courts were created on the model of colonial courts. A legislature of two houses was accepted because such legislatures had been common in colonial times. In the English Parliamentary system as it existed before 1760 the Americans had had no share; the later English system of Parliamentary responsibility was not yet developed, and had never been established in colonial governments; and they expressly excluded it from their new Constitution.

[Sidenote: State experience.]

They were little more affected by the experience of other European nations. Just before they assembled, Madison drew up an elaborate abstract of ancient, mediċval, and existing federal governments, of which he sent a copy to Washington. It is impossible to trace a single clause of the Constitution to any suggestion in this paper. The chief source of the details of the Constitution was the State constitutions and laws then in force. Thus the clause conferring a suspensive veto on the President is an almost literal transcript from the Massachusetts constitution. In fact, the principal experiment in the Constitution was the establishment of an electoral college; and of all parts of the system this has worked least as the framers expected. The Constitution represents, therefore, the accumulated experience of the time; its success is due to the wisdom of the members in selecting out of the mass of colonial and State institutions those which were enduring,

96

The real boldness of the Constitution is the novelty of the federal system which it set up. For the first time in history an elaborate written constitution was applied to a federation; and the details were so skilfully arranged that the instrument framed for thirteen little agricultural communities works well for forty-four large and populous States. A second novelty was a system of federal courts skilfully brought into harmony with the State judiciary. Even here we see an effect of the twelve years experience of imperfect federation. The convention knew how to select institutions that would stand together; it also knew how to reject what would have weakened the structure.

63. THE GREAT COMPROMISES (1787).

[Sidenote: State sovereignty.]

It was a long time before a compromise between the discordant elements could be reached. To declare the country a centralized nation was to destroy the traditions of a century and a half: to leave it an assemblage of States, each claiming independence and sovereignty, was to throw away the results of the Revolution. The convention finally agreed that while the Union should be endowed with adequate powers, the States should retain all powers not specifically granted, and particularly the right to regulate their own internal affairs.

[Sidenote: Representation of States.]

The next great question all but led to the breaking up of the convention. The New Hampshire delegate had not yet appeared, and Rhode Island was never represented in the convention; the large states had therefore a majority of one. On June 13 it was voted that the ratio of representation in both branches of the legislature should be in proportion to the population. Two days later, Patterson of New Jersey brought forward a plan satisfactory to the small States, by which the old plan of vote by States was to be retained, and the Confederation practically continued. For many days the two parties were unable to agree; the crisis was so serious that on June 28 Franklin, who was not renowned for piety, moved that thenceforward the sessions be opened with prayer. The deadlock was finally broken by the so-called Connecticut Compromise, adopted July 7: equal representation was to be preserved in the upper house, and proportional representation was to be granted in the lower.

[Sidenote: Representation of slaves.]

When it was proposed to levy taxes on the same basis, the Southern members objected that their negroes were not equal to freemen as producers of wealth. On July 12, the matter was adjusted by a compromise: the Southerners agreed to count slaves only at three fifths of their number, in apportioning both representatives and direct taxes. Since direct taxes have been but three times assessed in the history of the United States, the practical advantage was on the side of the North.

[Sidenote: Slave trade.]

It was otherwise in the third difficult question. Near the end of the convention the commercial and the agricultural States came into a disagreement. New England was anxious that Congress should have power to pass Acts protecting American shipping; on the other hand, the South desired to continue the slave-trade. Pinckney declared that "South Carolina can never receive the plan if it prohibits the slave-trade;" and Sherman of Connecticut cynically remarked, "The slave-trade is iniquitous; but inasmuch as the point of representation was settled, he should not object." On August 24 a third compromise left to Congress the power of passing Navigation Acts, but forbade it to prohibit the slave-trade during twenty years.

64. DETAILS OF THE CONSTITUTION (1787).

[Sidenote: Difficult questions.]

These difficult points out of the way, the convention arranged the details of the new government. One of the principal minor questions was the method of presidential election. Many members inclined towards an executive council; instead, it was agreed that there should be a President elected by Congress; but almost at the last moment, on September 7, the better plan of indirect election by the people was adopted. At one time the convention had agreed that Congress should have the right of veto upon State laws; it was abandoned, and instead was introduced a clause that the Constitution should be the supreme law of the land, and powerful courts were created to construe the law.

[Sidenote: Simplicity of the Constitution.]

In making up the list of the powers of Congress, the convention used brief but comprehensive terms. Thus all the difficulties arising out of the unfriendly commercial legislation of States, and their institution, with foreign treaties, were removed by the simple clause: "The Congress shall have Power ... to regulate Commerce with foreign Nations, and among the several States, and with the Indian Tribes." The great question of taxation was settled by fourteen words: "The Congress shall have Power ... To lay and collect Taxes, Duties,

Imposts, and Excises."

[Sidenote: Omissions.]

In a few respects the Constitution was deficient. It did not profess to be all-comprehensive, for the details of the government were to be worked out in later statutes. There was, however, no provision for future annexations of territory. No safeguards were provided for the proper appointment and removal of public officers. The growth of corporations was not foreseen, and no distinct power was conferred upon Congress either to create or to regulate them. Above all, the convention was obliged to leave untouched the questions connected with slavery which later disrupted the Union.

[Sidenote: The work finished.]

On Sept. 17, 1787, the convention finished its work. To the eloquent and terse phraseology of Gouverneur Morris we owe the nervous English of the great instrument. As the members were affixing their signatures, Franklin remarked, pointing to the picture of a sun painted behind the President's chair: "I have often and often,... in the vicissitudes of my hopes and fears, looked … without being able to tell whether it was rising or setting; but now, at length, I have the happiness to know that it is a rising and not a setting sun."

65. DIFFICULTIES OF RATIFICATION (1787, 1788).

[Sidenote: Action of Congress.]
[Sidenote: Action of legislatures.]

The text of the Constitution was printed and rapidly distributed throughout the Union. It was still but a lifeless draft, and before it could become an instrument of government the approving action of Congress, of the legislatures, and of State conventions was necessary. Congress, on Sept. 28, 1787, unanimously resolved that the Constitution be transmitted to State legislatures. The federal convention had determined that the consideration of its work should not depend, like the Articles of Confederation, upon the slow and unwilling humor of the legislatures, but that in each State a convention should be summoned solely to express the will of the State upon the acceptance of the Constitution. It had further avoided the rock upon which had been wrecked the amendments proposed by Congress; when nine State conventions should have ratified the Constitution, it was to take effect for those nine. On the same day that Congress in New York was passing its resolution, the Pennsylvania legislature in Philadelphia was fixing the day for the election of delegates; all the State legislatures followed, except in Rhode Island.

The next six months was a period of great anxiety and of national danger. The Constitution was violently attacked in every part of the Union: the President, it was urged, would be a despot, the House of Representatives a corporate tyrant, the Senate an oligarchy. The large States protested that Delaware and Rhode Island would still neutralize the votes of Virginia and Massachusetts in the Senate. The federal courts were said to be an innovation. It was known that there had been great divisions in the convention, and that several influential members had left, or at the last moment had refused to sign. "The people of this commonwealth," said Patrick Henry, "are exceedingly uneasy in being brought from that state of full security which they enjoyed, to the present delusive appearance of things." A special objection was made to the lack of a bill of rights, such as existed in State constitutions. The reply was that the framers of the Constitution had deliberately omitted it because Congress was in no case to have powers not conferred upon it by the Constitution. The argument was not conclusive: Rev. Mr. Caldwell, in the North Carolina convention, declared that "unalienable rights ought not to be given up if not necessary;" and another member of the same convention objected that "if there be no religious test required, Pagans, Deists, and Mahometans might obtain offices, And ... the senators and representatives might all be pagans." It was even suggested as a serious danger that the Pope of Rome might eventually be elected president.

[Sidenote: Federalists and Antifederalists.]

The friends of the measure, in order to deprecate the charge that they aimed at centralization, took upon themselves the name of Federalists. Their opponents called themselves antifederalists, corresponded with each other, and formed a short-lived national party. A shower of pamphlets on both sides fell upon the country. Of these the most famous and most efficacious was the "Federalist," successive numbers of which were contributed by Hamilton, Madison, and John Jay. With a calmness of spirit, a lucidity of style, and a power of logic which make it to this day one of the most important commentaries on the Constitution, the "Federalist" strove to show that the Constitution was safe for the people and advantageous for the States.

66. STATE CONVENTIONS (1787, 1788).

[Sidenote: First nine states.]

As the State conventions assembled, the excitement grew more intense. Four States alone contained within a few thousands of half the population of the

Union: they were Massachusetts, Virginia, New York, and North Carolina. In the convention of each of these States there was opposition strong and stubborn; one of them—North Carolina—adjourned without action; in the other three, ratification was obtained with extreme difficulty and by narrow majorities.

The first State to come under the "New Roof," as the Constitution was popularly called, was Delaware. In rapid succession followed Pennsylvania, New Jersey, Georgia, and Connecticut. In Massachusetts, the sixth State, there was a hard fight; the spirit of the Shays Rebellion was still alive; the opposition of Samuel Adams was only overcome by showing him that he was in the minority; John Hancock was put out of the power to interfere by making him the silent president of the convention. It was suggested that Massachusetts ratify on condition that a long list of amendments be adopted by the new government: the friends of the Constitution pointed out that the plan was simply to ratify a part of the Constitution and to reject the rest; each succeeding State would insist on a list of amendments, and the whole work must be done over. Feb. 6, 1788, the enthusiastic people of Boston knew that the convention, by a vote of 187 to 167, had ratified the Constitution; the amendments being added, not as a condition, but as a suggestion. Maryland, South Carolina, and New Hampshire brought the number up to nine.

[Sidenote: Virginia and New York.]

Before the ninth ratification was known, the fight had been won also in Virginia. Among the champions of the Constitution were Madison, Edmund Randolph, and John Marshall. James Monroe argued against the system of election which was destined twice to make him President. In spite of the determined opposition of Patrick Henry, and in spite of a proposition to ratify with amendments, the convention accepted. New York still held off. Her acquiescence was geographically necessary; and Alexander Hamilton, by the power of his eloquence and his reason, changed the vote of a hostile convention and added the eleventh State.

67. EXPIRATION OF THE CONFEDERATION (1788).

[Sidenote: The old Congress.]

During the session of the convention in Philadelphia Congress had continued to sit in New York, and the Northwest Ordinance was passed at this time (§ 52). On Sept. 13, 1788 Congress voted that the Constitution had been ratified, and that elections should proceed for the officers of the new government, which was to go into operation the first Wednesday in March, 1789.

Since Congress and the President must meet somewhere, it became the duty of the old Congress to fix, at least temporarily, the seat of government, Trenton, Lancaster, Princeton, and New York were suggested. Baltimore was voted; then, with its usual inconsistency, two days later Congress voted for New York. An attempt was made to settle the accounts of Congress; but all that could be ascertained was that they were in great confusion, and that vouchers had not yet been turned in for the expenditure of large sums. On October 23 is the last official record: "Two States attended." During the next five months the only evidences of national life were the perfunctory service of a few executive officers, the feeble movements of the army, now reduced to about six hundred men, and the steady accumulation of unpaid interest.

[Sidenote: Rhode Island and North Carolina.]

What, meantime, was the situation of the two States, Rhode Island and North Carolina, which had not ratified the Constitution, and which were, therefore, not entitled to take part in the elections? They had in 1781 entered into a constitution which was to be amended only by unanimous consent; their consent was refused; legally they had a right to insist on the continuance of the old Congress. The new Constitution was, strictly speaking, unconstitutional; it had been ratified by a process unknown to law. The situation was felt to be delicate, and the States were for the time being left to themselves. North Carolina came into the Union by a ratification of Nov. 21, 1789. It was suggested that the trade of States which did not recognize Congress should be cut off, and Rhode Island yielded. May 19, 1790, her ratification completed the Union.

68. WAS THE CONSTITUTION A COMPACT?

[Sidenote: The Constitution irregular.]

The third attempt to form an organic union was now successfully carried out. The irregular authority of the Continental Congress had been replaced by the legal but inefficient Confederation; to this was now to succeed an organized government, complete in all its departments, and well endowed with powers. How had this Constitution been adopted? What was the authority which had taken upon itself to diminish the powers of the States, and to disregard the clauses which required unanimous consent to amendments? Was the new Constitution an agreement between eleven States, or was it an instrument of government for the whole people? Upon this question depends the whole discussion about the nature of the Union and the right of secession.

[Sidenote: Compact theory.]

The first theory is that the Constitution was a compact made between sovereign States. Thus Hayne in 1830 declared that "Before the Constitution each state was an independent sovereignty, possessing all the rights and powers appertaining to independent nations.... After the Constitution was formed, they remained equally sovereign and independent as to all powers not expressly delegated to the federal government.... The true nature of the Federal Constitution, therefore, is ... a compact to which the States are parties." The importance of the word "compact" is that it means an agreement which loses its force when any one of the parties ceases to observe it; a compact is little more than a treaty. Those who framed the Constitution appeared to consider it no compact; for on May 30, 1787, Mr. Randolph moved that "-no treaty or treaties among the whole or part of the States, as individual sovereignties, would be sufficient." In fact, the reason for the violent opposition to the ratification of the Constitution was that when once ratified, the States could not withdraw from it.

[Sidenote: Constitution theory.]

Another view is presented by Webster in his reply to Hayne: "It is, sir, the people's Constitution, the people's government, made for the people, made by the people, and answerable to the people. The people of the United States have declared that this Constitution shall be the supreme law." It is plain that the Constitution does not rest simply upon the consent of the majority of the nation. No popular vote was taken or thought of; each act of ratification set forth that it proceeded from a convention of the people of a State.

[Sidenote: Basis of the Constitution.]

The real nature of the new Constitution appears in the light of the previous history of the country. The Articles of Confederation had been a compact. One of the principal reasons why the Confederation was weak was that there was no way of compelling the States to perform their duties. The new Constitution was meant to be stronger and more permanent. The Constitution was, then, not a compact, but an instrument of government similar in its origin to the constitutions of the States. The difference was that, by general agreement, it was not to take effect until it was shown that in at least nine States the people were willing to live under it. Whatever the defects of the Confederation, however humiliating its weakness to our national pride, it had performed an indispensable service; it had educated the American people to the point where they were willing to accept a permanent federal union. As the "Federalist" put it, "A nation without a national government is an awful spectacle."

CHAPTER VII.

ORGANIZATION OF THE GOVERNMENT (1789-1793).

69. REFERENCES.

BIBLIOGRAPHIES.—W. E. Foster, *References to Presidential Administrations*, 1-5; *References to the Constitution*, 18, 19; Justin Winsor, *Narrative and Critical History*, VII. 299-309, 323-329, 413-418, 446, 454, VIII. App.; P. L. Ford, *Bibliotheca Hamiltonia*; Channing and Hart, *Guide*, §§ 157-161.

HISTORICAL MAPS.—Nos. 1 and 3, this volume, and No. 1 in W. Wilson, *Division and Reunion* (*Epoch Maps*, Nos. 6, 7, and 8); T. MacCoun, *Historical Geography*; Scribner, *Statistical Atlas*, Plate 13.

GENERAL ACCOUNTS.—J. B. McMaster, *People of the United States*, I. 525-604, II. 1-88; R. Hildreth, *United States*, IV. 25-410; J. Schouler, *United States*, I. 74-220; H. Von Holst, *Constitutional History*, I. 64- 111; T. Pitkin, *Political and Civil History*, II. 317-355; Gen. Tucker, *United States*, I. 384-503; J. S. Landon, *Constitutional History*, 97- 119; Bryant and Gay, *Popular History*, IV. 100-123.

SPECIAL HISTORIES.—George Gibbs, *Memoirs of the Administrations of Washington and Adams*, I. 28-88; J. C. Hamilton, *History of the Republic*, IV.; W. G. Sumner, *Alexander Hamilton*; H. C. Adams, *Taxation in the United States* (1789-1816); W. G. Sumner, *Financier and Finances of the American Revolution*, II. chs. xvii.-xxxii.; J. T. Morse, *Life of Hamilton*, I. chs. vii.-xii.; M. P. Follet, *Speaker*; H. C. Lodge, *Hamilton*, 88-152, and *Washington*, II. 1-128; J. T. Morse, *John Adams*, 241-264, and *Jefferson*, 96-145; S. H. Gay, *Madison*, 128-192.

CONTEMPORARY ACCOUNTS.—W. Maclay, *Journal* (1789-1791) (a racy account of the Senate in the First Congress); Thomas Jefferson, *Anas*, in *Works*, ix. 87-185 (confessedly made up twenty-five years later); William Sullivan, *Familiar Letters on Public Characters*, 36-47 (written in reply to Jefferson); Joel Barlow, *Vision of Columbus*, 1787 (an epic poem); correspondence in works of Washington, Hamilton, Madison, Jefferson, and John Jay; newspapers, especially the *Columbian Centinel, Gazette of the United States, National Gazette.*—Reprints in *American History told by Contemporaries*, III.

70. GEOGRAPHY OF THE UNITED STATES IN 1789.

[Sidenote: Boundary questions.]

What were the physical, social, and political conditions under which the new government was to be established? In 1789 the exterior boundaries of the country were loosely defined by treaty (§ 46), but were not yet marked out, and there were several serious controversies. From the mouth of the St, Croix River to the head of the Connecticut the boundary was in confusion, and no progress had been made towards settling it. The water- line through the St. Lawrence and the Lakes was still unadjusted. It was found that the headwaters of the Mississippi lay to the south of the Lake of the Woods, so that there was a gap on the northwest. On the south Spain disputed the right of Great Britain to establish the boundary, insisted that her own undoubted settlements lay within the territory claimed by the United States, and declined to grant the free navigation of the lower Mississippi to the sea. Still more humiliating was the presence of British garrisons at Fort Niagara, Detroit, and other points within the undisputed boundaries of the United States.

[Sidenote: Interior boundaries.]

The interior boundaries of the country were in a like unsettled condition. Neither North Carolina nor Georgia had yielded up their western claims (§ 52). Vermont had not yet been recognized by New York as outside of her jurisdiction, and the Western Reserve lay along the southern shore of Lake Erie as an outlying part of Connecticut. No territorial government had been established for the Northwest territory, although settlement had begun to pour in. The southern territory was in complete confusion: Kentucky and the Tennessee valley were practically independent communities; and Georgia claimed the whole region south of them.

71. THE PEOPLE OF THE UNITED STATES IN 1789.

[Sidenote: Population.]

A census taken in 1790 gives us the number of inhabitants as a little under 4,000,000. Of these, 750,000—nearly one-fifth of the whole population— were negroes. Of the 3,170,000 whites, the ancestors of eight- tenths were probably English, and most of the others spoke English and were a homogeneous part of the community. Counting by sections, the States north of Maryland had a population of 1,968,000, and those south of Pennsylvania had 1,925,000; the States which were to be permanently slave- holding contained, therefore, a population about equal to that of New England and the

Middle States. Only a small part of this population was to be found west of the mountains. Settlement was working into central New York, southwest Pennsylvania, the neighboring parts of Virginia, and the upper waters of the Tennessee; but the only considerable western community was in Kentucky. These distant settlers had an important influence on the Union, since they lay within easy reach of the Spanish settlements, and occasionally threatened to withdraw.

[Sidenote: Intellectual life.]

The intellectual life of the people was little developed. Schools had not sensibly improved since colonial times. The graduating classes of all the colleges in 1789 count up to about 170. There were but two schools of medicine in the country, and no regular school of law. In one department of literature alone were the Americans eminent: the state papers of public men such as Washington, Hamilton, and Jefferson are written with the force and directness of the best school of English. Poetry there was; its character may be judged by a single quotation from Barlow's "Vision of Columbus," a favorite epic, published in 1787:—

"There stood stern Putnam, seamed with many a scar,
The veteran honours of an earlier war;
Undaunted Stirling, dreadful to his foes,
And Gates and Sullivan to vengeance rose;
While brave McDougall, steady and sedate,
Stretched the nerved arm to ope the scene of fate."

[Sidenote: Economic conditions.]

In economic conditions the United States were little more advanced than had been the colonies. The country abounded in natural resources: timber clad the whole Appalachian range, and spread far into the Mississippi valley; the virgin soil, and particularly the rich and untouched prairies of the West, were an accumulation of unmeasured wealth. Yet it was little easier to get from the sea to Lake Erie or to the Ohio than it had been forty years before. It seemed impossible that a country could be held together when it was so large that a courier might be two months on his way from the seat of government to the most distant frontier; and Jefferson predicted that it would be a thousand years before the country would be thickly settled as far west as the Mississippi. The chief resource of the country was agriculture; almost every State raised its own food, and there were considerable exports, particularly of wheat and flour. Manufactures were chiefly imported from England, the only widely known American industry being the distilling of New England rum. The chief source of wealth was still commerce; in 1790 the exports and imports were about twenty million dollars each, or five dollars per head of the population. The movement of vessels to foreign ports was tolerably free, but the vexatious restrictions and taxes imposed by England tended to throw an undue part of the profit into the hands of the English merchants. Business of every kind was much hampered by the want of bank capital and by the state of the currency.

72. POLITICAL METHODS IN 1789.

[Sidenote: Current political theories.]

The chief intellectual interest of the people was in politics. The State and the national constitutions both protected freedom of speech, and Americans were accustomed freely to discuss public men and public measures. Public opinion was, however, created by a comparatively small number of persons,—the leading planters of the South, merchants and great families in the Middle States, the gentlemen and clergy in New England. Already two different schools of political thought had appeared. The one is typified by John Adams's elaborate work, "The Defence of the American Constitutions," published in 1787. "The rich, the well-born, and the able," he says, "… must be separated from the mass and placed by themselves in a senate." The leading spirit in the other school was Thomas Jefferson. He wrote in 1787: "I am persuaded that the good sense of the people will always be found the best army. They may be led astray for a moment, but will soon correct themselves." The accepted principle of republican government was nevertheless that there should be a limited number of voters, following the lead of experienced statesmen of a higher social class.

[Sidenote: Political methods.]

A few symptoms of a change in political methods were visible. In 1788 a nominating convention was held in Harrisburg; this method of selecting candidates by representatives of the voters of their party was rapidly extended. In 1789 the secret Columbian Order, or Tammany Society, was formed in New York. At first benevolent and literary, the correspondent of the Massachusetts Historical Society, by 1800 it had become a political organization and was controlling local elections. In several States, and particularly in New York, factions had grown up about leading families of public men; in a few years they became political machines subject to the direction of a few leaders. Buying of votes was almost unknown, but there was much disorder at elections.

[Sidenote: Respect for authority.]

In many respects both the State and national governments were weak. The legislatures had, during the Revolution, been accustomed to ride roughshod over the minority, and they were still inclined to grant charters and privileges only to party friends; Federalist legislatures would charter only Federalist banks. Americans enjoyed their individual liberty, but resented the use of force either for collecting taxes or for upholding the authority of government; and the States were not accustomed unhesitatingly to accept the action of Congress. On the other hand, the Anglo-Saxon respect for law was recovering from the shock of the Revolution. There was a strong feeling of loyalty to the State governments, and the beginning of national interest and patriotism. By common consent the new Constitution was put quietly into effect by those who expected its success.

73. ORGANIZATION OF CONGRESS (1789).

[Sidenote: First congressional election.]

The first step in the organization of the government was to elect senators and representatives. The Senate was small, and was expected to be a kind of executive council. In due time John Adams was chosen vice-president, and became chairman. The Senate sat for several years in secret session; but from the journal of William Maclay, senator from Pennsylvania, we learn many interesting details, and know that the casting vote of the chairman was often necessary to settle important questions. The time and manner of electing members of the House was left to the States. In some cases all the members from a State were elected on one general ticket; in others the State was divided into districts. Among the distinguished members were Theodore Sedgwick and Elbridge Gerry of Massachusetts, Jonathan Trumbull of Connecticut, and James Madison of Virginia. From the first, the custom obtained that a member of the House should be a resident of the district from which he was chosen.

[Sidenote: Organization of Congress.]

The House organized April 6. In the Speaker appeared an officer until now unknown in the Federal system. At first he was only a moderator; after about a year he was given the power to appoint committees; and from that time dates the growth of those powers which have made him second in influence only to the President of the United States. The procedure was modelled partly on that of the old Congress, and partly upon that of the State legislatures: it is noticeable, however, that the system of permanent committees so familiar during the previous twelve years was not immediately readopted; It began to come in about 1794. The first act on the statute book was passed June 1, 1789, and prescribed a form of oath. Congress voted itself a moderate per diem of six dollars. The only other important question relative to the form of Congress was that of apportionment. On April 5, 1792, a bill allotting the members of the House to the States was the subject of the first executive veto.

[Sidenote: Amendments.]

One important function was performed before Congress adjourned, by submitting to the States twelve amendments to the Constitution. These were made up by comparison of the propositions submitted by the States at the time of ratification, and practically constituted a brief bill of rights. In due time all but two unimportant clauses were ratified by the States, and the great objection to the Constitution was thus removed.

The importance of the First Congress was that the general forms adopted for the transaction of its business have continued without serious change to the present day. Its officers have increased, its powers have developed, its political importance has expanded; but its parliamentary procedure is still much the same as in 1789.

74. ORGANIZATION OF THE EXECUTIVE (1789, 1790).

[Sidenote: The first President.]

While the senators and representatives were being selected, Presidential electors were also chosen in all the eleven States except New York. The States exercised their constitutional discretion: in some the electors were chosen by the legislatures, in others by general ticket, and in others by districts. In one thing they agreed: when quorums of both houses were obtained, so that the votes could be counted, April 6, 1789, it was found that every elector had cast a ballot for George Washington. On April 30 he took the oath of office in Federal Hall on Wall Street, New York, and Maclay records for the benefit of posterity that "he was dressed in deep brown, with metal buttons with an eagle on them, white stockings, a bag, and sword." As the presidency was an entirely new office, there was much difficulty and some squabbling over the details of his place. The question of title was raised; and it was understood that Washington would have liked to be called "His High Mightiness, the President of the United States and Protector of their Liberties." No action was taken, and the simple title of "Mr. President" was by common consent adopted.

[Sidenote: Executive departments.]
[Sidenote: Treasury Department.]

The duties of the President were clearly defined by the Constitution. It now became necessary to make some provision for subordinate executive officers. Here for the first time the importance of the legislation of the First Congress is visible. They had it in their power to put flesh and blood upon the dry bones of the Constitution: they might surround the President with a vigorous, active, and well-centred body of subordinates; or they might go back to the practice of the old Congress, and create executive officers who should be practically the servants of Congress. They resolved to trust the President. The first executive department to be established was the Department of Foreign Affairs, of which the name was a little latter changed to the Department of State. In due time Thomas Jefferson was appointed Secretary of State; among his successors have been John Marshall, James Madison, James Monroe, John Quincy Adams, Henry Clay, Martin Van Buren, Daniel Webster, John C. Calhoun, James Buchanan, and William H, Seward. The War Department bill passed August 7, and Henry Knox, who had been the head of the army under the old system, was reappointed. In establishing the Treasury Department a strong effort was made to create a Secretary of the Treasury as an agent of Congress rather than as the officer of the President. The details of the office were therefore carefully regulated by the statute, and specific duties were assigned to the Secretary. He was, however, appointed by the President, and the question was raised whether he was also removable by the President. The Senate insisted that the removal should not be valid without its approval; the House insisted that the President should be unrestrained by the casting vote of the Vice-President the latter system was adopted. The first Secretary of the Treasury was Alexander Hamilton.

[Sidenote: Relations with Congress.]

Then came the question of the relations of cabinet officers to Congress. Maclay records that on August 22, 1790, the President appeared in the Senate with Knox, and intimated that the Secretary of War would explain a proposed Indian treaty. The only remark that Knox seems to have made was: "Not till Saturday next;" but Maclay was convinced that he was there "to overawe the timid and neutral part of the Senate." With some displeasure, the Senate referred the matter to a committee. Hamilton desired an opportunity to address the House; but it was not accorded, nor does it appear that the privilege has ever been granted to any cabinet officer. Knox's speech is the nearest approach to the Parliamentary system which has been known in Congress.

75. ORGANIZATION OF THE COURTS (1789-1793).

[Sidenote: The Judiciary Act.]

By the Constitution there was to be a supreme court and such inferior courts as Congress should create. By the Act of Sept. 24, 1789 the federal judicial system was organized substantially as it now stands. Following the precedent of some of the States, two grades of inferior courts were created,—the district and the circuit. The judicial business of the country was small, and for the time being the supreme justices were to hold the circuit courts. Prosecuting officers and marshals were appointed, and here is to be found the germ of the present system of limited terms for public officials: they were to have commissions which should run four years; it seems to have been tacitly understood that they would be reappointed. A few brief clauses defined the manner in which suits could be appealed from the State courts to the national. This statute has made it possible to apply federal law in the same way throughout the Union: errors of construction, and divergencies of judgment involving the national Constitution, laws, and treaties, are corrected through this power of appeal to one central supreme tribunal. A little later an Act was passed defining crimes against the United States. The courts were speedily organized, and John Jay of New York was made the first chief justice.

[Sidenote: Important decisions.]

For a few years no important decisions were made by the court; but in February, 1793, a suit was entertained against the State of Georgia; soon after, one was entered against the State of Massachusetts. Georgia replied by passing a statute punishing with death any United States marshal who might attempt to serve a process upon her. Massachusetts urged the passing of an eleventh constitutional amendment; it was duly adopted in 1798, and prohibited suits before a federal court against a State, by a citizen of another State or of a foreign country.

76. REVENUE AND PROTECTION (1789-1792).

[Sidenote: Revenue scheme.]

The first necessity of the new government was to lay the taxes authorized under the new Constitution for its own support, for the payment of interest, and eventually for sinking the principal of the public debt. Two days after the House organized, Madison introduced a scheme, which eventually passed into the first tariff act. On May 13, 1789, after agreeing to a duty on "looking-glasses and brushes," it was moved to lay a tax of ten dollars each on imported slaves. A Georgia member protested against the tax as intended for the benefit of Virginia, and "hoped gentlemen would have some feeling for others;" the proposition failed.

[Sidenote: Question of protection.]

Another amendment, however, raised the most important political question connected with taxation. April 9, 1789, a Pennsylvania member wished to increase the list of dutiable articles, so as "to encourage the productions of our country and to protect our infant manufactures." A South Carolina member at once objected. Two days later a petition from Baltimore manufacturers asked Congress to impose on "all foreign articles which can be made in America such duties as will give a just and decided preference to our labors." New England opposed the proposed duties because molasses, hemp, and flax were included; molasses was a "raw material" for the manufacture of rum; and hemp and flax were essential for the cordage of New England ships. Lee of Virginia moved to strike out the duty on steel, since a supply could not be furnished within the United States, and he thought it an "oppressive, though indirect, tax on agriculture."

[Sidenote: The first tariff.]

The act as passed July 4, 1789, bore the title of "An Act for the encouragement and protection of manufactures;" yet the highest ad valorem duty was fifteen per cent. To be sure, the high rates of freight at that time afforded a very large additional protection; but no general revenue act ever passed by Congress has imposed so low a scale of duties.

[Sidenote: Hamilton's scheme.]

By the time the revenue had begun to come in under this Act, Secretary Hamilton had worked out in his mind a general financial system, intended to raise the credit and to strengthen the authority of the Union. The first step was to provide a sufficient revenue to pay running expenses and interest. Finding that the first tariff produced too little revenue, in 1790 and again in 1792 it was slightly increased, at Hamilton's suggestion. The second part of his scheme was to lay an excise, an internal duty upon distilled spirits. In 1791 a tax, in its highest form but twenty-five cents a gallon, was laid on spirits distilled from foreign or domestic materials. The actual amount of revenue from this source was always small; but Hamilton expected that the people in the interior would thus become accustomed to federal officers and to federal law. The effect of the revenue Acts was quickly visible: in 1792 the annual revenue of the government had risen to $3,600,000.

77. NATIONAL AND STATE DEBTS (1789, 1790).

[Sidenote: The debt funded.]

The third part of Hamilton's scheme was to fund the national debt into one system of bonds, and to pay the interest. When he assumed control of the Treasury he found, as nearly as could be calculated, ten millions of foreign debt with about two millions of accrued interest, and twenty-nine millions of domestic debt with eleven millions of accrued interest,—a total of more than fifty-two millions. So far as there was any sale for United States securities they had fallen to about twenty-five per cent of their par value. Jan. 14, 1790, Hamilton submitted one of a series of elaborate financial reports; it called on Congress to make such provision for principal and interest as would restore confidence. By this time an opposition had begun to rise against the great secretary, and Madison proposed to inquire in each case what the holder of a certificate of debt had paid for it; he was to be reimbursed in that amount, and the balance of the principal was to be paid to the original holder. Hamilton pointed out that in order to place future loans the Treasury must assure the public that bonds would be paid in full to the person holding a legal title. Congress accepted Hamilton's view, and an act was passed by which the interest was to be promptly paid, and an annual sum to be set apart for the redemption of the principal. The securities of the United States instantly began to rise, and in 1793 they were quoted at par. The credit of the government was reestablished.

[Sidenote: Assumption proposed.]

Now came a fourth part of Hamilton's scheme, upon which he laid great stress: he proposed that the outstanding State debts should likewise be taken over by the general government. The argument was that the States had incurred their debts for the common purpose of supporting the Revolution. There was strong opposition, particularly from States like Virginia, which had extinguished the greater part of their own debt. The House showed a bare majority in favor of the assumption project; on the appearance of members from North Carolina, which had just entered the Union, that majority was, on April 12, 1790, reversed.

[Sidenote: The seat of government.]
[Sidenote: Compromise.]

Meanwhile the old question of the permanent seat of the federal government had been revived, and, as in the days of the Confederation, it seemed impossible to agree. It was expected that the capital would lie somewhere in the Northern States; at one time Germantown was all but selected. The Virginia members suddenly took fire, and Lee declared that "he was averse to sound alarms or introduce terror into the House, but if they were well founded he thought it his duty;" and Jackson of Georgia declared that "this will blow the coals of sedition and injure the Union." The matter was laid over until the middle of 1790. It was evident that the friends of assumption were in a small minority, and the friends of a Northern capital in a small majority. Hamilton worked upon Jefferson to secure a compromise. The matter was adjusted at Jefferson's table: a few Northern votes were obtained for a Southern capital, and two Virginia members agreed to vote for assumption. By very narrow majorities it was therefore agreed that the national capital should be placed on the Potomac River, and that State debts amounting to $21,500,000 should be assumed. A few months later the President selected the site of the present national capital, and in due time the debts were taken up.

78. UNITED STATES BANK (1791, 1792).

[Sidenote: A bank proposed.]

Having thus reorganized the finances of the country, Hamilton now proposed the fifth part of his scheme,—the establishment of a national bank. In a report of Dec. 14, 1790, he presented the subject to the attention of Congress. He urged that it would benefit the public by offering an investment, that it would aid the government in making loans and by collecting taxes, and that its notes would be a useful currency. Hamilton drafted a bill, which was an adaptation of the charter of the Bank of England. The capital of $10,000,000, and the management of the bank, were to be private; but the government was to be a stockholder, and to have the right of requiring periodical statements of the bank's condition.

The Senate passed the bill without a division, substantially as drawn by Hamilton. Apparently it was on the point of going through the House, when Smith of South Carolina objected, and Jackson of Georgia declared that he had never seen a bank bill in the State of Georgia; "nor will they ever benefit the farmers of that State or of New York;" and he called it an unconstitutional monopoly.

[Sidenote: The question of implied powers.]

After a week's debate on the question whether the bank was authorized by the Constitution, it passed the House by a vote of 39 to 20, and was sent to the President. He called for the opinions of the members of his cabinet in writing, and the answers submitted by Hamilton and Jefferson are still among the most important documents on the construction of the Constitution. Jefferson's standpoint was simply that, since the Constitution nowhere expressly authorized the creation of a bank, Congress had gone beyond its powers. Hamilton asserted that if the bank were "necessary and proper to carry out any of the specific powers, such as taxation and the borrowing of money, then

Congress might create a bank, or any other public institution, to serve its ends." The President accepted Hamilton's view, and the act was signed. The capital of the bank was speedily subscribed, and it immediately entered on a prosperous and useful career.

79. SLAVERY QUESTIONS (1789-1798).

[Sidenote: Anti-slavery memorials.]

The question of the extent of the powers of Congress had already once been raised. On February 11 and 12, 1790, there were presented to Congress two memorials, the one the "Address of the People called Quakers, in their Annual Assembly convened;" the other the "Memorial of the Pennsylvania Society for Promoting the Abolition of Slavery." These memorials asked Congress to "exert upright endeavors, to the full extent of your power, to remove every obstruction to public righteousness," particularly in the matter of slavery. The motion to commit instantly roused Southern members. Jackson of Georgia said that "any extraordinary attention of Congress to the petition would hold their property in jeopardy." The matter was sent to a subcommittee, composed chiefly of Southern members. On March 8th that committee reported the principles under which Congress acted during the next seventy years. They said that Congress had no power to interfere with slavery or the treatment of slaves within the States; they might pass laws regulating the slave-trade, but could not then stop the importation of slaves from foreign countries into the United States. Another resolution, to the effect that Congress would exercise its powers for the humane principles of the memorial, was struck out by the House. The anti-slavery organizations from which these memorials had proceeded kept up a brisk fusillade of petitions. In some cases the House refused to receive them, but Congress did pass several laws reducing the evils of the slave-trade.

[Sidenote: Fugitive slaves.]

In 1793 the question came up, how fugitive slaves should be restored if they had fled and taken refuge in another State. An act was passed by which the United States assumed authority in the matter; the claimant was simply to satisfy any national or State magistrate that he was entitled to the person claimed. The act had hardly gone into effect before a fugitive was apprehended in Massachusetts. Josiah Quincy, who was employed to defend him, tells us that he "heard a noise, and turning round he saw the constables lying sprawling on the floor, and a passage opening through the crowd, through which the fugitive was taking his departure, without stopping to hear the opinion of the court." From the very first, therefore, we find in vigorous action the paraphernalia of the later anti- slavery movement,—societies, petitions, laws, and deliberate violation of laws.

80. THE SUCCESS OF THE NEW GOVERNMENT.

[Sidenote: The government established.]

The end of Washington's first administration in March, 1793, saw the government completely organized, and accepted throughout the Union. The distinction between friends and opponents of the Constitution had entirely disappeared. There was no longer any suggestion of substantial amendment. Two Congresses had gone through their work, and had accustomed the people to a national legislature. The President had made appointments, sent ambassadors, commanded the army, and vetoed bills, and yet there was no fear of a monarchy. The national courts were in regular and undisturbed session. The Union was complete, and two new States, Vermont and Kentucky, had been admitted.

This remarkable success was due in considerable part to the personal influence of a few men. Washington's great popularity and his disinterested use of his new powers had taken away a multitude of fears. The skill of Hamilton had built up a successful financial system. In Congress Madison had been efficient in working out the details of legislation. Washington, with his remarkable judgment of men, had selected an able staff of officials, representing all the sections of the country.

[Sidenote: Prosperity]

Yet, as Washington himself had said, "Influence is not government." One of the chief elements of the Union's strength was that it pressed lightly upon the people. For the first time in the history of America there was an efficient system of import duties. They were almost the sole form of taxation, and, like all indirect taxes, their burden was not felt. Above all, the commercial benefits of the new Union were seen from North to South. Trade between the States was absolutely unhampered, and a brisk interchange of products went on. The country was prosperous; its shipping increased, and foreign trade was also growing steadily.

[Sidenote: Relations with the States.]

So far the Union had met no violent resistance either from insurgents or from the States. In the Virginia convention of 1788 Patrick Henry had said: "I never will give up that darling word 'requisitions;' my country may give it up, the majority may wrest it from me, but I never will give it up till my grave."

Nevertheless, when the requisitions on the States were given up, the chief cause of dispute in the Union was removed. Up to this time the only distinctly sectional legislation had been the assumption of the State debts and the fixing of the national capital; and these two had been set off against each other. If peace continued, there was every prospect of a healthy growth of national spirit.

CHAPTER VIII.

FEDERAL SUPREMACY (1793-1801).

81. REFERENCES.

BIBLIOGRAPHIES.—W. E. Foster, *References to Presidential Administrations*, 1-8; Justin Winsor, *Narrative and Critical History*, VII. 294-314, 319, 320, 329-336, 454-456, 513-519; Channing and Hart, *Guide*, §§ 162, 166.

HISTORICAL MAPS.—Nos. 1, 4, this volume (*Epoch Maps*, Nos. 7, 9); MacCoun, *Historical Geography*; Scribner, *Statistical Atlas*, Plate 13; J. Morse, *American Geography*.

GENERAL ACCOUNTS.—J. B McMaster, *United States*, II. 89-557; H. Von Holst, *Constitutional History*, I. 112-167; J. Schouler, *United States*, I. 221-501; R. Hildreth, *United States*, IV. 411-704; V. 25-418; T. Pitkin, *United States*, II. 356-500 (to 1797); George Tucker, *United States*, I. 504-628, II. 21-145; Bryant and Gay, *Popular History*, IV. 123-144; Bradford, *Constitutional History*, 125-201.

SPECIAL HISTORIES.—Standard lives of Washington, especially Sparks, Marshall, and Irving; C. F. Adams, *Life of John Adams*; Henry Adams, *Albert Gallatin*; H. C. Lodge, *Washington*, II. 129-269; J. T. Morse, *Jefferson*, 146-208, and *John Adams*, 241-310; G. Pellew, *John Jay*, 262-339; S. H. Gay, *Madison*, 193-251; George Gibbs, *Administrations of Washington and Adams*, I., II.; W. H. Trescott, *Diplomatic History*; T. Lyman, *Diplomacy*; J. C. Hamilton, *Republic*, V., VI.

CONTEMPORARY ACCOUNTS.—Thomas Jefferson, *Anas* (*Works*, IX. 185-203);
William Sullivan, *Familiar Letters on Public Characters*, 48-187 (written in reply to Jefferson); Works of Washington, Jefferson, Fisher Ames, John Jay, Rufus King, Arthur St. Clair, John Adams, Madison, and Gallatin; Abigail Adams, *Letters*; W. Winterbotham, *Historical View* (1795); T. Cooper, *Some Information respecting America* (1793, 1794); Rochefoucault-Liancourt, *Voyage dans les États-Unis* (1795-1797) (also in translation); J. Weld, *Travels through the States* (1795-1797); newspapers, especially *General Advertiser* and *Aurora, Boston Gazette.*—Reprints in Alexander Johnston, *American Orations*, I.; *American History told by Contemporaries*, III.

82. FORMATION OF POLITICAL PARTIES (1792-1794).

[Sidenote: Origin of parties.]

During the four uneventful years from 1789 to 1793 two political parties had been slowly developed. Some writers have imagined that these two parties were a survival of the Revolutionary Whigs and Tories; some have traced them back to the debate on the assumption of State debts. John Adams, years later, went to the heart of the matter when he said: "You say our divisions began with Federalism and anti-Federalism. Alas! they began with human nature." The foundation for the first two great national parties was a difference of opinion as to the nature and proper functions of the new government.

During the second Congress, from 1791 to 1793, arose an opposition to Hamilton which gradually consolidated into a party. It came chiefly from the Southern and Middle States, and represented districts in which there was little capital or trade. Arrayed among his supporters were most of the representatives from New England, and many from the Middle States and South Carolina: they represented the commercial interests of the country; they desired to see the debt funded and the State debts assumed; they began to act together as another party.

[Sidenote: Hamilton and Jefferson.]

The final form taken by these two parties depended much upon the character of their leaders. Hamilton, a man of great personal force and of strong aristocratic feeling, represented the principle of authority, of government framed and administered by a select few for the benefit of their fellows. Jefferson, an advocate of popular government extended to a point never before reached, declared that his party was made up of those "who identified themselves with the people, have confidence in them, cherish and consider them as the most honest and safe, although not the most wise depositary of the public interest." Between two such men controversies were certain to arise. In May, 1792, Jefferson wrote that Hamilton had introduced speculation and a dangerous construction of the constitution; and Hamilton wrote that Jefferson was at the head of a hostile faction dangerous to the Union. Washington attempted to make himself an arbiter of this quarrel, but was unable to reconcile the two men. They both urged him to accept a second term for the presidency, and he was again unanimously elected in 1792. The quarrel between the two great chiefs had by this time got abroad. Hamilton was said to be a monarchist. His administration of the Treasury was attacked, and an investigation was held early in 1793; but no one was able to find any irregularity.

By this time the followers of Jefferson had begun to take upon themselves the name of Republicans. They held that the government ought to raise and spend as little money as possible; beyond that they rested upon the principles first definitely stated in Jefferson's opinion on the bank (§ 96) that Congress was confined in its powers to the letter of the Constitution; and that the States were the depositary of most of the powers of government. The other party took upon itself the name of Federal, or Federalist, which had proved so valuable in the struggle over the Constitution. Among its most eminent members were Hamilton, John Jay, Vice-President John Adams, and President Washington.

[Sidenote: Newspaper organs.]

Both parties now began to set in motion new political machinery. The "Gazette of the United States" became the recognized mouthpiece of the Federalists, and the "National Gazette," edited by Philip Freneau, translating clerk in Jefferson's department, began to attack Hamilton and other leading Federalists, and even the President. At a cabinet meeting Washington complained that "that rascal Freneau sent him three copies of his paper every day, as though he thought he would become a distributer of them. He could see in this nothing but an impudent design to insult him."

83. WAR BETWEEN FRANCE AND ENGLAND (1793).

[Sidenote: French Revolution.]
[Sidenote: War.]

So far the parties had been little more than personal followings; the mighty movements in Europe were now to crystallize them. Early in 1789 a revolution had come about in France; in 1791 a constitution was put in force under which the king became a limited monarch; in 1792 war broke out between France and a Prussian-Austrian alliance. Disasters on the frontier were followed by the overthrow of the monarchy, and in January, 1793, Louis the Sixteenth was executed. The anarchical movement, once begun, hurried on until the government of France fell into the hands of men controlled by the populace of Paris. On Feb. 3, 1793, the French Republic declared war against England: the issue was instantly accepted. As the two powers were unable conveniently to reach each other on land, great efforts were made on both sides to fit out fleets. The colonies of each power were exposed to attack, and colonial trade was in danger.

[Sidenote: Interest of America.]

From the first the sympathy of the United States had naturally been with France. The republic seemed due to American example; Jefferson was our minister at Paris in 1789, and saw his favorite principles of human liberty extending to Europe. The excesses of the Revolution, however, startled the Federalists, who saw in them a sufficient proof that Jefferson's "people" could not be trusted. The war brought up the question of the treaty of 1778 with France, by which the Americans bound themselves to guarantee the colonial possessions of France in case of defensive war.

[Sidenote: Danger to America.]

For the United States to enter the war as ally of either side meant to lose most of the advantages gained by the new Constitution: the Indians on the frontier had opposed and defeated a large body of United States troops; the revenue of the country derived from imports would cease as soon as war was declared; American ships would be exposed to capture on every sea. Trade with the West Indies, which proceeded irregularly and illegally, was now likely to be broken up altogether. The question was no longer one of international law, but of American politics: the Democrats were inclined to aid France, by war or by indirect aid,—such as we had received from France at the beginning of the Revolutionary War; the Federalists leaned toward England, because they wished English trade, and because they feared the spread of anarchical principles in America.

84. AMERICAN NEUTRALITY (1793).

[Sidenote: Neutrality proclamation.]

On April 5, 1793, the news of the outbreak of war was received at Philadelphia. Washington at once summoned his cabinet for the most important discussion which it had yet held. Was the United States to consider itself bound to enter the war and to defend the French West Indies against Great Britain? Should the President declare that the United States stood neutral in this contest? The question was new. For the first time in history there was an independent American power,—a nation so far removed by distance and by interest from European conflicts that it might reasonably ask that it should not be drawn into the struggle. Hamilton was inclined to hold the treaties abrogated by the change of government in France; Jefferson insisted that they were binding; both agreed that the President ought to issue a proclamation announcing that the United States would take no part on either side. The neutrality proclamation, issued April 22, was therefore an announcement to the world that the United States stood outside the European system, and might continue friendly relations with both belligerent powers.

This attitude was anything but what France had expected. On April 8 a French minister, Genet, landed in Charleston, armed with a quantity of blank commissions for privateers. He was a man twenty-eight years old, whose diplomatic experience had culminated in the disruption of one of the weaker neighbors of France. He had no doubt that the sympathy of the American people was with his country. He proposed, therefore, to act as though he stood upon his own soil: men were enlisted; privateers were commissioned; prizes were taken in American waters and brought into American ports for condemnation. Genet advanced northward in a kind of triumphal procession. Throughout the South and West, Democratic clubs were organized, modelled on the French Jacobin and other revolutionary clubs.

[Sidenote: Genet and Washington.]

He reached Philadelphia, to be confronted by the Neutrality Proclamation and by the firmness of the President. His privateers were checked. He does not appear to have demanded of the United States a fulfilment of the treaty of 1778, but he did ask for advance payment of money due to France, and for other favors. To his chagrin, Congress was not to meet until December, and he insisted in vain that there should be an extra session. In July Genet proceeded to fit out a captured British vessel, the "Little Sarah," as a privateer; and, contrary to the remonstrances of the government and his own implied promise, she was sent to sea. Encouraged by this success, he determined to make a public appeal to the people to override the President. His purpose was made known, and his career was at an end. When the United States asked for his recall, it was cheerfully accorded by the French government. In three months Genet had contrived to offend the principal officers of government and to insult the nation. The current of feeling was thus set toward England.

85. THE JAY TREATY (1794-1796).

[Sidenote: American grievances.]
[Sidenote: Neutral rights.]

Once more the English government neglected the favorable moment for securing the friendship of the United States. The grievances so much resented under the Confederation (§ 56) were continued: the Western posts were still occupied by the British; American vessels still paid unreasonable duties in British ports; the West India trade was still withheld. The war at once led to new aggressions. France and England throughout sought to limit American commerce by capturing vessels for violations of four disputed principles of international law. The first was that provisions are "contraband of war," and hence that American vessels carrying breadstuffs, the principal export of the United States, were engaged in an unlawful trade: the United States insisted that only military stores were "contraband of war." The second limiting principle was that, after notice of the blockade of a port, vessels bound to it might be taken anywhere on the high seas: the United States held that the notice had no validity unless there was an actual blockading force outside the port. The third principle was the so-called "Rule of 1756," that where a European country forbade trade with its colonies in time of peace it should not open it to neutrals in time of war: the United States denied the right of Great Britain to interfere in their trade with the French and Spanish colonies. The fourth principle was that a ship might be captured if it had upon it goods which were the property of an enemy. The United States asserted that "Free ships make free goods," that a neutral vessel was not subject to capture, no matter whose property she carried.

[Sidenote: Aggressions on the United States.]
[Sidenote: Impressment.]
[Sidenote: Danger of war.]

On May 9, 1793, the French ordered the capture of vessels loaded with provisions, although expressly excepted by the treaty of 1778. On June 8 the British issued a similar order; and in November the rule of 1756 was again put in force by the British government. Captures at once began by both powers; but the British cruisers were more numerous, did more damage, and thus inclined public sentiment in the United States against England. The pacific Jefferson now came forward as the defender of American interests: Sept. 16, 1793, he sent to Congress a report in which he set forth the aggressions upon American commerce, and recommended a policy of retaliation. Meantime a new grievance had arisen, which was destined to be a cause of the War of 1812. In time of war the commanders of British naval vessels were authorized to "impress" British seamen, even out of British merchant vessels. The search of American merchantmen on the same errand at once began, and was felt by the United States government to be humiliating to the national dignity. The whole country was outraged by the frequent seizure of native Americans, on the pretext that they were English born. Public feeling rose until on March 26, 1794, a temporary embargo was laid, forbidding vessels to depart from American ports. On April 17, a motion was introduced to cut off commercial intercourse with Great Britain. On April 19, therefore, the President appointed John Jay, Chief Justice of the United States, as a special envoy to make a last effort to adjust matters in England. Nevertheless, the non-inter course bill passed the House, and was defeated only by Adams's casting vote in the Senate.

[Sidenote: Jay's Treaty.]

Fortunately it was a time when communication with Europe was slow. Not until June did Jay reach England. A treaty was negotiated on November 19, but was not received by Washington until after the adjournment of Congress in March, 1795. The treaty had indeed removed some old grievances: the posts were to be evacuated; commissions were to settle the northeast boundary, and to adjust the claims for the British debts; but Jay got no indemnity for the negroes carried away by the British in 1783. The commercial clauses were far less favorable: the discriminating taxes against American shipping were at last withdrawn; but Jay was unable to secure any suitable guarantee for neutral trade, and could obtain no promise to refrain from searching American merchantmen, or seizing English-born sailors found thereon. Above all, the West India trade, which the United States so much desired, was granted only with the proviso that it should be carried on in vessels of less than seventy tons burden. In return for these meagre concessions, granted only for twelve years, the United States agreed not to export to any part of the world "molasses, sugar, coffee, cocoa, or cotton."

[Sidenote: Excitement in the United States.]

A special session of the Senate was summoned in June, 1795. and with great difficulty the necessary two-thirds majority was obtained. The twelfth article, containing the West India and the export clauses, was particularly objectionable, and the Senate struck it out. During the remainder of the year there was the fiercest popular opposition; the commercial and ship-building interest felt that it had been betrayed; Jay was burned in effigy; Hamilton was stoned at a public meeting; State legislatures declared the treaty unconstitutional. Washington was attacked so fiercely that he said the language used "could scarcely be applied to a Nero, to a notorious defaulter, or even to a common pickpocket." When Congress met in 1795 an effort was made to prevent the necessary appropriations for carrying out the treaty. It was only the great personal popularity of Washington that saved the country from a repudiation of the treaty and a war with England. Once in force, the treaty was found moderately favorable. Our commerce increased, and captures were much diminished.

86. THE WHISKEY REBELLION (1794).

[Sidenote: The excise unpopular.]
[Sidenote: Outbreak.]

During this year of excitement a serious outbreak had occurred in

Pennsylvania. Ever since the first Excise Act in 1791 (§ 76), there had been determined opposition to the collection of the whiskey tax. The people of southwestern Pennsylvania were three hundred miles from tide- water; and whiskey was the only commodity of considerable value, in small bulk, with which they could purchase goods. The tax, therefore, affected the whole community. In 1792 the policy pursued at the beginning of the Revolution was brought into action: mobs and public meetings began to intimidate the tax-collectors. In 1794 the difficulties broke out afresh, and on July 17 the house of Inspector-General Neville was attacked by a band of armed men; one man was killed, and the house was burned. Great popular mass meetings followed, and a few days later the United States mail was robbed.

[Sidenote: Suppression.]

As this violence was directed against the revenue laws, Hamilton made it his special task to suppress it. On September 25 the President called out the militia from Pennsylvania, New Jersey, Maryland, and Virginia. Hamilton himself accompanied the troops, fifteen thousand in number; they marched over the mountains, and reached the disaffected country at the end of October. The insurgents made no stand in the field, and the troops returned, after making a few arrests.

The matter now went to the courts. Six persons were indicted for treason, of whom two, Vigol and Mitchell, were convicted. They were rough and ignorant men, who had been led into the outbreak without understanding their own responsibility, and Washington pardoned them both. In July, 1795, a general amnesty was proclaimed.

[Sidenote: Effect.]

The effect of the whole movement was to make it evident throughout the nation that the United States had at its disposal a military force sufficient to put down any ordinary insurrection. In his message on the subject on Nov. 19, 1794, Washington alluded to "combinations of men who have disseminated suspicions, jealousies, and accusations of the whole government." The Senate applied these words to "self-created societies." The allusion was to the Democratic clubs, founded in 1793 when Genet came to the country (§ 84), and still in existence. The effect of Washington's criticism was to break down the societies and to check a movement which looked toward resistance to all constituted government. The opposition were compelled to take a less objectionable party name, and began to call themselves Republicans.

87. ELECTION OF JOHN ADAMS (1796).

On Sept. 17, 1796, Washington, in a public address, announced that he should not accept a re-election. The presidency had been irksome to Washington, and the personal attacks upon himself had grieved him; but he retired with the admiration and respect of the whole country. The selection of a successor at once became a party question. Jefferson, who had resigned the office of Secretary of State at the end of 1793, was the natural leader of the Republicans. John Adams, then Vice-President, had the largest Federalist following; but Hamilton hoped, by an electoral trick, to bring T. Pinckney, the candidate for Vice-President, in over his head. Adams candidly expressed his opinion of this intrigue: "That must be a sordid people indeed, a people destitute of a sense of honor, equity, and character, that could submit to be governed and see hundreds of its most meritorious public men governed by a Pinckney under an elective government."

[Sidenote: Adams and Jefferson.]

The danger was not, however, from Pinckney, but from Jefferson. When the votes were counted it was found that Adams had received the vote of the Northern States, with Delaware and a part of Maryland; but that Jefferson had received almost the whole vote of the South and of Pennsylvania. Adams became President by a vote of seventy-one, and Jefferson Vice-President by a vote of sixty-eight. The two men had been associated in early years, and were not unfriendly to each other. There was even a hint that Jefferson was to be taken into the cabinet. As soon as the administration began, all confidence between them was at an end. The same set of elections decided the membership of Congress to serve from 1797 to 1799; the Senate remained decidedly Federalist; in the House the balance of power was held by a few moderate Republicans.

[Sidenote: Adams's cabinet.]

Adams considered himself the successor to the policy of Washington, and committed the serious mistake of taking over his predecessor's cabinet. Hamilton retired in 1795; he had been replaced by his friend and admirer, Oliver Wolcott; the Secretary of State was Timothy Pickering of Pennsylvania: both these men looked upon Hamilton as their party chief. The administration began, therefore, with divided counsels, and with jealousy in the President's official household.

88. BREACH WITH FRANCE (1795-1798).

While the war-cloud with England was gathering and disappearing, new complications had arisen with France. The Jay treaty was received by that power as an insult, partly because it was favorable to her rival, partly because it removed the danger of war between England and the United States. In 1795 the first period of the Revolution was over, and an efficient government was constituted, with an executive directory of five. James Monroe, appointed minister to France, had begun his mission in September, 1794, just after the fall of Robespierre; he appeared in the National Convention, and the president of that body adjured him to "let this spectacle complete the annihilation of an impious coalition of tyrants." During Jay's negotiations he continued to assure the French of the friendship of America, although the Directory speedily declared that Jay's treaty had released France from the treaty of 1778. As Monroe made no effort to push the American claims for captured vessels, he was recalled in disgrace in 1796, and C. C. Pinckney was appointed as his successor.

Three weeks after his inauguration Adams received a despatch from Pinckney announcing that he had been treated as a suspected foreigner, and that official notice had been given that the Directory would not receive another minister from the United States until the French grievances had been redressed. A special session of Congress was at once summoned, and the President declared that "the action of France ought to be repelled with a decision which shall convince France and the world that we are not a degraded people, humiliated under a colonial spirit of fear and sense of inferiority." Headstrong behavior on the President's part would have immediately brought on war; but he had already made up his mind to send a special mission to France. In June, 1797, John Marshall and Elbridge Gerry, a Republican, but a personal friend of the President, were sent out to join Pinckney in a final representation.

It was nearly a year before news of the result was received. On April 2, 1798, the President communicated the despatches revealing the so-called "X. Y. Z. affair." It appeared that the envoys on reaching Paris, in October, 1797, had been denied an official interview, but that three persons, whose names were clouded under the initials X. Y. Z., had approached them with vague suggestions of loans and advances; these were finally crystallized into a demand for fifty thousand pounds "for the pockets of the Directory." The despatch described one conversation. "'Gentlemen,' said X., 'you do not speak to the point. It is money. It is expected that you will offer money.' We said that we had spoken to that point very explicitly, that we had given an answer. 'No,' he replied, 'you have not. What is your answer?' We replied, 'It is No, no, no; not a sixpence.'" The President concluded with a ringing paragraph which summed up the indignation of the American people at this insult. "I will never send another minister to France without assurances that he will be received, respected, and honored as the representative of a great, free, powerful, and independent nation."

[Sidenote: Naval war with France.]

The Republican opposition in Congress was overwhelmed and almost silenced. A succession of statutes in April, May, and June hurried on military and naval preparations, and on July 7, 1798, American vessels of war were authorized to attack French cruisers. On Feb. 9, 1799, the "Constellation" took the French frigate "Insurgente," and American cruisers and privateers had the satisfaction of retaliating for the numerous captures of American vessels by preying on French commerce. Measures were taken to raise land forces; but here again the rift in the Federal party appeared. Washington was made titular commander-in-chief. It was expected that operations would be directed by the second in command, and Hamilton's friends insisted that he should receive that appointment. With great reluctance Adams granted the commission, the result of which was the resignation of Knox, who had been third on the list.

89. ALIEN AND SEDITION ACTS (1798).

[Sidenote: Triumph of the Federalists.]
[Sidenote: Alien Act.]

For the first and last time in his administration John Adams found himself popular. From all parts of the country addresses were sent to the President approving his patriotic stand. The moderate Republicans in the House were swept away by the current, and thus there was built up a compact Federalist majority in both houses. It proceeded deliberately to destroy its own party. The newspapers had now reached an extraordinary degree of violence; attacks upon the Federalists, and particularly upon Adams, were numerous, and keenly felt. Many of the journalists were foreigners, Englishmen and Frenchmen. To the excited imagination of the Federalists, these men seemed leagued with France in an attempt to destroy the liberties of the country; to get rid of the most violent of these writers, and at the same time to punish American-born editors who too freely criticised the administration, seemed to them essential. This purpose they proposed to carry out by a series of measures known as the Alien and Sedition Acts. A naturalization law, requiring fourteen years residence, was hurried through. On April 25 a

Federalist introduced a temporary Alien Act, for the removal of "such aliens born, not entitled by the constitution and laws to the rights of citizenship, as may be dangerous to its peace and safety." The opposition, headed by Albert Gallatin, made a strong appeal against legislation so unnecessary, sweeping, and severe. The Federalists replied in panic fear: "Without such an act," said one member, "an army might be imported, and could be excluded only after a trial." To the details of the bill there was even greater objection. It conferred upon the President the power to order the withdrawal of any alien; if he refused to go, he might be imprisoned at the President's discretion, Nevertheless, the act, limited to two years, was passed on June 25, 1798. Adams seems to have had little interest in it, and never made use of the powers thus conferred.

[Sidenote: Sedition Act.]
[Sidenote: Sedition prosecutions.]

The Sedition Act was resisted with even greater stubbornness. It proposed to punish persons who should conspire to oppose measures of the government, or to intimidate any office-holder. The publishing of libels upon the government, or either house, or the President, was likewise made a crime. Against this proposition there were abundant arguments, on grounds both of constitutionality and expediency. It introduced the new principle of law that the United States should undertake the regulation of the press, which up to this time had been left solely to the States. That its main purpose was to silence the Republican journalists is plain from the argument of a leading Federalist: the "Aurora," a Republican organ, had said that "there is more safety and liberty to be found in Constantinople than in Philadelphia;" and the "Timepiece" had said of Adams that "to tears and execrations he added derision and contempt." It is impossible to agree with the member who quoted these extracts that "they are indeed terrible. They are calculated to freeze the blood in the veins." The Sedition Act was to expire in 1801. It was quickly put into operation, and one of the prosecutions was against Callender, known to be a friend of Jefferson; he was indicted and convicted for asserting among other things that "Mr. Adams has only completed the scene of ignominy which Mr. Washington began." So far from silencing the ribald journalists, the Act and its execution simply drew down worse criticism. On the other hand, the Federalist press, which had been hardly inferior in violence, was permitted to thunder unchecked. The Alien and Sedition Acts were party measures, passed for party purposes; they did not accomplish the purposes intended, and they did the party irreparable harm.

90. VIRGINIA AND KENTUCKY RESOLUTIONS (1798-1800).

[Sidenote: Danger of disunion.]
[Sidenote: Madison's and Jefferson's resolutions.]

The elections of 1798 in the excited state of public feeling assured a Federalist majority in the Congress to sit from 1799 to 1801. The Republicans felt that their adversaries were using the power of the federal government to destroy the rights of the people. June 1, 1798, Jefferson wrote to a friend who thought that the time was come to withdraw from the Union; "If on the temporary superiority of one party the other is to resort to a scission of the Union, no federal government can exist." The remedy which lay in his mind was an appeal to the people through the State legislatures. In November and December, 1798, two series of resolutions were introduced,—one in the Virginia legislature, the other in the Kentucky legislature; the first drawn by Madison, and the second by Jefferson's own hand. They set forth that the Constitution was a compact to which the States were parties, and that "each party has an equal right to judge for itself as well of infractions as of the mode and measure of redress." The Alien and Sedition Acts and some other statutes were declared by Kentucky "not law ... void and of no effect;" and the other States were called upon to unite in so declaring them void, and in protesting to Congress. For the first time since the Constitution had been formed, a clear statement of the "compact" theory of government was now put forth. It was a reasonable implication from these resolutions that if the Federalist majority continued to override the Constitution, the States must take more decisive action; but the only distinct suggestion of an attack on the Union is found in a second series of Kentucky resolutions, passed in 1799, in which it is declared that "nullification ... of all unauthorized acts ... is the rightful remedy."

[Sidenote: Purpose of the resolutions.]

The constitutional doctrine in these resolutions was secondary. The real purpose was to arouse the public to the dangerous character of the Federalist legislation. Madison, many years afterward, explained that he meant only an appeal to the other States to unite in deprecation of the measures. The immediate effect was to set up a sort of political platform, about which the opponents of the Federalists might rally, and by the presentation of a definite issue to keep up the Republican organization against the electoral year 1800.

91. ELECTION OF 1800-1801.

[Sidenote: Peace with France.]
[Sidenote: Breach in the party.]

The Alien and Sedition Acts had quickly destroyed all Adams's popularity in the Republican party; his later action deprived him of the united support of the Federalists. War with France was pleasing to them as an assertion of national dignity, as a protest against the growth of dangerous democracy in France, and as a step toward friendship or eventual alliance with England. Early in 1799 Talleyrand intimated that a minister would now be received from the American government. Without consulting his cabinet, with whom Adams was not on good terms, the President appointed an embassy to France. Early in 1800 they made a favorable treaty with France: better guarantees were secured for American neutral trade; the old treaties of 1778 were practically set aside; and the claims of American merchants for captures since 1793 were abandoned, This last action gave rise to the French Spoliation Claims, which remained unsettled for nearly a century thereafter, Adams's determination to make peace was statesmanlike and patriotic, but it gave bitter offence to the warlike Federalists. In May, 1800, Adams found his cabinet so out of sympathy that he removed Pickering, Secretary of State, and appointed John Marshall. This meant a formal breach between the Adams and the Hamilton wings of the party.

[Sidenote: Republicans successful.]

The campaign of 1800 thus began with the Federalists divided, and the Republicans hopeful. Hamilton was determined to force Adams from the headship, and prepared a pamphlet, for which materials were furnished by Oliver Wolcott, Secretary of the Treasury. Aaron Burr, a wily Republican leader, managed to get a copy, published it, and spread it broadcast. Adams was re-nominated by a caucus of Federalist members, and C. C. Pinckney was put on the ticket with him. Jefferson was, as in 1796, the candidate of his party for President. For Vice-President there was associated with him Burr, who was able to control the important vote of the State of New York. The result of this coalition was seen in May, 1800, when a New York legislature was elected with a Republican majority; and that legislature would, in the autumn, cast the vote of the State. The Federalists persevered, but South Carolina deserted them, so that both Jefferson and Burr received seventy-three votes, and Adams had only sixty- five. The Federalist supremacy was broken.

[Sidenote: Election by the House.]

Now arose an unexpected complication. There being a tie between Jefferson and Burr, the House of Representatives was called upon to decide between them, its vote being cast by States. Had the majority of the House been Republican, Jefferson would, of course, have received their votes; it was, however, Federalist, and the Federalists thought themselves entitled to choose that one of their enemies who was least likely to do them harm. Obscure intrigues were entered upon both with Jefferson and Burr. Neither would make definite promises, although Burr held out hopes of alliance with the Federalists. Hamilton now came forward with a letter in which he declared that of the two men Jefferson was less dangerous. "To my mind," said he, "a true estimate of Mr. Jefferson's character warrants the expectation of a temporizing rather than of a violent system." After a long struggle the deadlock was broken; Jefferson was chosen President of the United States, and Burr Vice-President.

92. CAUSES OF THE FALL OF THE FEDERALISTS.
[Sidenote: Unpopularity of the Federalists.]
[Sidenote: Judiciary Act.]

The electoral majority was small; the Federalists preserved their organization, and had the prestige of twelve years of administration; it was impossible to realize that there never again would be a Federalist president. In the election of 1804, however, they received but fourteen electoral votes altogether (§ 100). The reasons for this downfall are many, However popular the French war had been, the taxes made necessary by it had provoked great dissatisfaction; and in 1799 a little insurrection, the so-called Fries Rebellion, had broken out in Pennsylvania. The Sedition prosecutions were exceedingly unpopular, The last acts of the party left a violent resentment. In 1801, after it was known that there would be a Republican President with a large majority in both houses of Congress, the Federalists resolved to bolster up their power in the third department of government. A Judiciary Act was therefore passed, creating new courts, new judges, and new salaried officials. All the resulting appointments were made by Adams, and duly confirmed by the Senate, thus anticipating by many years any real needs of the country. A vacancy occurring in the chief-justiceship, Adams appointed John Marshall, one of the few Virginia Federalists; he had made his reputation as a politician and statesman: even Adams himself scarcely foresaw that he was to be the greatest of American jurists.

[Sidenote: Internal dissensions.]

Still more fatal were the internal dissensions in the party. In 1799 Washington died, and no man in the country possessed his moderating influence, The cabinet, by adhering to Hamilton and corresponding with him upon important public matters, had weakened the dignity of the President and of the party. In the election of 1800 Hamilton, besides his open attack on Adams, had again tried to reduce his vote sufficiently to bring Pinckney in over his head. Adams himself, although a man of strong national spirit, was in some respects too moderate for his party. Yet his own vanity and vehemence made him unfit to be a party leader.

[Sidenote: Republican theories.]

While these reasons may account for the defeat of the Federalists, they do not explain their failure to rise again. They had governed well: they had built up the credit of the country; they had taken a dignified and effective stand against the aggressions both of England and of France. Yet their theory was of a government by leaders. Jefferson, on the other hand, represented the rising spirit of democracy. It was not his protest against the over-government of the Federalists that made him popular, it was his assertion that the people at large were the best depositaries of power. Jefferson had taken hold of the "great wheel going uphill." He had behind him the mighty force of the popular will.

CHAPTER IX.

93. REFERENCES.

BIBLIOGRAPHIES.—W. E. Foster, *References to Presidential Administrations*, 8-12; Justin Winsor, *Narrative and Critical History*, VII. 310, 315-320, 336-341, 418-420, 519-522, 527-547; H. B. Tompkins, *Bibliotheca Jeffersoniana*; Channing and Hart, *Guide*, §§ 167-171.

HISTORICAL MAPS.—Nos. 1 and 4, this volume (*Epoch Maps*, Nos. 7 and 9); Labberton, *Atlas* Nos. lxvi., lxvii.; MacCoun, *Historical Geography*; Scribner, *Statistical Atlas*, Plates 13, 14.

GENERAL ACCOUNTS.—J. B. McMaster, *People of the United States*, II. 538-635; III. 1-338; J. Schouler, *United States*, II. 1-194; Bryant and Gay, *Popular History*, 1. 144-184; H. Von Holst, *Constitutional History*, I. 168-226; R. Hildreth, *United States*, V. 419-686; VI. 25- 148; Geo. Tucker, *United States*, II. 146-348; Bradford, *Constitutional History*, I. 202-329.

SPECIAL HISTORIES.—Henry Adams, *United States*, I.-IV., *John Randolph*, 48-267, and _Life of Gallatin; J. T. Morse, *Jefferson*, 209-300; George Tucker, *Life of Jefferson*; H. S. Randall, *Life of Jefferson*; J. A. Stevens, *Gallatin*, 176-311; S. H. Gay, *Madison*, 252-282; lives of Burr, Gerry, Plumer, Pickering; T. Lyman, *Diplomacy*; J. C. Hamilton, *Republic*, VII.

CONTEMPORARY ACCOUNTS.—Works of Jefferson, Madison, and Gallatin; J. Q. Adams, *Memoirs*, I. 248-551; William Sullivan, *Familiar Letters*, 187-289; Timothy Dwight, *Character of Thomas Jefferson*; S. G. Goodrich, *Recollections*, I. 106-137, 265-298; Basil Hall, *Voyages and Travels*; Timothy Dwight, *Travels* (1796-1813); Thomas Ashe, *Travels* (1806); John Mellish, *Travels* (1806-1811); John Davis, *Travels* (1798-1802); Isaac Weld, *Travels*; J. Stephens, *War in Disguise*.—Reprints in Mathew Carey, *The Olive Branch*; Henry Adams, *Documents Relating to New England Federalism; American History told by Contemporaries*, III.

94. THE POLITICAL REVOLUTION OF 1801.

To the mind of the Federalists the success of the Republicans, and particularly the elevation of Jefferson, meant a complete change in the government which they had been laboring to establish. Jefferson was to them the type of dangerous liberality in thought, in religion, and in government. In his tastes and his habits, his reading and investigation, Jefferson was half a century in advance of his contemporaries. Books and letters from learned men constantly came to him from Europe; he experimented in agriculture and science. Accused during his lifetime of being an atheist, he felt the attraction of religion, and, in fact, was not far removed from the beliefs held by the Unitarian branch of the Congregational Church in New England. Brought up in an atmosphere of aristocracy, in the midst of slaves and inferior white men, his political platform was confidence in human nature, and objection to privilege in every form. Although a poor speaker, and rather shunning than seeking society, he had such influence over those about him that no President has ever so dominated the two Houses of Congress.

[Sidenote: Jefferson's faults.]

Jefferson's great defect was a mistaken view of human nature: this showed itself in an unfortunate judgment of men, which led him to include among his friends worthless adventurers like Callender. As a student and a philosopher, he believed that mankind is moved by simple motives, in which self-interest is predominant: hence his disinclination to use force against insurrections; the people, if left to themselves, would, he believed, return to reason. Hence, also, his confidence in a policy of commercial restriction against foreign countries which ignored our neutral rights; this was set forth in his commercial report of 1793 (§ 85), and later was the foundation of his disastrous embargo policy (§ 103). He had entire confidence in his own judgment and statesmanship; his policy was his own, and was little affected by his advisers; and he ventured to measure himself in diplomacy against the two greatest men of his time,— William Pitt the younger and Napoleon Bonaparte.

[Sidenote: Moderate policy.]

Fortunately his administration began at a period when general peace seemed approaching. The treaty of Amiens in 1802 made a sort of armistice between France and Great Britain, and neutral commerce was relieved from capture. The national income was steadily rising (§ 52), the Indians were quiet, the land dispute with Georgia—the last of the long series—was on the point of being settled, the States showed no sign of insubordination. In his inaugural address the new President took pains to reassure his fellow- citizens. "We have called by different names brethren of the same principle," said he; "we are all Republicans, we are all Federalists." Among the essential principles of government which he enumerated, appeared "absolute acquiescence in the decisions of the majority,—the vital principle of republics,—from which is no appeal but to force, the vital principle and immediate parent of despotism."

[Sidenote: Purpose to win the Federalists.]

The studied moderation of this address shows clearly the policy which Jefferson had in his mind. In a letter written about this time he says: "To restore that harmony which our predecessors so wickedly made it their object to break, to render us again one people, acting as one nation,... should be the object of every man really a patriot." Jefferson was determined to show the Federalists that there would be no violent change in his administration; he hoped thus to detach a part of their number so as to build up the Republican party in the Northern States. Even in forming his cabinet he avoided violent shocks; for some months he retained two members of Adams's cabinet; his Secretary of State was Madison, who in 1789 was as much inclined to Federalism as to Republicanism; and he shortly appointed as his Secretary of the Treasury Albert Gallatin, the Parliamentary leader of the party, but in financial principles and policy much like Hamilton.

95. JEFFERSON'S CIVIL SERVICE (1801-1803).

[Sidenote: Jefferson's principles.]

In a few weeks the disposition to conciliate was severely tried by the pressure of applicants for office. Jefferson's principles on this subject were summed up in a letter written March 24, 1801: "I will expunge the effects of Mr. A.'s indecent conduct in crowding nominations after he knew they were not for himself.... Some removals must be made for misconduct.... Of the thousands of officers, therefore, in the United States a very few individuals only, probably not twenty, will be removed: and these only for doing what they ought not to have done." Gallatin heartily supported him in this policy of moderation. Jefferson then laid down the additional principle that he would fill all vacancies with Republicans until the number of officeholders from each party was about equal. "That done, I shall return with joy to that state of things when the only questions concerning a candidate shall be, Is he honest? Is he capable? Is he faithful to the Constitution?"

[Sidenote: Political removals.]

Adams was promptly rebuked by the removal of twenty-four persons appointed in the two months previous. Other removals were made for what would now be called "offensive partisanship." Then came a third group of removals, in order, as Jefferson said, "to make some room for some participation for the Republicans." At the time he acknowledged that there had been sixteen cases,—in fact, there were many more; at the end of about two years after his inauguration, out of 334 officers occupying important places, 178 were new appointments, and of their predecessors at least 99 had been removed. These officers in many cases carried with them a staff of subordinates. It is safe to say that one half the persons who had been in the civil service of the United States in March, 1801, were out of it in March, 1805.

[Sidenote: Appointments.]

Nor did Jefferson adhere to his purpose to appoint Federalists and Republicans indiscriminately after the balance should have been reached. He appointed none but members of his own party; many Federalists in office came over to the Republicans; and by 1809 the civil service was practically filled with Republicans.

96. ATTACK ON THE JUDICIARY (1801-1805).

[Sidenote: Repeal of the Judiciary Act.]

Moderation in Jefferson's mind did not extend to the judiciary which had been forced upon the country by the Federalists in 1801. At his suggestion Breckenridge, in 1802, moved to repeal the recent Act, and thus to get rid at once of the new courts and of the incumbents. The Federalists protested that the Constitution was being destroyed. "I stand," said Gouverneur Morris, "in the presence of Almighty God and of the world, and I declare to you that if you lose this charter, never, no, never, will you get another. We are now, perhaps, arrived at the parting point." The repeal was plainly intended to remove the last bulwark of the Federalist party in the government. It was made more obnoxious by a clause suspending the sessions of the Supreme Court until February, 1803. It was passed by a majority of one in the Senate, and by a party vote of fifty-nine to thirty-two in the House. The President signed it, and all the new circuit judges and judicial officers were thus struck from the roll of the government.

[Sidenote: Impeachments.]
[Sidenote: Marbury vs. Madison.]

The narrow majority in the Senate warned Jefferson not to proceed farther with such statutes; but the judiciary could be affected in another way. Several of the supreme and district judges were ardent Federalists, and had expressed strong political opinions from the bench. In February, 1803, the House impeached John Pickering, district judge in New Hampshire; his offence was drunkenness and violence on the bench; but the purpose to intimidate the other judges was unmistakable. Two of them accepted the issue. The Supreme Court had resumed its session only a few days, when, in 1803, Marshall made a decision in the case of Marbury *vs.* Madison. Marbury was one of Adams's "midnight appointments;" the suit was brought for his commission, which had not been delivered, and was retained by Madison when he became Secretary of State. Marshall decided that "to withhold his commission is an act deemed by the court not warranted by law, but violative of a legal vested right." Upon a technical point, however, the complaint was dismissed.

[Sidenote: Chase trial.]
[Sidenote: Appointments.]

Further defiance came from another justice of the Supreme Court, Samuel Chase of Maryland. His prejudice against Callender on his trial for sedition had exasperated the Republicans (§ 89), and on May 2, 1803, while the Pickering impeachment was impending, Chase harangued the grand jury as follows: "The independence of the national judiciary is already shaken to its foundation, and the virtue of the people alone can restore it…. Our republican constitution will sink into a mobocracy,… the worst of all possible governments." Pickering was convicted March 12, 1804, and on the same day the House impeached Chase. By this time the Republicans had overshot the mark, and notwithstanding Chase's gross partisanship, on March 1, 1805, the impeachment failed for want of a two-thirds vote. The only hope of controlling the Supreme Court was therefore to fill vacancies, as they occurred, with sound Republicans. Three such opportunities occurred in Jefferson's administration. To his great chagrin, the new judges showed themselves as independent, though not as aggressive, as Marshall.

97. THE POLICY OF RETRENCHMENT (1801-1809).

[Sidenote: Federal finance.]

Although the effort to check the power of the judiciary failed, in another direction Jefferson struck out a new and popular policy. Under the Federalists the taxes had increased from $3,600,000 in 1792 to $10,700,000 in 1800. This increase had been more than balanced by the growth of expenditures. The Indian and French wars had brought unexpected expenses upon the government, and the construction of a little navy was still going on, In 1793 the government spent $3,800,000. In 1800 it spent $10,800,000. Of this amount $6,000,000 went for the army and navy, and $3,000,000 for interest. The deficits had been obscured by a funding system under which payments to the sinking fund were practically made out of borrowed money, so that the debt had risen from $80,000,000 in 1793 to nearly $83,000,000, in 1800.

[Sidenote: Gallatin's finance.]

If peace could be guaranteed, a considerable part of the expenditure could be cut down; and thus taxes might be reduced, and still a surplus be left, out of which to pay instalments on the public debt. In his first annual message the President accordingly advised the reduction of the military and naval forces, and also of the civil officers. Gallatin proceeded to draw up a financial plan: the annual revenue was to be $10,800,000, military expenses were to be cut down to $2,500,000, and the civil expenses to about $1,000,000; the remainder, $7,300,000, was to be devoted to the reduction of the debt.

[Sidenote: Success of the system.]

Neither part of this scheme worked precisely as had been expected. The army indeed underwent what Jefferson called a "chaste reformation;" it was cut down from 4,000 to 2,500 men, to the great discontent of the officers. The number of vessels in commission was reduced from about twenty-five to seven, and the construction of vessels on the stocks was stopped, so that in 1802 less than $1,000,000 was spent on the navy. Nevertheless, the civil and miscellaneous expenses of the government grew steadily. Under the Federalist administration, the total expenditures in time of peace, exclusive of interest, had never been more than $3,000,000; in 1802 Gallatin spent $3,700,000, and in 1809 $7,500,000. The debt was, however, rapidly diminished, and in 1809 stood at only $45,000,000; nearly half of the interest charge was thus cut off, and for the first time the government found itself with more money than it knew how to use. The taxes had been reduced by a million and a half, by striking off the unpopular direct tax and excise; the loss was more than met by an unexpected increase in the revenue from customs, which in 1808 stood at $16,000,000,

[Sidenote: Drawbacks.]

To reach this result Jefferson and Gallatin deliberately neglected to make ordinary preparations against attack; fortifications were abandoned, skilled officers dismissed, ships allowed to decay at the wharves or on the stocks, and the accumulation of military material ceased. The only offset to this neglect was the creation of a military school at West Point in 1802, and the training gained by the naval wars against the Barbary powers.

98. BARBARY WARS (1801-1806).

[Sidenote: The navy.]

The Peace Establishment Act of March 3, 1801, authorized the President to sell all the vessels of the navy except thirteen frigates, of which only six were to be kept in commission; and the number of naval officers was reduced from five hundred to two hundred. "I shall really be chagrined," wrote Jefferson, "if the water in the Eastern Branch will not admit our laying up the whole seven there in time of peace, because they would be under the immediate eye of the department, and would require but one set of plunderers to take care of them." Events were too much for Jefferson's genial intention. Ever since the Middle Ages the petty Moorish powers on the north coast of Africa had made piracy on the Mediterranean trade their profession. In accordance with the custom of European nations, in 1787 the United States had bought a treaty of immunity with Morocco, and later with Algiers, Tripoli, and Tunis. Every payment to one of these nests of pirates incited the others to make increased demands. In May, 1800, the Pasha of Tripoli wrote to the President of the United States: "We could wish that these your expressions were followed by deeds, and not by empty words.... If only flattering words are meant, without performance, every one will act as he finds convenient." Receiving no satisfaction, he declared war upon the United States.

[Sidenote: The pirates subdued.]

One of the first acts of Jefferson's administration was, therefore, to despatch a squadron to blockade Tripoli, and in 1802 he was obliged to consent to a declaration of war by the United States. The frigates were unsuitable, and in 1803 Congress resumed the hated Federalist policy of building a navy. Four new vessels, of a small and handy type, were constructed, and under Commodore Preble, Tripoli was compelled in 1805 to make peace and to cease her depredations. The other Barbary powers were cowed by this exhibition of spirit, and for some years our commerce was undisturbed. The first result of the war was, therefore, that the corsairs were humbled. A far greater advantage to the United States was the skill in naval warfare gained by the officers of the navy. Thenceforward it was impossible to think of shutting the navy up in the Eastern Branch of the Potomac. Naval expenditures slowly increased, and seven years later the good effect was seen in the War of 1812.

99. ANNEXATION OF LOUISIANA (1803).

[Sidenote: Jefferson's political principles.]

Jefferson came into power as a stickler for a limited government, confined chiefly to foreign and commercial affairs. He now entered upon the most brilliant episode of his administration,—the annexation of Louisiana; and that transaction was carried out and defended upon precisely the grounds of loose construction which he had so much contemned.

[Sidenote: Napoleon's colonial system.]

In 1763 France had two flourishing American colonies,—Louisiana and Hayti, the western end of the island of San Domingo. The former province was ceded to Spain (§ 18); the latter, the centre of the French colonial system, was nearly destroyed by a slave insurrection in 1791. When, in 1800, Napoleon Bonaparte became First Consul and virtual dictator, he formed a brilliant scheme of reviving the French colonial empire. The first step was to recover Louisiana; the second was to make peace with England, so as to stop the naval war and release the French resources; the third step was to occupy, first Hayti, and then Louisiana. The three plans were pursued with characteristic rapidity. In October, 1800, the secret treaty of San Ildefonso was negotiated, by which Spain agreed to return Louisiana to France, the condition being that Napoleon should create a kingdom of Etruria for the son-in-law of the king of Spain. In 1802 the Peace of Amiens was made with England.

[Sidenote: Toussaint Louverture.]

A combined French and Spanish squadron had already, October, 1801, carried a great expedition to occupy the whole island of San Domingo, with secret orders to re-establish slavery. Then came an unexpected check: the fleet and the army of ten thousand experienced French troops were unable to break down the resistance of Toussaint Louverture, a native black general who aimed to be the Napoleon of the island. Toussaint was taken; but the army was forced back into a few sea-ports, and almost swept away by disease. The blacks were still masters of the island.

[Sidenote: Alarm of the United States.]

The next step was to have been the occupation of Louisiana. By this time, April, 1802, the news of the cession reached the United States, and drew from Jefferson a remarkable letter. "The day that France takes possession of New Orleans," said he, "fixes the sentence which is to restrain her forever within her low-water mark. From that moment we must marry ourselves to the British fleet and nation." As though to justify this outburst of anti-Gallican zeal on the part of the old friend of France, the Spanish Intendant of Louisiana, Oct. 16, 1802, withdrew the so-called "right of deposit" under which Americans on the upper Mississippi had been able to send goods to the sea and to receive return cargoes without the payment of Spanish duty. If the province were to pass to France with the Mississippi closed, it seemed to Jefferson essential that we should obtain West Florida, with the port of Mobile; and in January, 1803, James Monroe was sent as special envoy to secure this cession. [Sidenote: Louisiana treaty.]

The day after he reached Paris, Livingston, the resident minister, had closed a treaty for the cession, not of West Florida, but of all Louisiana. The inner history of this remarkable negotiation has been brought to light by Henry Adams in his History of the Administration of Jefferson. The check in San Domingo had dampened the colonial ardor of Napoleon; war was about to break out again with England; Napoleon's ambition turned toward an European empire; and he lightly offered the province which had come to him so cheaply. Neither Livingston, Monroe, nor Jefferson had thought it possible to acquire New Orleans; with 880,000 square miles of other territory it was tossed into the lap of the United States as the Sultan throws a purse of gold to a favorite.

[Sidenote: Indefinite boundaries.]

The treaty, dated April 30, 1803, gave to the United States Louisiana, "with the same extent that it now has in the hands of Spain, and that it had when France possessed it." The two phrases, instead of explaining each other, were contradictory: Louisiana as it was when France possessed it had included settlements as far east as the Perdido River; Louisiana in the hands of Spain had extended only to the Iberville. The United States had therefore annexed a province without knowing its boundaries. We are now aware that Napoleon had issued orders to occupy the country on the north only as far as the Iberville, but on the south as far as the Rio Grande; at the time France refused to give any information on either point. Hence the United States gave up the claim to Texas, in which there was reason, and insisted on the title to West Florida, which was nowhere to be found in the treaty.

100. FEDERAL SCHEMES OF DISUNION (1803-1809).

[Sidenote: Anger of the Federalists.]
[Sidenote: Arguments for annexation.]

The annexation of Louisiana aroused a storm in both hemispheres. The Spanish government vehemently protested, the more because the promised kingdom of Etruria proved to be but a mock principality. In the United States the Federalists attacked both the annexation and the method of annexation with equal violence. The treaty promised that the people should as soon as possible be admitted as a State into the Union; the balance of power in the government was thus disturbed, and the Federalists foresaw that the influence of New England must diminish. Their constitutional arguments were just such as had been heard from the Republican writers and legislatures in 1798: the constitution, they said, nowhere gives express power to annex territory, and therefore there is no such power; the Union is a partnership, and new members cannot be admitted except by unanimous consent. The Republicans furnished themselves with arguments drawn from the Federal arsenal: the right to annex territory, they said could be implied from the power to make treaties, from the power to regulate territory, and from the "necessary and proper" clause. Jefferson was not so ready to give up his cherished principles, and proposed a constitutional amendment to approve and confirm the cession. His party friends scouted the idea. The treaty was duly ratified, fifteen millions were appropriated for the purchase, and on Dec. 20, 1803, possession of the territory was given,

[Sidenote: Intrigues with Burr.]

The cup of the Federalists was now full, and a few violent spirits, of whom Timothy Pickering was the leader, suggested that the time had come to withdraw from the Union. They found no hearing among the party at large. In 1804, therefore, they tried to form a combination with a wing of the New York Republicans controlled by Burr, who had been read out of his party by the Jeffersonian wing. He came forward as an independent candidate for Governor, and asked for the support of the New York Federalists. Hamilton stood out against this movement, and wrote a letter urging his friends not to vote for him. Burr received the Federalist vote, but was defeated, and in his humiliation sent Hamilton a challenge, and killed him in the duel. The affair still further weakened the Federalists; in the national election of 1804 they cast but fourteen votes,—those of Connecticut, Delaware, and Maryland. Even Massachusetts voted for Jefferson.

[Sidenote: The Federalists weakened.]

Commerce was still increasing; the Union was growing in extent and importance; neither the interests nor the principles of the people had suffered. The Federalist predictions of danger from Jefferson had not been fulfilled. There were still a few leaders who brooded over a plan of separation; but the strength of the Federalists was now so broken that in 1807 John Quincy Adams, son of the ex-President, and senator from Massachusetts, went over to the Republican party.

101. THE BURR CONSPIRACY (1806-1807).

[Sidenote: Burr's schemes.]

The election of 1804 was the last attempt of Aaron Burr to re-enter public life. His private character, already sufficiently notorious, had been destroyed by the murder of Hamilton, and he was a desperate man. In 1805 Burr went West, and was well received by many prominent men, including General Wilkinson, the senior officer of the United States army, and Andrew Jackson, then a lawyer in Nashville, Tennessee. His purposes were vague: he planned the establishment of a colony on the new Western lands; he had relations with certain Spanish adventurers who wished the independence of Mexico; he hinted at securing the secession of the Western States, with the aid of the British government. His chief purpose seems to have been to head a revolution in the newly acquired Louisiana.

[Sidenote: Burr's expedition.]

To the rumors that Burr had some desperate and treasonable intention Jefferson paid no attention. In December, 1806, Burr mustered a party of men at Blennerhasset's Island, in the Ohio River, and with them floated down the river. Twice attempts were made by local authorities to stop him and prosecute him, but he was allowed to continue, with about a hundred men, till in January, 1807, while on the lower Mississippi, he learned from a newspaper that the President had issued a proclamation directing his capture. He abandoned his men, and shortly afterwards fell into the hands of the authorities, and was sent to Washington for trial.

[Sidenote: Wilkinson's treachery.]
[Sidenote: Burr's Trial.]

Meanwhile steps had been taken to prevent the expected rising in Louisiana. Wilkinson was then on the extreme western frontier. He received a cipher message from Burr, and after waiting for some hours to make up his mind, concluded to betray him, sent the letters to the government, went to New Orleans, and there arrested several of Burr's adherents, by military authority. The danger to the Union had been slight, the laxity on Jefferson's part unpardonable. Having Burr in his power, he now relentlessly pursued him with a prosecution for treason. The trial was held in Richmond, Chief Justice Marshall presiding, and ended on Sept. 1, 1807. The indictment had set forth the mustering of the men at Blennerhasset's Island: since the only acts which could be called treasonable had occurred elsewhere, the court declared the evidence insufficient, and there was nothing for the jury to do but to bring him in not guilty. The President had shown that he could use force, if necessary; and the courts had again shown their independence of the President. Burr disappeared from public notice.

102. AGGRESSIONS ON NEUTRAL TRADE (1803-1807).

[Sidenote: American trade.]
[Sidenote: Admiralty decisions.]

The renewal of the war between England and France in May, 1803, at first was advantageous to the United States; it precipitated the cession of Louisiana and it gave new employment for American shipping. French West Indian products were freely imported, re-shipped, and exported, thus avoiding the rule of 1756 (§ 85); as a result, the customs revenue leaped in one year from fourteen to twenty millions. In 1805 these favorable conditions were reversed. In May the British admiralty courts decided that goods which had started from French colonies could be captured, even though they had been landed and re-shipped in the United States. Captures at once began; English frigates were stationed outside the port of New York, and vessels coming in and going out were insolently stopped and searched; impressments were revived. In 1804 thirty-nine vessels had been captured by the British; in 1805 one hundred and sixteen were taken; and probably a thousand American seamen were impressed.

[Sidenote: Continental System.]

On Oct. 21, 1805, the combined French and Spanish fleets were overwhelmed at Trafalgar. Thenceforward England had the mastery of the seas, while France remained supreme on land. Napoleon, who had in 1804 taken the title of Emperor, was determined to destroy English trade with the Continent, and had no scruples against ruining neutrals in the attempt. He resolved upon a "Continental System,"—to shut against the importation of English goods the ports of France and her dependencies and allies, including, as the result of recent conquests, almost the whole northern coast of the Mediterranean, and a considerable part of the coast of the German Ocean and the Baltic Sea.

[Sidenote: Orders and decrees.]

The English retaliated with an Order in Council, dated May 16, 1806, by which the whole coast from Brest to the river Elbe was declared blockaded. There was no blockading squadron; yet American vessels were captured as they left their own ports bound for places within the specified limit. Napoleon retorted with the Berlin Decree of Nov. 21, 1806, in which he declared the whole British Islands in a state of blockade; the trade in English merchandise was forbidden, and no vessel that had touched at a British port could enter a French port. These measures were plainly intended to cut off the commerce of neutrals; and as the European wars had now swept in almost every seafaring power, on one side or the other, the Americans were the great neutral carriers. In January, 1807, Great Britain announced that neutral vessels trading from one port under French influence to another were subject to capture, and that all French ports were blockaded. The Milan Decree of December, 1807,

145

completed the structure of injustice by ordering the capture of all neutral vessels which had been searched by an English vessel. In 1806 the Jay Treaty expired, and the Americans lost its slight protection. The effect of this warfare of proclamations was at once seen in the great increase of captures: one hundred and ninety-four American vessels were taken by England in 1807, and a large number by the French.

103. POLICY OF NON-RESISTANCE (1805-1807).

[Sidenote: Prosperity of American trade.]

The wholesale seizure of American property was exasperating to the last degree. The disdainful impressment of American seamen, and still more the unofficial blockade of the ports, would have justified war. Yet notwithstanding the loss of American shipping, trade continued to prosper, and vessels engaged in foreign commerce increased; freights were so high that an annual loss by capture of ten per cent could be made up out of the profits. The New Englanders, therefore, who suffered most were not most anxious for war, nor could Jefferson bear to give up his policy of debt-reduction and of peaceful trade. Toward France, indeed, he showed remarkable tenderness, because that power controlled Spain, from which Jefferson was eagerly seeking the cession of West Florida.

[Sidenote: Gunboat system.]

Some American policy must be formulated. War seemed to Jefferson unnecessary, and he therefore attempted three other remedies, which in a measure neutralized each other. The first was to provide some kind of defence. To build new vessels seemed to him an invitation to the English navy to swoop down and destroy them. To fortify the coasts and harbors properly would cost fifty millions of dollars. He proposed, therefore, to lay up the navy and to build a fleet of gunboats, to be hauled up under sheds in time of peace, but if war came, to be manned by a naval militia and to repel the enemy. Between 1806 and 1812 one hundred and seventy-six gunboats were built. They never rendered any considerable service, and took $1,700,000 out of Gallatin's surplus.

[Sidenote: Pinkney treaty.]

The second part of Jefferson's policy was to negotiate with England for a new treaty. The conditions upon which he insisted were impossible, and Pinkney and Monroe, therefore, in December, 1806, made the best terms they could: there was no article against impressment; they surrendered the principle that free ships make free goods; they practically accepted the rule of 1756. The treaty was so unacceptable that Jefferson never submitted it to the Senate; and thenceforward to the War of 1812 we had only such commercial privileges as England chose to grant.

[Sidenote: Non-importation act.]

The only remaining arrow in Jefferson's quiver was the policy of commercial restriction. On April 18, 1806, an act was Passed by which, after November 15, the importation of manufactured goods from England and English colonies was forbidden. Even this was suspended on December 29.

[Sidenote: "Leopard" and "Chesapeake."]
[Sidenote: The Americans aroused.]

The effect of these feeble efforts to secure fair treatment was seen on June 27, 1807. The only excuse for the impressment of American seamen was that sailors from the British men-of-war were apt to desert when they reached an American port, and frequently shipped on board American vessels. The chief reason was the severity of naval discipline and the low wages paid by the British government. The American frigate "Chesapeake," about leaving Norfolk for a Mediterranean cruise, had several such deserters on board without the commander's knowledge. When outside the capes the British frigate "Leopard" suddenly bore down on her, hailed her, and her captain announced that he was about to search the ship for these deserters. Commander Barron was taken by surprise; his guns were not ready for action, his crew was not yet trained. He refused to permit the search, was fired upon, and was obliged to surrender. Four men were taken off, of whom three were American citizens, and the "Chesapeake" carried back the news of this humiliation. The spirit of the nation was aflame. Had Jefferson chosen, he might have gone to war upon this issue, and would have had the country behind him. The extreme point which he reached was a proclamation warning British armed vessels out of American waters; he preferred a milder sort of warfare.

104. THE EMBARGO (1807-1808).

[Sidenote: Jefferson's recommendations.]

The Non-importation Act, which up to this time had had no force, finally went into effect Dec. 14, 1807. Two days later news was received that the king had ordered British naval officers to exercise their assumed right of impressment. Forthwith Jefferson sent a message to Congress, hinting that England was about to prohibit American commerce altogether, and recommending an embargo so as to prevent the loss of our ships and seamen.

The Senate hurried a bill through all its stages in a single day; and the House, by nearly two to one, accepted it. No foreign merchant vessel could leave an American port, except in ballast, or with a cargo then on board; no American merchantman could leave for a foreign port on any terms.

[Sidenote: The embargo evaded.]

The embargo was not really intended to save American shipping, for the owners were willing to run their own risks. The restriction was so new, so sweeping so little in accordance with the habits of the people, and so destructive to the great interests of commerce that it was systematically evaded. Vessels left port on a coasting voyage, and slipped into a West Indian port, and perhaps returned with a West Indian cargo. Severe supplementary acts were therefore necessary. A great trade sprang up across the border into Canada, followed by new restrictions, with severe penalties and powers of search hitherto unknown in the law of the United States. On Lake Champlain, on June 13, 1808, a band of sixty armed men fired upon United States troops, and carried a raft in triumph over the border. A prosecution for treason against one of the men involved was a failure.

[Sidenote: No settlement with England.]

The expectation was that the President, backed up by the embargo, would now succeed in a negotiation with England, that atonement would be made for the "Chesapeake" outrage, and that a commercial treaty would at last be gained. Mr. George Rose came over as British minister in December, 1807; but he took the unfortunate attitude that the American government owed England an apology for action growing out of the "Chesapeake" outrage, and he returned in March without accomplishing anything: the two countries remained in an attitude of hostility throughout the year.

105. REPEAL OF THE EMBARGO (1809).

[Sidenote: Effect on England.]

When Congress assembled in December, 1808, the effect of the embargo was manifest. English merchants engaged in the American trade protested, and asked the British government to withdraw its Orders in Council. Lord Castlereagh declared that the embargo was "operating at present more forcibly in our favor than any measure of hostility we could call forth, without war actually declared;" English trade to the amount of $25,000,000 was, indeed, cut off; but notwithstanding this loss, the total exports of England increased. "The embargo," says Henry Adams, "served only to lower the wages and the moral standard of the laboring classes throughout the British empire, and to prove theirhelplessness."

[Sidenote: Effect on France.]

The reception of the embargo by France was even more humiliating. On April 17, 1808, Napoleon issued a decree at Bayonne directing that all American vessels which might enter the ports of France, Italy, and the Hanse towns should be seized, "because no vessels of the United States can now navigate the seas without infracting the law of the said States." "The Emperor applauds the embargo," said the French foreign minister.

[Sidenote: Effect on the United States.]

In America the embargo, which was intended to cut off the profits of foreign merchants and the provisions needed in foreign countries, had crippled the shipping interests, had destroyed the export trade, and had almost ruined the farmers. Exports dropped in one year from one hundred and ten millions to twenty-two millions; import duties were kept up during 1808 by returning vessels, but in 1809 sank from sixteen millions to seven millions; shipbuilding fell off by two-thirds; shipping in foreign trade lost 100,000 tons; wheat fell from two dollars to seventy-five cents a bushel. The South, from which the majority in favor of the embargo had been drawn, suffered most of all: tobacco could not be sold, and Virginia was almost bankrupt.

[Sidenote: The embargo a failure.]
[Sidenote: The embargo repealed.]

The money loss did not measure the injury to the country. New England ingenuity was devoted to new methods of avoiding the law of the land, and a passionate feeling of sectional injury sprang up. In the election of 1808 the Federalists carried all New England except Vermont, and had a few Southern votes; and the Republican majority in Congress was much cut down. The embargo had plainly failed, and the only alternative seemed to be war. Even Jefferson was obliged to admit that the embargo must end a few months later; "But I have thought it right," he wrote, "to take no part myself in proposing measures, the execution of which will devolve on my successor." It became known that Madison, the President-elect, favored the repeal of the embargo in June, and that Jefferson was only anxious that it should last out his administration. The discontent of New England was so manifest that a South Carolina member said: "You have driven us from the embargo. The excitement in the East renders it necessary that we should enforce the embargo with the bayonet, or repeal it. I will repeal it,—and I could weep over it more than over a lost child." On Feb. 2, 1809, the House, by a vote of 70 to 40, decided upon immediate repeal. The only question now was what policy should be substituted. On February 28 an agreement was reached: the embargo was replaced by a non-intercourse law which forbade British or French vessels to enter American ports; but there was no threat against the captors of American vessels.

[Sidenote: Jefferson humiliated.]

Throughout his whole administration Jefferson had never before been confronted with an offensive bill. He had been practically the leader in both houses of Congress, and until this moment his followers had never deserted him. He could not end his administration with a veto, and he signed the act, although it was a tacit condemnation of his whole policy with reference to neutral trade. The defence of the embargo was that it prevented war: but it had inflicted on the country the material losses and excited the factional spirit which would have resulted from war; and the danger of war was greater at the end than at the beginning of the experiment.

CHAPTER X.

106. REFERENCES.

BIBLIOGRAPHIES.—W. E. Foster, *References to Presidential Administrations*, 12-15; J. Winsor, *Narrative and Critical History*, VII. 320-323, 341-343, 420-437, 457-460, 522-524; Channing and Hart, *Guide*, §§ 170-173.

HISTORICAL MAPS.—Nos. 1 and 4, this volume (*Epoch Maps*, Nos. 7 and 9); T. MacCoun, *Historical Geography*; Henry Adams, *United States*, VI, VII., VIII., *passim*; Anderson, *Canada* (1814); Arrowsmith, *Map of the United States* (1813); Scribner, *Statistical Atlas*, Plate 14; school histories of Channing, Johnston, Scudder, and Thomas.

GENERAL ACCOUNTS—R. Hildreth, *United States*, VI. 149-674; H. Von Hoist, *Constitutional History*, I 226-272; J. Schouler, *United States*, II. 194-444; J. B. McMaster, *United States*, III. 339-560 (to 1812), IV.; Bryant and Gay, *Popular History*, IV. 185-244; Geo. Tucker, *United States*, II. 349-515, III. 21-145; Bradford, *Constitutional History*, I. 330-410.

SPECIAL HISTORIES.—Henry Adams, *History of the United States*, V.- IX.; C. Schurz, *Henry Clay*, I. 38-137; S. H. Gay, *James Madison*, 283- 337; C. J. Ingersoll, *Historical Sketch of the Second War*; T. Roosevelt, *Naval War of 1812*; J. Armstrong, *Notices of the War of 1812*; B. J. Lossing, *Pictorial Field-book of the War of 1812*; H. M Brackenridge, *History of the Late War*; William Jones, *Military Occurrences* and *Naval Occurrences*; E. S. Maclay, *United States Navy*.

CONTEMPORARY ACCOUNTS—J. Q. Adams, *Memoirs*, II, III. (ch. ix); S. G Goodrich, *Recollections*, I. 435-514, II. 9-60; Dolly Madison, *Memoirs and Letters*; John Randolph, *Letters to a Young Relative*; S. Leech, *Thirty Years from Home* (by a seaman of the Macedonian); W. Cobbett, *Pride of Britannia Humbled*(1815); Coggeshall, *History of the American Privateers*; William Sullivan, *Familiar Letters on Public Characters*, 290-355; Timothy Dwight, *History of the Hartford Convention*. Works of Jefferson, Madison, Gallatin, Dallas, Clay.— Reprints in M. Carey, *Olive Branch*; A. Johnston, *American Orations*, I, *American History told by Contemporaries*, III.

107. NON-INTERCOURSE LAWS (1809, 1810).

[Sidenote: Madison's administration.]

James Madison, who became President March 4, 1809, felt that his administration was to be a continuation of that of Jefferson; and he took over three members of Jefferson's cabinet, including Gallatin. The Secretary of State, Robert Smith, was incapable, and Madison was practically his own foreign minister.

[Sidenote: The situation abroad.]

The condition of European affairs was, on the whole, favorable to America. In 1807 Russia had formed an alliance with France and had accepted the Continental System, thus cutting off American trade; but in 1808 the French lost ground in Spain, and the Spanish and Portuguese ports were thus opened to American commerce. Nevertheless a hundred and eight merchantmen were captured by England in 1808.

[Sidenote: Non-intercourse Act.]
[Sidenote: Favorable trade.]

To defend American commerce and the national honor, the administration possessed but three weapons,—war, retaliatory legislation, and diplomacy. War meant both danger and sacrifice; there was already a deficit in the Treasury. Congress, therefore, continued to legislate, while at the same time attempts were made to negotiate with both France and England. The Non-intercourse Act continued in force throughout 1809, and hardly impeded American commerce; trade with England and France went on through a few intermediary ports such as Lisbon and Riga, and there was a brisk direct trade under special license of one or the other of the powers. The shipping engaged in foreign trade now reached a higher point than ever before. The profits of American vessels were so great that forged American papers were openly sold in England. The defection of New England was stayed, and the President was supported by a fair majority in both Houses. It remained to be seen whether non-intercourse would have any effect in securing a withdrawal of the offensive orders and decrees.

108. FRUITLESS NEGOTIATIONS (1809-1811).

[Sidenote: The Erskine treaty.]

On April 19, 1809, Madison obtained what seemed a diplomatic triumph; Erskine, the new British envoy, signed a formal agreement that the British government should withdraw the Orders in Council. A proclamation was then issued, announcing that trade might be renewed with Great Britain. As France had from the first protested that her Decrees were simply retaliatory, it was expected that they would in due time also be annulled. The satisfaction of the country was short-lived: Erskine had gone beyond his instructions. Once more the opportunity to conciliate the United States was thrown away by England; his agreement was formally disavowed; and on August 9 the President had the mortification of issuing a second proclamation, announcing that the Orders had not been withdrawn, and that trade with England was still forbidden.

[Sidenote: Jackson's negotiation.]

Another British minister, James Jackson, was received October 1, and began his negotiation by asserting that Madison had tricked Erskine into signing an agreement which the American government knew he was not authorized to make. The charge was denied, and his relations were finally closed on November 8 by a note in which he was informed that inasmuch as he "had used a language which cannot be understood but as reiterating and even aggravating the same gross insinuation, no further communications will be received." Having thus practically been dismissed for brutally insulting the government to which he was accredited, Jackson made a tour of the Eastern States, and was received with hospitality and enthusiasm by the leading New England Federalists.

[Sidenote: Macon Bill No. 2.]
[Sidenote: Anger of France.]
[Sidenote: Pretended revocation by France.]

From France no satisfaction could be obtained during 1809. To remove all restrictions on commerce was to give up everything; but Congress was tired of resistance, and on May i, 1810, passed the "Macon Bill No. 2," which was practically a surrender of all the principles at stake. It provided that commerce should be free, but that if either England or France should withdraw her Orders or Decrees, intercourse should be prohibited with the nation which retained them. The probable effect on France was speedily seen by the publication of a Decree which had been issued March 23, 1810: it declared that all American vessels which had entered French ports after the date of the Non-Intercourse Act of 1809 were to be seized. This was practically an act of war. The Macon bill now suggested to the Emperor that the Americans might be entrapped into another ambush: on August 5 his foreign minister wrote to Armstrong, the American minister, that "the Emperor loves the Americans," and that he would revoke the Milan and Berlin Decrees from November 1, provided England would withdraw her Orders in Council. Five days earlier the secret Decree of the Trianon had ordered the seizure of all American vessels that might reach French ports. The object of these measures was to entice American vessels within the reach of the French, and the ruse was successful. November 1 the President issued a proclamation declaring trade with England suspended because France had withdrawn her Decrees. Then ensued a long diplomatic discussion: since captures of American vessels by French cruisers continued, the British government refused to admit that the Decrees had been withdrawn, and complained of the prohibition of English trade. On December 25 Napoleon drew in his net by a general order for the seizure of all American vessels in French ports; and property to the value of about ten million dollars was thus confiscated.

[Sidenote: Fruitless negotiation with England.]

The British ministry kept its promise to Jackson, not to recall him till the end of a year. In February, 1811, Pinkney, our minister in London, demanded his passports, and left England with a tacit threat of war. The British government instantly sent a fourth minister, Mr. Foster, to the United States, and on June 13, 1811, reparation was made for the "Leopard- Chesapeake" outrage. This tardy act was received with coldness: four weeks earlier the English corvette "Little Belt" had fired upon the American frigate "President;" the fire was returned, and the "Little Belt" captured.

109. THE WAR PARTY (1811).

[Sidenote: Madison's first Congress.]

The responsibility for peace or war was now thrown upon the Congress which assembled Nov. 4, 1811. It had been elected at a time when it was believed that France had at last withdrawn the Decrees, and it had a strong Republican majority in both branches; there were but six Federalists in the Senate, and thirty-seven in the House. Even Massachusetts had chosen a Republican senator.

[Sidenote: The young Republicans.]

The new Congress had little of the timid spirit of its predecessor. It contained an unusual number of vigorous young men. Among the members who appeared for the first time in the House were John C. Calhoun, Langdon Cheves, and William Lowndes; two years later Daniel Webster took his seat. The first act of the new House Was to elect as its Speaker Henry Clay of Kentucky,—a young man for the first time a member of the House, and known to be in favor of war. His selection meant a change of counsels; the committees were reorganized, and Calhoun was made a leading member of the committee on Foreign Relations.

For the first time since 1807 war seemed likely. The controlling element in Congress had no longer the traditions of the Revolutionary War and the influence of Revolutionary statesmen. Many of these members represented interior States, having no sea-coast, and subject to no danger from invasion. These States were too new to command the affectionate support of their people; to their members the United States government represented the power and dignity of America; they chafed under the humiliations which had so long been suffered. The growth of the South and West enabled Congress to override the Federalists of New England and the peace Republicans of the Middle States.

[Sidenote: Madison's attitude.]

The President was a peaceful man, but he was unable to manage Congress, and was weary of the long series of offensive measures against his country. The annual message bore a distinctly warlike tone, especially toward England; and Gallatin suggested increased import duties and new war taxes.

[Sidenote: Who was the enemy?]

The grievances of the United States were heavy, but to go to war was difficult. The government was hampered by the fact that the New England ship-owners, in whose behalf the government was negotiating and threatening, preferred an irregular and hazardous trade to war. A more serious difficulty was that France had notoriously been a worse enemy than England; she had done all the open injury in her power, and had then treacherously entrapped our vessels. Madison had taken the untenable ground that our trade was respected by France, and that the British government was therefore bound to withdraw its Orders. The New England Federalists had a corresponding partisan friendship for England, and could see no offence in the blockade of our coasts, or even in impressment.

[Sidenote: Designs on Canada.]

Yet the war spirit against England was steadily rising. The reason is to be found in a speech delivered by Henry Clay some months later: "An honorable peace is obtainable only by an efficient war. My plan would be to call out the ample resources of the country, give them a judicious direction, prosecute the war with the utmost vigor, strike wherever we can reach the enemy at sea or on land, and negotiate the terms of peace at Quebec or Halifax." The immediate object of the war was, therefore, not to secure the rights of vessel-owners: war would instantly make all American commerce subject to capture; the evident purpose was to take Canada, and by the occupation of British territory to force England to make a favorable peace.

[Sidenote: Preliminaries of war.]

On Jan. 6, 1812, a bill for raising twenty-five thousand troops was passed, and fifty thousand volunteers were authorized. The enthusiasm of Congress was chilled by new action of the French government, which proved its friendliness by capturing American merchantmen wherever found upon the sea. Nevertheless, on April 1 the President recommended an embargo, which was understood to be preliminary to war with England. As the time for Presidential nominations came on, the New York Republicans bolted, and nominated De Witt Clinton.

[Sidenote: War declared.]

Still the war was delayed. Although on May 19 news was received that the British government would not yield the Orders in Council, it was June 1 before Madison sent to Congress a message recommending war, and not until June 18 did the declaration pass. Nearly forty Republican members refused to vote for it, and the test vote was seventy-nine to forty-nine in the House, and nineteen to thirteen in the Senate.

[Sidenote: Causes of the war.]

The causes of the war, as set forth in the messages of the President and in contemporary speeches, were four. The first was that the British had tampered with the Indians and urged them to hostilities: it was true, and it was trying; but the breaking out of war simply aggravated that difficulty. The second charge was the interference with neutral trade by the Orders in Council; but the injury from the French Decrees had been more humiliating. The third complaint was perhaps the most serious and exasperating: it was the virtual blockade of American ports by British cruisers, and their interference with arriving and departing vessels. Finally came the impressment of American seamen.

[Sidenote: Orders in Council withdrawn.]

Of these grievances the last two had not up to this time been put forward as cause for war. On June 16, two days before the declaration of war, the British government reluctantly withdrew the Orders in Council against which the United States had for six years protested. Before hostilities had fairly begun, notice was sent to the American government: it insisted on prosecuting the war, which was therefore undertaken ostensibly for the protection of the coast and the prevention of impressments.

110. STRENGTH OF THE COMBATANTS (1812).

In every respect except in the numbers available for land operations the Americans seemed inferior to the English. It was a war between a people of eight millions and a people of nearly twenty millions. The United States had been deceived by eleven years of great prosperity, and failed to see that the revenues of the government rose almost entirely from import duties, which would be cut off by war; and Congress showed a decided unwillingness to supplement these with other taxes. In 1811 the customs produced $13,000,000, in 1812 but $9,000,000; and the total revenue of the government was less than $10,000,000. The war, once begun, cost about $30,000,000 a year. The government was therefore thrown back upon loans, and it borrowed $98,000,000 during the war. As the credit of the government began to diminish, those loans were sold at prices much less than their face, and the country was obliged to issue $37,000,000 of Treasury notes. Meanwhile, England was raising by taxation nearly Ł70,000,000 a year, and in 1815 was successfully carrying a debt of Ł860,000,000. The remnant of Republican prejudice against Federalist finances was just sufficient to prevent the re-chartering of the United States Bank in 1811. The country, therefore, entered on the war with insufficient means, impaired credit, and a defective financial organization.

In national spirit, also, the United States was the weaker. The British had for twenty years been carrying a popular war with France, in which they had shown themselves far superior at sea, and had gained great military experience. In the United States sectional spirit was more violent than at any time since 1798. We now know that some of the leading Federalists were, up to the outbreak of the war, in confidential communication with British envoys. In 1809 and 1810 the Republican governor and legislature in Pennsylvania were opposing with military violence the service of the writs of the United States District Court in the Olmstead Case. The disaffection of the Federalists was publicly expressed by Josiah Quincy, of Massachusetts, in a Speech in 1811 on the admission of Louisiana: "If this bill passes, it is my deliberate opinion that it is virtually a dissolution of this Union; that it will free the States from their moral obligation; and, as it will be the right of all, so it will be the duty of some, definitely to prepare for a separation, amicably if they can, violently if they must."

[Sidenote: The two armies.] Nor did the military and naval preparation of the country make up for its political weakness. The regular army of the United

States was composed of 6,700 men. The service was so unpopular that two proclamations were issued in 1812 promising pardons to deserters. The highest number of officers and men in the regular army was during the war but 34,000. The dependence of the government, therefore, for offensive operations was upon the State militia. The general officers were old Revolutionary soldiers or men who had seen no service; the military organization was defective; and the Secretary of War, Eustis, was incompetent. In this very year, 1812, the British regular troops under Wellington were steadily beating back the French, who had been supposed to be the best soldiers in the world.

[Sidenote: The two navies.]

In naval affairs comparison between the two powers was almost impossible. The American navy consisted of twelve vessels, the largest of which were the three 44-gun frigates "United States", "Constitution," and "President". The number of men was 4,000, with 1,500 marines. The British navy was composed of eight hundred and thirty vessels, of which two hundred and thirty were larger than any of the American ships; they had 150,000 seamen, and unlimited power of impressing sailors.

[Sidenote: The theatre of the war.]

The theatre of war was to be much the same as in the French and Indian war (§ 14). The lines stretched from Nova Scotia to the Great Lakes, but settlement had extended so far westward that Detroit marked the flank of both powers, and Lake Erie was included in the field of operations. Like Braddock in 1755 (§ 16), the Americans expected to roll the enemy's line up from west to east; and at the same time they meant to penetrate where Loudon and Abercrombie had attacked, through Lake Ontario and Lake Champlain. For harbor and coast defence they relied chiefly on the fleet of gunboats.

111. WAR ON THE NORTHERN FRONTIER (1812, 1813).

[Sidenote: Campaign of 1812.]

For the beginning of the campaign two expeditions were planned,—one across the river from Detroit, the other across the Niagara from Buffalo. The experience of the Revolution threw little light on the problem of conveying large bodies of men, with the necessary stores, across such stretches of wild country. General Hull, in command at Detroit, after a single effort to invade Canada, was forced back, and on Aug. 16, 1812, was brought to a disgraceful capitulation. Fort Dearborn, now Chicago, and Mackinac were captured at about the same time. In October and November two attempts were made to cross the Niagara into Canada. Owing to the incapacity of the commanders, Van Rensselaer and Smythe, six thousand American troops were held in check, and smaller bodies of them defeated, by one thousand British. The military authorities in the centre waited for the reduction of western Canada before attempting to advance northward to Montreal.

[Sidenote: Campaign of 1813.]

The campaign of 1813 was little more fortunate. The British, with their savage allies, held Detroit; but a fresh-water navy had been constructed by both parties on Lake Erie, and the victory of Commodore Perry gave the control of Lake Erie, and thus of Detroit, to the Americans. On the Niagara frontier the Americans were successful in occupying the British forts on the western side of the river, but could not penetrate the country. A northern expedition descended the St. Lawrence, but was obliged to retire into American territory without result; and in the last days of the year the Niagara posts were again abandoned.

112. NAVAL WARFARE (1812-1815).

[Sidenote: The first cruise.]
[Sidenote: English cruisers captured.]

When the war broke out, the purpose of the administration was to keep the vessels of the United States navy in Port for harbor and coast defence. An order was sent to New York authorizing a brief preliminary cruise, and within one hour Commodore Rodgers, with the frigates "President", and "Congress", the ship "Hornet" and brig "Argus", had got to sea. Within two days the little squadron attacked the British frigate "Belvidera," which had made herself obnoxious by her blockade of American ports, but lost her. On August 19 the frigate "Constitution", Captain Hull, met the British frigate "Guerriere", renowned for its unauthorized search of American vessels: in thirty minutes the "Guerriere" was taken; and the "Constitution" returned in triumph to Boston. The effects of this brilliant victory were immediately felt: New England shared in it; British naval prestige had received a damaging blow; and the Navy Department could no longer hope to keep the navy at home for police duty. Meantime the sloop-of-war "Wasp" had captured the British brig "Frolic" of equal force; and Decatur, in the frigate "United States", on October 25 took the British frigate "Macedonian". A few weeks later the frigate "Constitution" captured the British frigate "Java".

[Sidenote: Effect of the victories.]

The result of six months naval warfare was the capture of three British frigates and two smaller vessels, besides large numbers of merchantmen. American commerce had been almost driven from the seas, but only three small American cruisers had been taken. The victories were more than unexpected, they were astounding In nearly every fight the American vessel was of heavier tonnage, and threw a heavier broadside; but the sailors were fighting the most renowned naval power in the world, The British captains in every case sought the encounter, and they were defeated by the superior tactical skill, and especially the superior gunnery, of the Americans, Congress was obliged by the force of public sentiment to begin the construction of new vessels. At the same time American privateers ranged the seas and brought in British merchantmen. In 1813 there was a minor naval warfare on Lakes Erie, Ontario, and Champlain, Two small armed vessels, the "Peacock" and the "Boxer," were captured at sea by the Americans; and the ship "Essex," under Captain Porter, ranged the Pacific and captured thirteen vessels,

[Sidenote: The American navy subdued.]

The tide had now begun to turn, In June, 1813, Captain Lawrence, of the frigate "Chesapeake," was challenged by Captain Broke, of the "Shannon," to fight him near the harbor of Boston. People assembled on Marblehead Neck to see the English cruiser made a prize; after a hard fight the "Chesapeake" was captured and towed into Halifax. It was the victory of disciplined courage over courage less trained, and perhaps less well handled. By this time large blockading squadrons had been sent out, and most of the American fleet was shut up in the harbors of Boston, New London, and New York. The frigate "President" was captured while endeavoring to escape from New York; the "Essex" was taken in a neutral port; and for a time there was no American cruiser on the sea.

[Sidenote: American privateers.]

The defence of the newly acquired American reputation at sea was thus left to the privateers. They were small, handy vessels, apt at striking, and quick to run away. In 1813 they captured four hundred prizes, while the national cruisers took but seventy-nine. The "True-Blooded Yankee" alone in thirty-seven days took twenty-seven vessels, some of them in Dublin Bay, and was not captured. The loss of property and of prestige was so great that in 1814 insurance on vessels crossing the Irish Channel was rated at thirteen per cent. During two and a half years of war the privateers took fourteen hundred prizes, and the cruisers took three hundred more. On the other hand, about seventeen hundred American merchantmen had been captured by the British. The flag of the United States on unarmed vessels had at the end of 1814 almost ceased to float on the ocean.

113. DISASTROUS CAMPAIGN OF 1814.

[Sidenote: The situation abroad.]

Nothing but a total want of understanding of the conditions in Europe could have brought about the War of 1812. In 1811 the Continental System (§ 102) had broken down, because Russia would no longer cut off the trade in American ships. The result of this breach was Napoleon's Russian campaign of 1812; his success would have totally excluded American commerce from the Baltic, and would probably have resulted in the overthrow of England. The Americans were assisting the cause of a great tyranny and a great commercial monopoly.

[Sidenote: Fall of Napoleon.]

During 1812 and 1813, while the Americans were vainly struggling to capture a few petty forts on the Canadian frontier, Napoleon was falling back step by step; and on April 6, 1814, he abdicated his throne, and a general European peace was made.

[Sidenote: Lundy's Lane.]
[Sidenote: English invasion.]
[Sidenote: Capture of Washington.]

The result was new energy in the American war. Twelve thousand English veteran troops were despatched to Canada, and expeditions were planned to harass the American coast. The struggle was renewed on the Niagara frontier under the efficient command of Jacob Brown, a New York militia general. An American force penetrated into Canada and fought the successful battle of Lundy's Lane; but Brown was wounded, and his forces abandoned the field. The British now attempted to invade the United States; the Maine coast was occupied, almost without resistance, as far south as the Penobscot; the Americans were attacked at Fort Erie, on the west side of the Niagara; and a force of eighteen thousand men moved up Lake Champlain to Plattsburg. On September 11 its advance was checked by a field-work and an American fleet under Macdonough. Both at Fort Erie and at Plattsburg the veteran British troops were beaten off by the Americans behind their breastworks. Meanwhile the nation had been overwhelmed with terror and shame by the capture of Washington. Five thousand British troops landed from the Chesapeake, marched fifty miles across a populous country, and coolly took the national capital. The defence made by General Winder is characterized in his order to the artillery when, with seven thousand militia, he was about to make a stand: "When you retreat, take notice that you must retreat by the Georgetown road." The President and cabinet fled, and the public buildings were burned, in alleged retaliation for destruction of buildings in Canada; and the assailing force withdrew to its ships without molestation. Encouraged by this success, a similar attack was made upon Baltimore; here a spirited resistance from behind intrenchments once more beat the British off.

[Sidenote: Attack on New Orleans.]

Now came the news that an expedition was preparing to attack the Gulf coast. Andrew Jackson, who had been engaged in Indian wars in the southwest, was put in command. Still, he made no preparation for the defence of New Orleans, until, on December 10, the British expedition of fifty sail was sighted. Jackson now showed his native energy; troops were hurried forward, and militia were brought together. A want of common watchfulness suffered the British to reach a point within seven miles of New Orleans before they met any resistance. Then Jackson made such defence as he could. He formed an intrenched line with artillery; and here, with about forty-five hundred men, he awaited the advance of eight thousand of the British. They attacked him Jan. 8, 1815, and were repulsed.

114. QUESTION OF THE MILITIA (1812-1814).

[Sidenote: New England disaffected.]

As at New Orleans, so throughout the war, the greater part of the fighting was done by State militia hastily assembled, imperfectly disciplined, and serving only for short terms. From the beginning, however, the New England States had refused to furnish militia on the call of the general government. They did not interfere with volunteer recruiting, and Massachusetts alone supplied as many troops as came from Virginia and North and South Carolina; but they declined officially to take part in offensive military operations. The war was very unpopular to the New Englanders because of the great losses to their commerce, and because they paid more than half the expense; nor had New England any sympathy with that invasion of Canada which was so popular in the West.

[Sidenote: Militia refused.]

As soon as war broke out, the Secretary of War authorized General Dearborn to summon twenty thousand militia from the New England States. Care was taken in sending the call to ask for small detachments of the militia, so as to rid the United States of the general militia officers appointed by the States. The result of these combined causes was that the Governor of Connecticut refused to send militia, declaring that he must "yield obedience to the paramount authority of the Constitution and the laws." The Massachusetts House voted that the "war is a wanton sacrifice of our best interests;" and the Governor of Massachusetts informed the President that since there was no invasion, there was no constitutional reason for sending the militia. New Hampshire took similar ground, and the governor of Rhode Island congratulated the legislature on the possession of two cannon, with which that State might defend itself against an invader. On Nov. 10, 1813, Governor Chittenden of Vermont ordered the recall of a brigade which had been summoned outside the boundary of the State, declaring it to be his opinion that "the military strength and resources of this State must be reserved for its own defence and protection exclusively."

[Sidenote: National government hampered.]
[Sidenote: New England attacked.]

The general government had no means of enforcing its construction of the Constitution. It did, however, withdraw garrisons from the New England forts, leaving those States to defend themselves; and refused to send them their quota of the arms which were distributed among the States. This attitude was so well understood that during the first few months of the war English cruisers had orders not to capture vessels owned in New England. As the war advanced, these orders were withdrawn, and the territory of Massachusetts in the District of Maine was invaded by British troops. An urgent call for protection was then made upon the general government; but even in this crisis Massachusetts would not permit her militia to pass under the control of national military officers.

115. SECESSION MOVEMENT IN NEW ENGLAND (1814).

[Sidenote: Federalist successes.]
[Sidenote: Opposition to the war.]

More positive and more dangerous opposition had been urged in New England from the beginning of the war. Besides the sacrifice of men, Massachusetts furnished more money for the war than Virginia. In the elections of 1812 and 1813 the Federalists obtained control of every New England State government, and secured most of the New England members of Congress. The temper of this Federalist majority may be seen in a succession of addresses and speeches in the Massachusetts legislature. On June 15, 1813, Josiah Quincy offered a resolution that "in a war like the present, waged without justifiable cause and prosecuted in a manner which indicates that conquest and ambition are its real motives, it is not becoming a moral and religious people to express any approbation of military or naval exploits which are not immediately connected with the defence of our sea-coast and soil." As the pressure of the war grew heavier, the tone in New England grew sterner. On Feb. 18, 1814, a report was made to the Massachusetts legislature containing a declaration taken almost literally from Madison's Virginia Resolution of 1798 (§ 90), that "whenever the national compact is violated, and the citizens of the State oppressed by cruel and unauthorized laws, this legislature is bound to interpose its power and wrest from the oppressor his victim."

[Sidenote: Impotence of Congress.]
[Sidenote: Resistance threatened.]

The success of the British attacks in August and September, 1814, seemed to indicate the failure of the war. Congress met on September 19 to confront the growing danger: but it refused to authorize a new levy of troops; it refused to accept a proposition for a new United States Bank; it consented with reluctance to new taxes. The time seemed to have arrived when the protests of New England against the continuance of the war might be made effective. The initiative was taken by Massachusetts, which, on October 16 voted to raise a million dollars to support a State army of ten thousand troops, and to ask the other New England States to meet in convention.

[Sidenote: A convention called.]

On Dec. 15, 1814, delegates assembled at Hartford from Massachusetts, Connecticut, and Rhode Island, with unofficial representatives from New Hampshire and Vermont. The head of the Massachusetts delegation was George Cabot, who had been chosen because of his known opposition to the secession of that State. As he said himself: "We are going to keep you young hot-heads from getting into mischief." The expectation throughout the country was that the Hartford convention would recommend secession, Jefferson wrote: "Some apprehend danger from the defection of Massachusetts. It is a disagreeable circumstance, but not a dangerous one. If they become neutral, we are sufficient for one enemy without them; and, in fact, we get no aid from them now."

[Sidenote: Hartford Convention.]
[Sidenote: Secession impending.]

After a session of three weeks, the Hartford Convention adjourned, Jan. 14, 1815, and published a formal report. They declared that the Constitution had been violated, and that "States which have no common umpire must be their own judges and execute their own decisions." They submitted a list of amendments to the Constitution intended to protect a minority of States from aggressions on the part of the majority. Finally they submitted, as their ultimatum, that they should be allowed to retain the proceeds of the national customs duties collected within their borders. Behind the whole document was the implied intention to withdraw from the Union if this demand were not complied with. To comply was to deprive the United States of its financial power, and was virtually a dissolution of the constitution. The delegates who were sent to present this powerful remonstrance to Congress were silenced by the news that peace had been declared.

116. THE PEACE OF GHENT (1812-1814).

[Sidebar: Russian mediation.]
[Sidebar: American commissioners sent.]

Three months after the war broke out, the Russian government had offered mediation; it regretted to see the strength of the English allies wasted in a minor contest with America. Madison eagerly seized this opportunity, and on May 9, 1813, Gallatin and Bayard were sent as special commissioners. On arriving in Russia they found that the British government had refused the offer of mediation. The immediate effect was to take Gallatin out of the Treasury, and he was followed by Secretary Campbell, to whose incompetence the financial impotence of the war is partly due. Toward the end of 1813 an offer of direct negotiation was made by the British government, and John Quincy Adams, Jonathan Russell, and Henry Clay were added to the negotiators. The absence of Clay, who had exercised such influence as Speaker of the House, accounts for the apathy of Congress in 1814.

[Sidebar: The effect of European peace.]
[Sidenote: Impressment.]

It was not until Aug. 8, 1814, that the commissioners finally met English commissioners at Ghent. Of the grievances which had brought on the war, most had been removed by the European peace: neutral vessels were no longer captured; the blockade of American ports in time of peace was not likely to be resumed; and the impressment of American seamen ceased because the English navy was reduced. The two countries were therefore fighting over dead questions. The Americans, however, naturally desired, in making peace, to secure a recognition of the principles for which they had gone to war; and the British had now no other enemy, and were incensed at the temerity of the little nation which had attempted to invade Canada and had so humiliated England at sea. Gradually, the commissioners began to find common ground. Gallatin reported to the home government that in his judgment no article could be secured renouncing the right to impress British subjects wherever found. With a heavy heart, Madison consented that that point should be omitted from the treaty.

[Sidenote: The war unpopular in England.]

During 1814 great pressure was put upon the British government to make peace, on account of the loss inflicted by American privateers. The war was costing England about ten million pounds sterling a year, and no definite result had been gained except the capture of a part of Maine and of the American post of Astoria in Oregon. The Americans were unable to make headway in Canada; the English were equally unable to penetrate into the United States. Wellington was consulted, and reported that in his judgment the British could hope for no success without naval superiority on the lakes. The brave resistance of the Americans at Fort Erie and Plattsburg had won the respect of the great military commander. The ministry, therefore, resolved upon peace.

[Sidenote: Territory.]
[Sidenote: Fisheries.]
[Sidenote: The treaty signed.]

The first question to settle was that of territory. The British consented to restore the territory as it had been before the war; some attempt was made to create a belt of frontier neutral territory for the Indians who had been allies of the British, but that point was also abandoned. Next came the question of the fisheries: the British held that the American rights had been lost by the war; Clay insisted that the British right of navigation of the Mississippi had also been forfeited, and that the fisheries might therefore be sacrificed as a "matter of trifling moment." Adams stood out for the fisheries, and the result was that neither question was mentioned in the treaty. In 1818 a special convention was negotiated, defining the fishery rights of the United States. Upon these general lines agreement was at last reached, and the treaty was signed Dec. 24, 1814, several weeks before the battle of New Orleans.

117. POLITICAL EFFECTS OF THE WAR (1815).

[Sidenote: No gain from the war.]
[Sidenote: National pride.]

After nearly three years of war, the expenditure of one hundred millions of dollars, the loss of about thirty thousand lives, the destruction of property, and ruinous losses of American vessels, the country stood where it had stood in 1812, its boundary unchanged, its international rights still undefined, the people still divided. Yet peace brought a kind of national exaltation. The naval victories had been won by officers and men from all parts of the Union, and belonged to the nation. The last struggle on land, the battle of New Orleans, was an American victory, and obliterated the memory of many defeats. President Madison, in his annual message of 1815, congratulated the country that the treaty "terminated with peculiar felicity a campaign signalized by the most brilliant successes."

[Sidenote: Training of soldiers.]

One noteworthy effect of the war had been the development of a body of excellent young soldiers. Winfield Scott distinguished himself in the Niagara campaigns, and rose eventually to be the highest officer of the American army. William Henry Harrison's military reputation was based chiefly on the Indian battle of Tippecanoe in 1811, but it made him President in 1840. Andrew Jackson's victory at New Orleans brought him before the people, and caused his choice as President in 1828. The national pride was elated by the successes of American engineers, American naval architects, American commodores, and volunteer officers like Jacob Brown, who had finally come to the front.

[Sidenote: Extrication from European politics.]

The end of the war marks also the withdrawal of the United States from the complications of European politics. From 1775 to 1815 the country had been compelled, against its will, to take sides, to ask favors, and to suffer rebuffs abroad. During the long interval of European peace, from 1815 to 1853, the United States grew up without knowing this influence. Furthermore, the field was now clear for a new organization of American industries. The profits of the shipping trade had not been due so much to American enterprise as to the greater safety of foreign cargoes in neutral bottoms. When this advantage was swept away, American shipping languished, and its place was taken by manufacturing.

[Sidenote: Decay of the Federalist party.]
[Sidenote: Persistence of Federalist principles.]
[Sidenote: Gain in national spirit.]

The most marked result of the war was the absorption of the Federalist Party, which at once began, and in five or six years was complete. In the election of 1812 eighty-nine votes had been cast for the Federalist candidate (§ 109); in 1816 there were but thirty-four (§ 123); in 1820 there was not one. This did not mean that Federalist principles had decayed or been overborne; the real reason for the extinction of that party was that it lived in the ranks of the Republican party. When Jefferson in 1801 said, "We are all Republicans, we are all Federalists," he expressed what had come to be true in 1815. The great principles for which the Federalists had striven were the right of the federal government to exercise adequate powers, and its duty to maintain the national dignity: those principles had been adopted by the Republicans. John Randolph was almost the only leader who continued to stand by the Republican doctrine enunciated by Jefferson when he became President. Jefferson himself had not scrupled to annex Louisiana, to lay the embargo, and to enforce it with a severity such as Hamilton would hardly have ventured on. Madison had twice received and used the power to discriminate between the commerce of England and of France; and during the war the nation had reimposed federal taxes and adopted Federalist principles of coercion. James Monroe, Secretary of State at the end of Madison's administration, and candidate for the Presidency in 1816, was in his political beliefs not to be distinguished from moderate Federalists like James A. Bayard in 1800. The Union arose from the disasters of the War of 1812 stronger than ever before, because the people had a larger national tradition and greater experience of national government, and because they had accepted the conception of government which Washington and Hamilton had sought to create.

CHAPTER XI

118. REFERENCES.

BIBLIOGRAPHIES.—W. E. Foster, *References to Presidential Administrations*, 15-19; Justin Winsor, Narrative and Critical History_,
VII. 344, 345, 437-439; J.F. Jameson, *Bibliography of Monroe* (Appendix to Oilman's *Monroe*); Channing and Hart, *Guide*, §§ 174-178.

HISTORICAL MAPS.—Nos. 1 and 5, this volume, and No. 1, Wilson, *Division and Reunion* (*Epoch Maps* Nos. 7, 8, and 10); Labberton, *Atlas*, lxvii.; T. MacCoun, *Historical Geography, Scribner, Statistical Atlas*, Plate 14.

GENERAL ACCOUNTS.—H. Von Holst, *Constitutional History*, I. 273-408; R.
Hildreth, *United States*. VI. 575-713 (to 1821); James Schouler, *United States*, II. 444-463, III. 1-335; Bryant and Gay, *Popular History*. IV. 244-281; J. B. McMaster, *People of the United States*, IV. (to 1820); Geo. Tucker, *United States*, III. 146-408; J. T. Morse, *John Quincy Adams*, 102-164; Ormsby, *Whig Party*, 129-172.

SPECIAL HISTORIES.—Henry Adams, *History of the United States*, IX.; Carl Schurz, *Henry Clay*, I. 137-202; N. P. Gilman, *James Monroe*, 125- 174; F. W. Taussig, *Tariff History*, J. L. Bishop, *American Manufactures*, II. 146-298; G. F. Tucker, *Monroe Doctrine*, Payne, *European Colonies*, E. Stanwood, *Presidential Elections*, H. L. Carson, *Supreme Court*, I. chs. xii.-xiv.; A C. McLaughlin, *Cass*, chs. ii., iv.

CONTEMPORARY ACCOUNTS.—J. Q. Adams, *Memoirs*, IV.-VI.; Josiah Quincy, *Figures of the Past, Niles Register*, T. H. Benton, *Thirty Years' View*, I. 1-44; Nathan Sargent, *Public Men, and Events*, I. 17-56; R. Rush, *Residence at the Court of London*, J. Flint, *Recollections of the last Ten Years* (1826); R. Walsh, *Appeal from the Judgment of Great Britain* (1819); D. Warden, *Statistical, Political, and Historical Account of the United States* (1819); S. G. Goodrich, Recollections, II. 393-436; *The National Intelligencer*; Featon, *Sketches of America, Fifth Report*; works of Clay, Calhoun, Webster, Madison, Woodbury.— Reprints in F. W. Taussig, *State Papers and Speeches on the Tariff, American History told by Contemporaries*, III.

119. CONDITIONS OF NATIONAL GROWTH (1815).

[Sidenote: Prosperity.]

The population of the United States at the end of the war was about eight million five hundred thousand, and it was increasing relatively faster in the South and West than near the seaboard. The return of peace seemed also a return of prosperity. Short crops abroad revived the demand for American cereals, so that the surplus accumulated during the war could be sold at fair prices, and the exports in 1816 ran up to $64,000,000. In 1815, American shipping recovered almost to the point which it had reached in 1810. The revenue derived from taxation in 1814 was but $11,000,000; in 1816 it was $47,000,000. More than twenty thousand immigrants arrived in 1817. Wealth seemed increasing both in the North and the South.

[Sidenote: National literature.]
[Sidenote: The Clergy.]

Another evidence of the quickening of national life was the beginning of a new national literature. In 1815 was founded the "North American Review," and in an early number appeared Bryant's "Thanatopsis." Already in 1809 had appeared the first work of an American which was comparable with that of the British essayists,—Washington Irving's "Knickerbocker" History of New York. His quaint humor was not less appreciated from his good-natured allusions to the Jeffersonian principle of government "by proclamation." The hold of the clergy had been much weakened in New England; there had been a division of the Congregational Church, with the subsequent founding of the Unitarian branch; and the Jeffersonian principle of popular government was gaining ground. The people were keen and alert.

[Sidenote: Means of transportation.]
[Sidenote: Steamboats.]

In two respects the war had taught the Americans their own weakness: they had had poor facilities for transportation, and they had lacked manufactures of military material. There was a widespread feeling that the means of intercommunication ought to be improved. The troops on the northern frontier had been badly provisioned and slowly reinforced because they could not readily be reached over the poor roads. A system had been invented which was suitable for the rapid-running rivers of the interior and for lake navigation: in 1807 Fulton made the first voyage by steam on the Hudson River. Nine years later a system of passenger service had been developed in various directions from New York, and a steamer was running on the Mississippi.

Manufactures had sprung up suddenly and unexpectedly in the United States. The restrictive legislation from 1806 to 1812, though it had not cut off foreign imports, had checked them; and shrewd ship-owners had in some cases diverted their accumulated capital to the building of factories. In 1812 commerce with England was totally cut off, and importations from other countries were loaded down with double duties. This indirect protection was enough to cause the rise of many manufactures, particularly of cotton and woollen goods. In 1815, the capital invested in these two branches of industry was probably $50,000,000. On the conclusion of peace in England and America an accumulated stock of English goods poured forth, and the imports of the United States instantly rose from $12,000.000 in 1814, to $106,000,000 in 1815. These importations were out of proportion to the exports and to the needs of the country, and they caused the stoppage of a large number of American factories. Meanwhile, American ships had begun to feel the competition of foreign vessels in foreign trade. Without intending it, the country had drifted into a new set of economic conditions.

120. THE SECOND UNITED STATES BANK (1816).

[Sidenote: Banks and currency.]

The first evidence of this change of feeling was a demand for the renewal of the bank which had been allowed to expire in 1811 (§ 110). The country had been thrown entirely upon banks chartered by the States; the pressure of the war had caused their suspension, and the currency and banking capital of the United States had thus been thrown into complete confusion. For example, the Farmers Exchange Bank of Gloucester, R. I., was started, with a capital of $3,000; accumulated deposits so that one of the directors was able to steal $760,000; and then it failed, with specie assets of $86.46. In 1811 there were eighty-eight State banks; in 1816 there were two hundred and forty-six.

[Sidenote: Bank bill of 1814.]
[Sidenote: The Bank Act.]

Since the re-charter bill of 1811 had failed by only one vote, Dallas, Secretary of the Treasury in 1814, again proposed a national bank. Congress accepted the principle, but an amendment proposed by John C. Calhoun so altered the scheme that upon Dallas's advice Madison cast his first important veto against it on Jan. 30, 1815. What Dallas desired was a bank which would lend money to the government; what Congress planned was a bank which would furnish a currency based on specie. In the next session of Congress Madison himself urged the creation of a bank, and this time Calhoun supported him. The Federalists, headed by Daniel Webster,— remnants of the party which had established the first national bank,— voted against it on the general principle of factious opposition. A small minority of the Republicans joined them, but it was passed without much difficulty, and became a law on April, 10, 1816.

[Sidenote: Bank charter.]

The bank was modelled on its predecessor (§ 78), but the capital was increased from $10,000,000 to $35,000,000, of which the United States government held $7,000,000. It was especially provided that "the deposits of the money of the United States shall be made in said bank or branches thereof." In return for its special privileges the bank agreed to pay to the government $1,500,000. The capital was larger than could safely be employed; it was probably intended to absorb bank capital from the State banks. The prosperity of the country, aided by the operations of the bank, secured the renewal of specie payments by all the sound banks in the country on Feb. 20, 1817.

[Sidenote: Loose construction accepted.]

The striking feature in the bank was not that it should be established, but that it should be accepted by old Republicans like Madison, who had found the charter of a bank in 1791 a gross perversion of the Constitution. Even Henry Clay, who in 1811 had powerfully contributed to the defeat of the bank, now came forward as its champion.

121. INTERNAL IMPROVEMENTS (1806-1817).

[Sidenote: Local improvements.]
[Sidenote: Cumberland road.]
[Sidenote: Gallatin's scheme.]

Side by side with the bank bill went a proposition for an entirely new application of the government funds. Up to this time internal improvements— roads, canals and river and harbor improvements—had been made by the States, so far as they were made at all. Virginia and Maryland had spent considerable sums in an attempt to make the Potomac navigable, and a few canals had been constructed by private capital, sometimes aided by State credit. In 1806 the United States began the Cumberland Road, its first work of the kind; but it was intended to open up the public lands in Ohio and the country west, and was nominally paid for out of the proceeds of those public lands. Just as the embargo policy was taking effect, Gallatin, encouraged by the accumulation of a surplus in the Treasury, brought in a report, April 4, 1808, suggesting the construction of a great system of internal improvements: it was to include coastwise canals across the isthmuses of Cape Cod, New Jersey, upper Delaware and eastern North Carolina; roads were to be constructed from Maine to Georgia, and thence to New Orleans, and from Washington westward to Detroit and St. Louis. He estimated the cost at twenty millions, to be provided in ten annual instalments. Jefferson himself was so carried away with this prospect of public improvement that he recommended a constitutional amendment to authorize such expenditures. The whole scheme disappeared when the surplus vanished; but from year to year small appropriations were made for the Cumberland road, so that up to 1812 more than $200,000 had been expended upon it.

[Sidenote: Calhoun's Bonus Bill.]
[Sidenote: Madison's veto.]

The passage of the bank bill in 1816 was to give the United States a million and a half of dollars (Section 120). Calhoun, therefore, came forward, Dec. 23, 1816 with a bill proposing that this sum be employed as a fund "for constructing roads and canals and improving the navigation of watercourses." "We are" said he, "a rapidly—I was about to say a fearfully—growing country…. This is our pride and danger, our weakness and our strength." The constitutional question he settled with a phrase: "If we are restricted in the use of our money to the enumerated powers, on what principle can the purchase of Louisiana be justified?" The bill passed the House by eighty-six to eighty-four; it was strongly supported by New York members, because it was expected that the general government would begin the construction of a canal from Albany to the Lakes; it had also large support in the South, especially in South Carolina. In the last hours of his administration Madison vetoed it. His message shows that he had selected this occasion to leave to the people a political testament; he was at last alarmed by the progress of his own party, and, like Jefferson, he insisted that internal improvements were desirable, but needed a constitutional amendment. The immediate effect of the veto was that New York, seeing no prospect of federal aid, at once herself began the construction of the Erie Canal, which was opened eight years later. [Sidenote: State improvements.] Other States attempted like enterprises; but the passes behind the Susquehanna and Potomac rivers were too high, and no permanent water way was ever finished over them.

122. THE FIRST PROTECTIVE TARIFF (1816).

[Sidenote: Increase of duties.]

The protection controversy had hardly appeared in Congress since the memorable debate of 1789 (Section 76). From time to time the duties had been slightly increased, and in 1799 a general administrative tariff act had been passed. The wars with the Barbary powers had necessitated a slight increase of the duties, known as the Mediterranean Fund, and this had been allowed to stand. Up to the doubling of the duties in 1812 the average rate on staple imports was only from ten to fifteen per cent, and the maximum was about thirty per cent. The whole theory of the Republican administration had been that finance consisted in deciding upon the necessary expenses of government, and then in providing the taxes necessary to meet them. This theory had been disturbed by the existence of a debt which Jefferson was eager to extinguish; and he therefore permitted the duties to remain at a point where they produced much more than the ordinary expenditure of the government.

[Sidenote: The manufacturers.]
[Sidenote: The West.]

A change had now come over the country. The incidental protection afforded by the increase of duties, and then by the war, had built up manufactures, not only in New England, but in New York and Pennsylvania. In these strongholds of capital and trade there was a cry for higher duties, and it was much enforced by the attitude of the Western members. There were a few staple crops, particularly hemp and flax, which could not be produced in the face of foreign competition, and for which Western States were supposed to be adapted. Hence a double influence was at work in behalf of a protective tariff: the established industries pleaded for a continuance of the high duties which had given them an opportunity to rise; and the friends of young industries asked for new duties, in order that their enterprises might be established.

[Sidenote: Dallas's tariff bill.]
[Sidenote: Opponents.]
[Sidenote: Advocates.]

Accordingly, in February, 1816, Secretary Dallas made an elaborate report in favor of protective duties. John Randolph, who still posed as the defender of the original Republican doctrine, protested. "The agriculturist," said he, "has his property, his lands, his all, his household gods to defend;" and he pointed out what was afterward to become the most effective argument against the tariff: "Upon whom bears the duty on coarse woollens and linens and blankets, upon salt and all the necessaries of life? Upon poor men and upon slaveholders." Webster, representing the commercial interest of New England, decidedly opposed the tariff, especially the minimum principle, and succeeded in obtaining a slight reduction. One of the strongest defenders of the tariff was Calhoun. Manufactures, he declared, produced an interest strictly American, and calculated to bind the widespread republic more closely together. The chief supporter of the system was Henry Clay of Kentucky, the Speaker of the House. His argument was that the country ought to be able to defend itself in time of war, It was not expected at this time that a protective tariff would become permanent. In a few years, said a committee of the House, the country would be in a condition to bid defiance to foreign competition.

[Sidenote: Protective policy.]
[Sidenote: The minimum.]

The act as passed April 27, 1816, had favorable votes in every State in the Union except Delaware and North Carolina. The opposition was strong in the South and in New England. Madison signed the bill and accepted the policy, and even Jefferson declared that "We must now place the manufacturer by the side of the agriculturist." The act imposed duties of twenty-five per cent upon cotton and woollen goods, and the highest ad valorem duty was about thirty per cent. In addition, no duty was to be less than six and a quarter cents a yard on cottons and woollens: hence as improvements in machinery caused a rapid lowering of the cost of production abroad, the duty grew heavier on coarse goods, in proportion to their value, till it was almost prohibitory. The act was accepted without any popular demonstrations against it, and remained in force, with some unimportant modifications, until 1824. One purpose undoubtedly was to show to foreign governments that the United States could discriminate against their trade if they discriminated against ours.

123. MONROE'S ADMINISTRATION (1817-1825).

[Sidenote: Monroe's election.]
[Sidenote: The cabinet.]

The election of 1816 proved that the Federalists could no longer keep up a national organization. They were successful only in Massachusetts, Connecticut, and Delaware. On March 4, 1817, therefore, James Monroe took his seat as the President of a well-united people. Although he had been the friend and candidate of Randolph, he represented substantially the same principles as Jefferson and Madison. His cabinet was the ablest since Washington's; he gathered about him four of the most distinguished public men in the country. His Secretary of State was John Quincy Adams, one of the negotiators of the treaty of Ghent. His Secretary of the Treasury was

William H. Crawford of Georgia, who had shown financial ability in Congress and in Madison's cabinet. For Secretary of War he chose John C. Calhoun, who had in the six years of his national public service become renowned as an active and almost a passionate advocate of the use of large national powers. His Attorney-General was William Wirt of Virginia.

[Sidenote: Party strength.]

These young men represented an eager policy, and in their national principles had advanced far beyond the old Federalists; but the people had been somewhat startled by the boldness of the preceding Congress, and many of the members who would have agreed with the President had lost their seats. Throughout the whole administration Jefferson at Monticello, and Madison at Montpelier, remained in dignified retirement; from time to time Monroe asked their advice on great public questions.

[Sidenote: Commercial treaties.]

One of the first tasks of the administration was to restore the commercial relations which had been so disturbed by the Napoleonic wars. Algiers had taken advantage of the War of 1812 to capture American vessels. In 1815 the Dey was compelled on the quarter-deck of Decatur's ship to sign a treaty of peace and amity. All our commercial treaties had disappeared in the war, and had to be painfully renewed. In 1815 a commercial convention was made with Great Britain, and in 1818 the fishery privileges of the United States were reaffirmed. The West India trade was still denied, but a retaliatory act brought Great Britain to terms, and it was opened in 1822.

124. TERRITORIAL EXTENSION (1805-1819).

[Sidenote: Northern boundary.]
[Sidenote: Oregon.]
[Sidenote: Boundary treaty.]

The administration inherited two serious boundary controversies, one with England, and another with Spain. Some progress had been made toward running the northeast boundary, till in 1818 the commissioners disagreed. The northwest boundary had now come to be more important. A few months before the annexation of Louisiana, Jefferson had sent an expedition to explore the country drained by the Columbia River, which had been discovered by a Boston ship in 1791. This expedition, under Lewis and Clark, in 1805 reached tributaries of the Columbia and descended it to its mouth, anticipating a similar English expedition. Nevertheless, the Hudson's Bay Company established trading-posts in the region. Monroe settled the difficulty for the time being by a treaty with Great Britain in 1818, providing that the disputed region lying between the Rocky Mountains and the Pacific Ocean and extending indefinitely northward should be jointly occupied by both countries. At the same time the northern boundary was defined from the Lake of the Woods to the Rocky Mountains.

[Sidenote: West Florida.]
[Sidenote: Spanish treaty.]

A year later another treaty with Spain gave to the United States a region which Jefferson had longed for in vain. Ever since 1803 the United States had asserted that West Florida had come to it as a part of Louisiana (§ 99). Spain steadfastly refused to admit this construction or to sell the province. In 1810 Madison by proclamation took possession of the disputed region, and a part of it was soon after added to Louisiana. East Florida could not possibly be included within Louisiana, but as a detached peninsula it was of little value to Spain. John Quincy Adams now undertook a negotiation for the settlement of all outstanding difficulties with Spain, and on Feb. 22, 1819, a treaty was signed: East Florida was ceded for a payment of about $6,500,000, and at the same time the western boundary of Louisiana was settled. An irregular line was described from the Gulf to the forty-second parallel; it was not far distant from the watershed south and west of the tributaries of the Mississippi. Then came the triumph of the whole negotiation: Adams obtained from Spain a renunciation of all claims north of the forty-second parallel, as far west as the Pacific. Our hold upon Oregon was thus much strengthened.

125. JUDICIAL DECISIONS (1812-1824).

[Sidenote: New judges.]
[Sidenote: Authority asserted.]

Two departments of the federal government had now shown their belief that the United States was a nation which ought to exercise national powers How did it stand with the judiciary department? Of the judges of the Supreme Court appointed by Washington and Adams but two remained in office in 1817; but the new justices, as they were appointed, quietly accepted the constitutional principles laid down by Marshall, their Chief Justice and leader. Among them was Joseph Story of Massachusetts, whose mastery of legal reasoning and power of statement gave him unusual influence. After the Marbury case in 1803 (§ 96) the Court refrained for some years from delivering decisions which involved important political questions. In 1809, however, it sustained Judge Peters of the Pennsylvania District Court in a struggle for authority against the governor and legislature of that State (§

110). The courts were victorious, and the commander of the militia, who had opposed them with armed force, was punished.

[Sidenote: Appeals taken.]
[Implied powers affirmed.]

The legislation of 1815 and 1816 showed to the Court that its view of the Constitution was accepted by the people; and it now began a series of great constitutional decisions, which put on record as legal precedents the doctrines of implied powers and of national sovereignty. In the great cases of Martin *vs.* Hunter's Lessee, and Cohens *vs.* Virginia, in 1816 and 1821, it asserted the right of the Supreme Court to take cases on appeal from the State courts, and thus to make itself the final tribunal in constitutional questions. At about the same time, in two famous cases, McCullough *vs.* Maryland in 1819, and Osborn et al. *vs.* Bank of the United States in 1824, the doctrine of implied powers was stated in the most definite manner. Both cases arose out of the attempt of States to tax the United States Bank, and the final issue was the power of Congress to charter such a bank. The doctrine laid down by Hamilton in 1791 (§ 78) was reaffirmed in most positive terms. "A national bank," said Marshall, "is an appropriate means to carry out some of the implied powers, a usual and convenient agent.... Let the end be within the scope of the Constitution, and all means which are ... plainly adapted to that end, which are not prohibited,... but consistent with the letter and spirit of the Constitution, are constitutional." Although the tariff act was not tested by a specific case, the spirit of the decision reached it also.

[Sidenote: State powers limited.]
[Sidenote: Impairment of contracts.]

Having thus asserted the authority of the nation on one side, the Court proceeded to draw the boundary of the powers of the States on the other side. In a question arising out of grants of land by the Georgia legislature in the Yazoo district, it had been claimed that any such grant could be withdrawn by a subsequent legislature. The Court held in Fletcher *vs.* Peck, in 1810, that such a withdrawal was in contravention of the constitutional clause which forbade the States to impair the obligation of contracts. In 1819, in the celebrated case of Dartmouth College *vs.* Woodward, this principle was pushed to an unexpected conclusion. The legislature of New Hampshire had passed an act modifying a charter granted in colonial times to Dartmouth College. Webster, as counsel for the Board of Trustees which had thus been dispossessed, pleaded that a charter granted to a corporation was a contract which could not be altered without its consent. Much indirect argument was brought to bear upon Marshall, and eventually the Court held that private charters were contracts. The effect of this decision was to diminish the power and prestige of the State governments; but the general sentiment of the country sustained it. So united did all factions now seem in one theory of national existence that in the election of 1820 Monroe received every vote but one.

126. THE SLAVERY QUESTION REVIVED (1815-1820).

[Sidenote: Silent growth of slavery.]

Out of this peace and concord suddenly sprang up, as Jefferson said, "like a fire-bell in the night," a question which had silently divided the Union, and threatened to dissolve it. It was the question of slavery. During the whole course of the Napoleonic wars the country had been occupied in the defence of its neutral trade; since 1815 it had been busy in reorganizing its commercial and political system. During this time, however, four new States had been admitted into the Union: of these, two—Ohio and Indiana— came in with constitutions prohibiting slavery; two—Louisiana and Mississippi—had slaves. This balance was not accidental; it was arranged so as to preserve a like balance in the Senate.

[Sidenote: Slavery profitable.]
[Sidenote: Slave-trade forbidden.]

The movement against slavery had by no means spent itself: there were still emancipation societies both North and South. In 1794 Jay appeared to suppose that cotton was not an American export (§ 85); but since the invention of the cotton-gin in 1793 the cultivation of cotton by slave labor had grown more and more profitable, and in 1820 that export was valued at nearly twenty millions. The planters of the northern belt of slaveholding States did not share in this culture, but they found an increasing sale for their surplus blacks to their Southern neighbors; they had, therefore, joined with members from the Northern States in the act of March 2, 1807, to prohibit the importation of slaves. The act was insufficient, inasmuch as the punishment provided was slight, and slaves captured while in course of illegal importation were sold for the benefit of the States into which they were brought, In 1820 the slave-trade was made piracy, so that the nominal penalty was death.

[Sidenote: Schemes of colonization.]

One evidence of the uneasiness of the country on the slavery question was the formation of the American Colonization Society in 1816. Its purpose was to encourage emancipation, and thus to reduce the evils of slavery, by drawing off the free blacks and colonizing them in Africa. It had a large membership throughout the country; James Madison and Henry Clay were among its presidents. Some States made grants of money in its aid, and after 1819 the United States assisted it by sending to the African colony slaves captured while in course of illegal importation. The whole scheme was but a palliative, and in fact rather tended to strengthen slavery, by taking away the disquieting presence of free blacks among the slaves. The Society, however, never had the means to draw away enough negroes sensibly to affect the problem; the number which they exported was replaced many times over by illegal importations from Africa.

[Sidenote: Fugitive slaves.]
[Sidenote: District of Columbia.]

In two other directions the nation had power over slavery, but declined to exercise it The Fugitive Slave Act (Section 79) was found to be ineffective. From 1818 to 1822 three bills to strengthen it were introduced and strongly pressed, but nothing could be accomplished. In the District of Columbia, where the United States had complete legislative power, slavery existed under a very harsh code. Washington was a centre for the interstate slave-trade, and John Randolph, himself a slaveholder, could not restrain his indignation that "we should have here in the very streets of our metropolis a depot for this nefarious traffic;" but Congress took no action.

[Sidenote: Status of Louisiana.]

A question had now arisen which must be decided. The whole of the Louisiana cession was slaveholding territory, and settlers had gone up the Mississippi River and its western tributaries with their slaves. In 1819 it was found necessary to provide a territorial government for Arkansas; and the people living about the Missouri River applied to be admitted as a State with a slaveholding constitution.

127. THE MISSOURI COMPROMISES (1818-1821),

[Sidenote: Arkansas debate.]

The first step in the great slavery contest was a bill introduced into the House in December, 1818, providing a territorial government for Arkansas. Taylor of New York proposed that slavery be prohibited in the Territory; McLane of Delaware suggested the "fixing of a line on the west of the Mississippi, north of which slavery should not be tolerated." The test vote on the exclusion of slavery was a tie, and Clay, as Speaker, cast his vote against it. The new Territory lay west of the Mississippi, and adjacent to Louisiana. The Northern members were, therefore, not disposed to make the issue at that point, and on March 2, 1819, an Act was passed organizing Arkansas, with no mention of slavery. Meanwhile, Illinois had been admitted, making eleven free States.

[Sidenote: Proposed restriction on Missouri.]

Side by side with this debate had proceeded a discussion on the admission of Missouri as a State. On Feb. 13, 1819, Talmadge of New York proposed as an amendment "that the further introduction of slavery or involuntary servitude be prohibited, ... and that all children of slaves born within the said State after the admission thereof into the Union shall be free." Missouri lay west of Illinois, which had just been admitted into the Union as a Free State; the Northern members, therefore, rallied, and passed the Talmadge amendment by a vote of eighty-seven to seventy-six. The Senate, by a vote of twenty-two to sixteen, refused to accept the amendment; there was no time for an adjustment, and Congress adjourned without action.

[Sidenote: Missouri bill.]
[Sidenote: Maine bill.]
[Sidenote: Compromise line.]

During 1819 the question was discussed throughout the Union. Several legislatures, by unanimous votes, protested against admitting a new Slave State, and when the new Congress assembled in 1819 it became the principal issue of the session. Alabama was at once admitted, restoring the balance of Slave and Free States. The people of Maine were now about to separate from Massachusetts, and also petitioned for entrance into the Union. A bill for this purpose passed the House on December 30, and a month later a bill for the admission of Missouri, with the Talmadge amendment, was also introduced into the House. The Senate, on Feb. 16, 1820, voted to admit Maine, provided Missouri was at the same time admitted as a Slave State. The House still refused to comply. Thomas of Illinois now proposed as a compromise the principle suggested by McLane a year earlier,—that an east and west line be drawn across the Louisiana cession, north of which slavery should be prohibited. Fourteen Northern members united with the seventy-six Southern members to form a bare majority against prohibiting slavery in Missouri; the principle was thus abandoned, and the only question was where the line should be drawn: the parallel of 36° 30' was selected, but it was expressly provided that Missouri should be slaveholding. On March 3 the compromise became a law.

[Sidenote: Missouri constitution.]

A year later a third difficulty arose. The people of Missouri had formed a constitution which provided that free colored men should not be allowed to enter the State under any pretext. Nearly the whole Northern vote in the House was cast against admitting the State with this provision. Clay brought about a compromise by which the Missourians were to agree not to deprive of his rights any citizen of another State. Upon this understanding Missouri was finally admitted.

[Sidenote: Friends of disunion.]
[Sidenote: Advantage to the South.]
[Sidenote: Advantage to the North.]

In form the compromises were a settlement of difficulties between the two Houses; in fact they were an agreement between the two sections, by which the future of slavery in every part of the Louisiana purchase was to be settled once for all. Threats were freely made that if slavery were prohibited in Missouri, the South would withdraw. Calhoun told Adams that if the trouble produced a dissolution of the Union, "the South would be from necessity compelled to form an alliance, offensive and defensive, with Great Britain." Adams retorted by asking whether, in such a case, if "the population of the North should be cut off from its natural outlet upon the ocean, it would fall back upon its rocks bound hand and foot to starve, or whether it would not retain its powers of locomotion to move southward by land?" The compromise was, as Benton says, "conceived and passed as a Southern measure," although Randolph called it a "dirty bargain;" nevertheless, on the final test vote thirty-five Southern members refused to admit the principle that Congress could prohibit slavery in the Territories. The South gained Missouri, and a few years later Arkansas came in as a slave State; but in the long run the advantage was to the North. The South got the small end of the triangle; the North the whole region now occupied by the States of Kansas, Nebraska, Iowa, the Dakotas, and Montana, and parts of Colorado, Wyoming, and Minnesota; and the final struggle over slavery was postponed for thirty years.

128. RELATIONS WITH THE LATIN-AMERICAN STATES (1815-1823).

[Sidenote: The Spanish colonies.]
[Sidenote: Revolutions.]

While the attention of the country was absorbed by the Missouri struggle, a new question of diplomacy had arisen. In 1789 almost every part of the two American continents south of the United States, except Brazil, was subject to Spain. The American Revolution had given a shock to the principle of colonial government by European powers; the Spanish colonies refused to acknowledge the authority of the French usurpers in Spain, and in 1808 a series of revolts occurred. At the restoration of the Spanish Bourbons in 1814, the colonies returned to nominal allegiance. The new king attempted to introduce the old regime: the colonies had too long enjoyed the sweets of direct trade with other countries, and they resented the ungentle attempts to restore them to complete dependence; between 1816 and 1820 the provinces on the Rio de la Plata, Chile, and Venezuela again revolted; and by 1822 there was a revolutionary government in every continental Spanish province, including Mexico.

[Sidenote: The Holy Alliance.]
[Sidenote: Intervention proposed.]

When Europe was reorganized, after the fall of Napoleon, almost all the powers entered into a kind of a treaty, known as the Holy Alliance, framed Sept. 26, 1815. They announced the future principle of international relations to be that of "doing each other reciprocal service, and of testifying by unalterable good will the mutual affection with which they ought to be animated," and that they considered themselves "all as members of one and the same Christian nation." Within this pious verbiage was concealed a plan of mutual assistance in case of the outbreak of revolutions. When Spain revolted against her sovereign in 1820, a European Congress was held, and by its direction the French in 1823 a second time restored the Spanish Bourbons. The grateful king insisted that the revolution of the Spanish colonies ought to be put down by a common effort of the European powers, as a danger to the principle of hereditary government.

[Sidenote: American interests.]
[Sidenote: Russian colonization.]
[Sidenote: English proposals.]

Here the interests of the United States became involved: they were trading freely with the Spanish Americans; they sympathized with the new governments, which were nominally founded on the model of the North American republic; they felt what now seems an unreasonable fear that European powers would invade the United States. At the same time the Russians, who had obtained a foothold on the northwest coast fifty years earlier, were attempting to establish a permanent colony, and on Sept. 24, 1821, issued a ukase forbidding all foreigners to trade on the Pacific coast north of the fifty-first parallel, or to approach within one hundred Italian miles of the shore. John Quincy Adams, who had a quick eye for national rights, protested vigorously. Now came most gratifying evidence that the United States was the leading power in America: in September, 1823, the British government proposed to our minister in England that the two countries should unite in a declaration against European intervention in the colonies. The invitation was declined, but the good will of Great Britain was assured.

129. THE MONROE DOCTRINE (1823).

[Sidenote: Monroe's message.]
[Sidenote: Colonization clause.]
[Sidenote: Intervention Clause.]

John Quincy Adams had succeeded in bringing the President to the point where he was willing, in behalf of the nation, to make a protest against both these forms of interference in American affairs. When Congress met, in December, 1823, Monroe sent in a message embodying what is popularly called the Monroe Doctrine. He had taken the advice of Jefferson, who declared that one of the maxims of American policy was "never to suffer Europe to meddle with cis-Atlantic affairs." Madison, with characteristic caution, suggested an agreement with Great Britain to unite in "armed disapprobation." In the cabinet meeting, Adams pointed out that intervention would result, not in restoring the colonies to Spain, but in dividing them among European nations, in which case Russia might take California. His views prevailed, and the message contained, in the first place, a clause directed against Russia: "The American continents, by the free and independent condition which they have assumed and maintained, are henceforth not to be considered as subjects for future colonization by any European powers." Against intervention there was even a stronger protest: "With the governments who have declared their independence and maintained it,... we could not view any interposition for the purpose of oppressing them, or controlling in any other manner their destiny, by any European power, in any other light than as a manifestation of an unfriendly disposition toward the United States."

[Sidenote: Effect.]

In every way this dignified protest was effectual: the news caused an immediate rise in the funds of the revolted States in European markets; projects of European intervention were at once abandoned; and Great Britain followed the United States in recognizing the independence of the new countries. In 1824 Russia made a treaty agreeing to claim no territory south of 54° 40', and not to disturb or restrain citizens of the United States in any part of the Pacific Ocean.

When Monroe retired from the Presidency on March 4, 1825, the internal authority of the national government had for ten years steadily increased, and the dignity and influence of the nation abroad showed that it had become one of the world's great powers.

CHAPTER XII.

130. REFERENCES.

BIBLIOGRAPHIES.—W. E. Foster, *References to Presidential Administrations*, 20-22; Justin Winsor, *Narrative and Critical History*, VII. 346-348; Channing and Hart, *Guide*, §§ 179-180.

HISTORICAL MAPS.—No. 5, this volume (*Epoch Maps*, No 10); *Scribner's Statistical Atlas*, Plates 14, 15; school histories of Channing and Johnston.

GENERAL ACCOUNTS.—H. Von Hoist, *Constitutional History*, I. 409-458; James Schouler, *United States*, III. 336-450; Geo. Tucker, *United States*, III. 409-515.

SPECIAL HISTORIES.—Josiah Quincy, *Life of John Quincy Adams*, chap. vii.; J. T. Morse, *John Quincy Adams*, 164-225; W. H. Seward, *Life of John Quincy Adams*, 137-201; C. Schurz, *Henry Clay*, I. 203-310; W. G. Sumner, *Andrew Jackson*, 73-135; E. M. Shepard, *Martin Van Buren*, 84- 150; H. C. Lodge, *Daniel Webster*, 129-171; J. L. Bishop, *History of American Manufactures*, II. 298-332.

CONTEMPORARY ACCOUNTS.—J. Q. Adams, *Memoirs*, VII., VIII. (chapter xiv.); H. Niles, *Weekly Register*; T. H. Benton, *Thirty Years's View*, I. 44-118; Josiah Quincy, *Figures of the Past*; N. Sargent, *Public Men and Events*, I. 56-160; Ben Perley Poore, *Perley's Reminiscences*, 1-87; John Trumbull, *Autobiography*; J. French, *Travels*, Mrs. Trollope, *Domestic Manners of the Americans*.—Reprints in *American History told by Contemporaries*, III.

131. POLITICAL METHODS IN 1824.

[Sidenote: Old statesmen gone.]

The United States was in 1825 half a century old, and the primitive political methods of the early republic were disappearing. Most of the group of Revolutionary statesmen were dead; Jefferson and John Adams still survived, and honored each other by renewing their ancient friendship; on July 4, 1826, they too passed away. The stately traditions of the colonial period were gone: since the accession of Jefferson, the Presidents no longer rode in pomp to address Congress at the beginning of each session; and inferior and little-known men crept into Congress.

[Sidenote: New constitutions.]

The constitutions framed during or immediately after the Revolution had been found too narrow, and one after another, most of the States in the Union had adopted a second, or even a third. Each change was marked by a popularization of the government, especially with regard to the suffrage. Immigrants had begun to have a sensible effect upon the community. In 1825 there were ten thousand, and the number more than doubled in five years. These changes were reflected in the management of State politics; the greater the number of voters, the greater the power of organization. Hence there had sprung up in the States a system of political chiefs, of whom Aaron Burr is a type.

[Sidenote: Political proscription.]
[Sidenote: Four Years' Tenure Act.]

Three new political devices had now become general among the States. The first was the removal of administrative officers because they did not agree in politics with the party which had elected a governor. This system was in use in Pennsylvania as early as 1790; it was introduced into New York by 1800, and gradually spread into other States. At first it was rather a factional weapon: when the adherents of the Livingstons got into power, they removed the friends of the Clintons; when the Clintonians came in, they turned out the Livingstons. Later, it was a recognized party system. In 1820 Secretary Crawford secured the passage by Congress of an apparently innocent act, by which most of the officers of the national government who collected and disbursed public money were to have terms of four years. The ostensible object was to secure more regular statements of accounts; it was intended and used to drop from the public service subordinates of the Treasury department who were not favorable to Crawford's Presidential aspirations.

[Sidenote: The Gerrymander.]

The second device appears to have been the invention of Elbridge Gerry, when governor of Massachusetts in 1812, and from him it takes the name of Germander, The Federalists were gaining in the State; the Republican legislature, before it went out, therefore redistricted the State in such fashion that the Republicans with a minority of votes were able to choose twenty-nine senators, against eleven Federalists. No wonder that the "New England Palladium" declared this to be "contrary to republicanism and to justice."

[Sidenote: Political organization.]

A third and very effective political device was the caucus. The term was applied particularly to a conference of the members of each party in Congress, which had taken upon itself the nomination of the Presidents. The influence of the extending suffrage, and of political tricks and devices, had as yet little effect in national politics. It was evident, however, that the principles of political manipulation could be applied in national elections. The Republican party of New York was in 1825 managed by a knot of politicians called the Albany Regency. Of these, the ablest was Martin Van Buren, and four years later he succeeded in building up a national political machine.

132. THE TARIFF OF 1824 (1816-1824).

[Sidenote: Effect of the tariff.]

An evidence of political uneasiness was the Tariff Act of May 22, 1824. The tariff of 1816 had not brought about the good that was expected of it: importations of foreign goods were indeed cut down from $129,000,000 in 1816 to $50,000,000 in 1823; but the balance of trade was still rather against the United States, and in 1819 there was a financial crisis. In 1820 an act to raise the duties passed the House, but was lost in the Senate by a single vote. Manufactures had been growing, although profits were not large, and public sentiment was beginning to change in New England. The Western vote was now larger than eight years earlier, and was in favor of protection. Exports of agricultural products had fallen off, and the agricultural States hoped to find a better market among the manufacturers.

[Sidenote: Act of 1824.]

It was a favorable time for a tariff act, inasmuch as the friends of none of the Presidential candidates were willing to commit themselves against it. Clay came forward as the champion of the protective system: "The object of this bill," said he, "is to create thus a home market, and to lay the foundation of a genuine American policy." The South now strongly and almost unanimously opposed the tariff; even Webster spoke against it, declaring "freedom of trade to be the general principle, and restriction the exception." A combination of the Middle and Western States with a part of New England furnished the necessary majority. The tariff increased the duties on metals like iron and lead, and on agricultural products like wool and hemp, but gave little additional protection to woollen and cotton goods. As the bill approached its passage, John Randolph violently protested: "There never was a constitution under the sun in which by an unwise exercise of the powers of the government the people may not be driven to the extremity of resistance by force."

133. THE ELECTION OF 1824.

[Sidenote: Era of good feeling.]
[Sidenote: Presidential candidates.]

The ground was now cleared for the choice of a successor to Monroe. The Federalist organization had entirely disappeared, even in the New England States; all the candidates called themselves Republicans or Democrats,— the terms were considered synonymous,—and there was little difference in their political principles. The second administration of Monroe has been called the "Era of Good Feeling," because there was but one party; in fact it was an era of ill feeling, because that party was broken up into personal factions. Three of the cabinet ministers and the Speaker of the House of Representatives were candidates for the succession to Monroe. Calhoun, Secretary of War, who still believed that it was to the interest of the nation and of the South to have a strong national government, came forward early, but quietly accepted an undisputed nomination for the Vice- Presidency. John Quincy Adams, Secretary of State, was nominated by New England legislatures early in the year 1824. William H. Crawford of Georgia, Secretary of the Treasury, succeeded in obtaining the formal nomination of the party caucus on Feb. 14, 1824; less than a third of the Republican members were present, and the character of the nomination rather injured than aided Crawford. Henry Clay was nominated by the legislatures of Kentucky and four other States; he was very popular in Congress and throughout the West. All three of the candidates just mentioned were in ability and experience well qualified to be President.

[Sidenote: Andrew Jackson.]

A fourth candidate, at that time a Senator from Tennessee, was Gen. Andrew Jackson. He was a rough frontiersman, skilled in Indian wars, but so insubordinate in temper that in 1818 he had invaded Florida without instructions; and Calhoun as Secretary of War had suggested in the cabinet that he be court-martialed. Jackson himself at first held back, but in 1822 he received the nomination of the Tennessee legislature, and in 1824 that of the legislature of Pennsylvania. Benton has called him "the candidate of the people, brought forward by the masses;" he was really brought forward by one of his neighbors, Major Lewis, who was convinced that he had the elements of popularity, and who managed his campaign with great skill. But no combination could be made for him with the Albany Regency; Van Buren's organ, the "Argus," said of him: "He is respected as a gallant soldier, but he stands, in the minds of the people of this State, at an immeasurable distance from the Executive Chair."

[Sidenote: Electoral vote.]

The election showed that Jackson had ninety-nine electoral votes, Adams eighty-four, Crawford forty-one, and Henry Clay thirty-seven, The popular vote, so far as it could be ascertained, was 150,000 for Jackson, and about 110,000 for Adams. There was no clear indication of the people's will, and under the Constitution the House of Representatives was to choose the President from the three candidates who had received most electoral votes. Several Clay electors had changed their votes to Crawford; the result was that Crawford, and not Clay, was third on the list, and that Clay was made ineligible.

134. THE ELECTION OF 1825.

[Sidenote: Clay favors Adams.]

Crawford's influence had now much declined, so that Clay and his friends held the balance of power between Jackson and Adams. On Jan. 8, 1825, Clay advised his friends to vote for Adams, who was in every way the more suitable candidate; he represented principles acceptable to the large majority of voters; he favored a tariff; he was an enthusiastic advocate of internal improvements; he desired to make the influence of the United States felt in South and Central America.

[Sidenote: Election in the House.]

The vote in the House showed thirteen States for Adams, seven for Jackson, and four for Crawford. Jackson accepted the result calmly,—indeed Adams had always shown a friendly spirit toward him, and had defended him in 1818. Within a few days a rumor went abroad that Clay had sold his support of Adams for the appointment as Secretary of State.

[Sidenote: "Corrupt bargain."]

He denied it, Adams denied it, and there has never been any proof to show that there had been an understanding between them or their friends. Jackson's supporters, however, were quick to see the damaging effect of such a charge, and began to publish abroad the assertion that there had been a corrupt bargain, or, as John Randolph put it, "a coalition of Blifil and Black George, —a combination, unheard of until now, of the Puritan and the blackleg." Once persuaded that the charge was true, it was impossible to disabuse Jackson's mind, and during the next four years his friends continued to assert that he had been deprived of the Presidency by a trick.

[Sidenote: "Demos Krateo".]

Another equally baseless and equally injurious charge was that the House had violated the spirit of the Constitution by selecting a candidate who had a less number of electoral votes than Jackson. "The election of Mr. Adams," said Benton, "was also a violation of the principle, Demos Krateo." In consequence, many members of Congress who had voted for Adams lost their seats.

135. THE PANAMA CONGRESS (1825-1826).

[Sidenote: Adam's cabinet.]

The new President was handicapped from the beginning of his administration by his inability to make up a strong cabinet. Clay was eager and venturesome; the other members, except Wirt, were not men of great force. Adams manfully withstood the pressure put upon him to remove the adherents of Crawford and of Jackson in the public service; a high-minded and magnanimous man, he was determined that his administration should not depend upon the political services of office-holders.

[Sidenote: Proposed Spanish-American Congress.]

In December, 1824, Gen. Simon Bolivar had issued invitations to the Spanish American governments to send delegates to a Congress at Panama, and the invitation was later extended to the United States. One of the questions to be discussed was "resistance or opposition to the interference of any neutral nation" (§ 129). Another was "the manner in which the colonization of European Powers on the American continent shall be resisted." The evident purpose of the proposed meeting was to secure some kind of joint agreement that the Monroe Doctrine should be enforced. In such a meeting the United States might naturally expect to have a preponderating influence; and Clay accepted the invitation a few days before the first Congress under Adams's administration assembled.

[Sidenote: Objections to the Congress.]

The proposition was taking, and it was undoubtedly in line with the policy of the preceding administration. Nevertheless it was resolved by the opponents of Adams to make a stand against it, and it was not until March 14, 1826, that the nominations of the envoys were confirmed by the Senate. The first objection to the scheme was that it would commit the United States to a military defence of its neighbors. To this, Adams replied that he intended only an "agreement between all the parties represented at the meeting, that each will guard by its own means against the establishment of any future European colony within its borders." Among the powers invited to send delegates was Hayti, a republic of revolted slaves as yet unrecognized by the United States government. To Southern statesmen, association with Hayti meant an encouragement to slave-insurrection in the United States.

[Sidenote: Connection with Monroe Doctrine.]

The controversy was now transferred to the House, where an informal resolution was passed that the United States "ought not to become parties ... to any joint declaration for the purpose of preventing the interference of any of the European powers." The necessary appropriations were with difficulty secured, and the envoys despatched Before they reached Panama the Congress had adjourned, and it never reassembled. The instability of the Spanish-American governments was such that any joint agreement must have obliged the United States to assume great responsibilities, without any corresponding advantage.

136. INTERNAL IMPROVEMENTS (1817-1829).

[Sidenote: Monroe's veto.]

The failure of the bonus bill in 1817 (Section 121) had only checked the progress of internal improvements. The Cumberland road had been slowly extended westward, and up to 1821 $1,800,000 had been appropriated for it;

but on May 4, 1822, Monroe vetoed a bill for its preservation and repair. The technical objection was that tolls were to be charged; in fact, the veto was, like Madison's, a warning to Congress not to go too far.

[Sidenote: First harbor bill.]
[Sidenote: Preliminary surveys.]
[Sidenote: Stock subscriptions.]

Nevertheless, on March 3, 1823, a clause in a lighthouse bill appropriated $6,150 for the improvement of harbors. Up to this time the States had made such improvements, reimbursing themselves in part out of dues laid by consent of Congress on the shipping using the harbor. The next year another step in advance was taken by appropriating $30,000 for preliminary surveys: the expectation was that the whole ground would be gone over, and that the most promising improvements would be undertaken and finished first. A third step was the act of March 3, 1825, by which the United States subscribed $300,000 to the stock of the Chesapeake and Delaware Canal.

[Sidenote: Opposition.]

At the beginning of Adams's administration, therefore, the country seemed fully committed to the doctrine that, under the Constitution as it stood, Congress might build works, or subscribe money to aid in their construction, and ought to look forward to completing a general system. Clay had declared, Jan. 17, 1825, that he considered the question of carrying into effect "a system of internal improvements as amounting to the question whether the union of these States should be preserved or not;" and in his inaugural address, March 4, 1825, Adams urged the continuance of the system. Here again appeared opposition, partly sectional, and partly intended to embarrass Adams. The Virginia legislature declared internal improvements unconstitutional; and on Dec. 20, 1826, Van Buren introduced a resolution denying the right of Congress to construct roads and canals within the States.

[Sidenote: Land grants.]
[Sidenote: Distribution.]

An effort was now made to avoid the question of appropriating money by setting apart public lands. Grants of eight hundred thousand acres of land were made for the construction of canals in Indiana, Ohio, and Illinois, and such gifts continued at irregular intervals down to 1850. Since the debt was rapidly disappearing, another suggestion was that the surplus revenue should be periodically divided among the States. It satisfied no one. As Hayne of South Carolina said: "We are to have doled out to us as a favor the money which has first been drawn from our own pockets,… keeping the States forever in a state of subserviency."

Although $2,310,000 were appropriated for internal improvements during Adams's administration, on the whole the system was growing unpopular. Calhoun, who as Secretary of War in 1819 had recommended a judicious system of roads and canals, in 1822 said that on mature consideration he did not see that the requisite power was given to Congress in the Constitution. On the whole, Adams's enemies opposed the appropriations.

137. THE CREEK AND CHEROKEE QUESTIONS (1824-1829).

[Sidenote: Tribal governments.]
[Sidenote: Difficulty with Georgia.]

Another difficulty inherited by Adams's administration arose out of the promise of the United States in 1802 to remove the Indians from within the limits of Georgia as soon as possible. The two principal tribes were the Creeks and the Cherokees, both partially civilized and settled on permanent farms, and both enjoying by treaty with the United States a tribal government owing no allegiance to Georgia. On Feb. 12, 1825, a treaty had been signed by a few Creek chiefs without the authority or consent of the nation, by which they purported to give up lands of the tribe in Georgia. In defiance of the government at Washington, the Georgia authorities proceeded to survey the lands, without waiting to have the treaty examined; and Governor Troup called upon the legislature to "stand to your arms," and wrote to the Secretary of War that "President Adams makes the Union tremble on a bauble." In a sober report to the legislature it was urged that the time was rapidly approaching when the Slave States must "confederate."

[Sidenote: Conflict of authority.]

The survey was suspended; but on Nov. 8, 1825, Governor Troup advised the legislature that "between States equally independent it is not required of the weaker to yield to the stronger. Between sovereigns the weaker is equally qualified to pass upon its rights." On Jan. 24, 1826, a new treaty was negotiated, by which a considerable part of the disputed territory was given to Georgia. Again the State attempted to survey the lands before the transfer was completed, and again Adams interposed. On Feb. 17, 1827, Governor Troup called out the State militia to resist the United States troops. Congress was rather pleased at the humiliation to the President, and declined to support him; he was obliged to yield.

[Sidenote: The Cherokees subdued.]

The Cherokees, more highly civilized and better organized than the Creeks, could not be entrapped into any treaty for surrendering their lands. Georgia, therefore, proceeded to assert her jurisdiction over them, without reference to the solemn treaties of the United States. Each successive legislature from 1826 passed an Act narrowing the circle of Indian authority. In December, 1826, Indian testimony was declared invalid in Georgia courts. The Cherokees, foreseeing the coming storm, and warned by the troubles of their Creek neighbors, proceeded to adopt a new tribal constitution, under which all land was to be tribal property. The Georgia legislature replied, in 1827, by annexing part of the Cherokee territory to two counties; the purpose was to drive out the Cherokees by making them subject to discriminating State laws, and by taking away the land not actually occupied as farms. The issue raised was whether the United States or Georgia had governmental powers in Indian reservations. By a close vote the House intimated its sympathy with Georgia, and in December, 1828, Georgia proposed to annex the whole Cherokee country. Adams was powerless to defend the Indians; in order to humiliate the President, the national authority had successfully been defied.

138. THE TARIFF OF ABOMINATIONS (1828).

[Sidenote: Commercial treaties.]
[Sidenote: Woollen bill.]

In one respect Adams was successful; he negotiated almost as many commercial treaties as had been secured during the previous fifty years. Trade had sprung up with the Spanish American States. England had meanwhile begun to relax her system of protection, and encouraged manufactures by importing raw materials on very low duties; woollens were therefore so cheapened that they could again be sold in the United States in competition with American manufacturers. In October, 1826, the Boston woollen manufacturers asked "the aid of the government." A bill was accordingly introduced, which Adams would doubtless have signed, increasing the duties on coarse woollens. It passed the House in 1827, but was lost in the Senate by the casting vote of the Vice-President, Calhoun. His change of attitude is significant; it showed that the most advanced Southern statesman had abandoned the policy of protection, as he had abandoned the policy of internal improvements. The Boston petition marked another change. New England had at last settled down to manufacturing as her chief industry, and insisted on greater protection.

[Sidenote: Tariff agitation.]

The narrow failure of the Woollens Bill in 1827 encouraged a protectionist convention at Harrisburg, which suggested very high duties; but the main force behind the movement was a combination of the growers and manufacturers of wool, including many Western men. It is probable that Clay was glad to make the tariff a political issue, hoping thus to confound the anti-Adams combination.

[Sidenote: Tariff on raw materials.]
[Sidenote: The act passed.]

A new bill was reported, introducing the novel principle that the raw materials of manufactures should be highly protected; the purpose was evidently to frame a tariff unacceptable to New England, where Adams had his chief support, and to draw the votes of the South and West. The Western Jackson men favored it because it raised the tariff; and the Southern anti-tariff men expected to kill Adams with the bill, and then to kill the bill. They therefore voted for enormous duties: the duty on hemp was raised from $35 to $60 a ton; on wool from about thirty per cent to about seventy per cent. In vain did the Adams men attempt to reframe the bill: when it came to a vote, sixteen of the thirty-nine New England members felt compelled to accept it, with all its enormities, and it thus passed the House. Even Webster voted for it in the Senate, and his influence secured its passage. On May 24, 1828, Adams signed it. Throughout the debate the influence of the approaching campaign was seen. John Randolph said of it: "The bill referred to manufactures of no sort or kind except the manufacture of a President of the United States."

[Sidenote: Southern protests.]

Notwithstanding these political complications the South saw clearly that the act meant a continuance of the protective system. Five States at once protested in set terms against the law and against the passage by Congress of protective acts. Calhoun came forward as the champion of this movement, and he put forth an argument, known as the South Carolina Exposition, in which he suggested a convention of the State of South Carolina. "The convention will then decide in what manner they [the revenue acts] ought to be declared null and void within the limits of the State, which solemn declaration would be obligatory on our own citizens." The period of the Virginia and Kentucky Resolutions seemed to have returned.

139. ORGANIZED OPPOSITION TO ADAMS (1825-1829).

It has been seen that on most of the great questions which arose in Adams's administration there was a division, not so much on principle, as between the friends and opponents of the President. The four years of his administration were really a long drawn Presidential campaign. The friends of Jackson sought in every possible way to make Adams odious in the public mind.

[Sidenote: Executive patronage.]
[Sidenote: Retrenchment.]

One of the early evidences of this personal opposition was a report brought in, May 4, 1826, by a Select Committee on Executive Patronage; it included Benton and Van Buren, who had heartily given in his adhesion to Jackson. They reported that the exercise of great patronage by one man was dangerous, and they proposed that a constitutional amendment be secured, forbidding the appointment of senators or representatives to office. In the next Congress, from 1827 to 1829, the Jackson men had a majority in both Houses, and an attempt was made to prejudice Adams by showing that the government was extravagant. Resolutions were adopted calling for a retrenchment; but no misuse of the public money could be brought home to the President.

The so-called investigations were only political manoeuvres: a President who permitted his political enemies to remain in office was upbraided for abusing the appointing power, a President who had never removed one person for political reason was accused of a misuse of the removing power. Nevertheless, the steady waning of Adams's popularity shows that he was not in accord with the spirit of the people of his time.

[Sidenote: Jackson's campaign.]
[Sidenote: The Democrats.]

Meanwhile, a formidable combination had been formed against him. In October, 1825, Jackson had been re-nominated by the Tennessee legislature. Crawford's health had failed, and his followers, chiefly Southern men, threw in their lot with Jackson. Van Buren prepared to renew the combination of Southern and Middle State votes which had been so successful in 1800. His organizing skill was necessary, for the Jackson men lacked both coherence and principles. Strong bank men, anti-bank men, protectionists, and free-traders united in the support of Jackson, whose views on all these points were unknown. Towards the end of Adams's administration the opposition began to take upon itself the name of the Democratic party; but what the principles of that party were to be was as yet uncertain.

140. THE TRIUMPH OF THE PEOPLE (1828).

[Sidenote: Adams's policy.]
[Sidenote: New political forces.]

John Quincy Adams's principles of government were not unlike those of his father: both believed in a brisk, energetic national administration, and in extending the influence and upholding the prestige of the United States among foreign powers. John Adams built ships; John Quincy Adams built roads and canals. Both Presidents were trained statesmen of the same school as their English and French contemporaries. The outer framework of government had little altered since its establishment in 1789; within the nation, however, a great change had taken place. The disappearance of the Federalists had been followed by a loss of the political and social pre-eminence so long enjoyed by the New England clergy; and in 1835 the Congregational Church was disestablished in Massachusetts. The rise of manufactures had hastened these changes, both by creating a new moneyed class, and by favoring the increase of independent mill-hands having the suffrage and little or no property. Cities were growing rapidly, especially in the Middle States: in 1822 Boston gave up the town-meeting; in 1830 New York had two hundred thousand inhabitants, and Philadelphia one hundred and seventy thousand; and the voters in the cities were more easily controlled by a few master minds. In the South alone was the old principle of government by family and influence preserved; but even here the suffrage was widely extended, and the small planters had to be tenderly handled.

[Sidenote: Power of the West.]

The West was the most important new element in the government. The votes of the States west of the mountains elected Jefferson in 1800, and Madison in 1812, and gave Jackson his preponderance of electoral votes over Adams in 1824. The West was at this time what the colonies had been half a century earlier,—a thriving, bustling, eager community, with a keen sense of trade, and little education. But, unlike the colonies, the West was almost without the tradition of an aristocracy; in most of the States there was practically manhood suffrage. Men were popular, not because they had rendered the country great services, but because they were good farmers, bold pioneers, or shrewd lawyers. Smooth intriguers, mere demagogues, were not likely to gain the confidence of the West, but a positive and forcible character won their admiration. It was a people stirred by men like Henry Clay, great public speakers, leaders in public assemblies, impassioned advocates of the oppressed in other lands. It was a people equally affected by the rough and ruthless character of men like Jackson. An account which purports to come from Davy Crockett illustrates the political horse-play of the time. In 1830 he was an anti-Jackson candidate for re-election to Congress. He was beaten, by his opponents making unauthorized appointments for him to speak, without giving him notice. The people assembled, Crockett was not there to defend himself, his enemies said that he was afraid to come, and no later explanations could satisfy his constituents.

[Sidenote: General ticket system.]

The political situation was still further complicated by the adoption in nearly all the States of the general ticket system of choosing electors; a small majority in New York and Pennsylvania might outweigh large majorities in other States. In a word, democracy was in the saddle; the majority of voters preferred a President like themselves to a President of superior training and education. Sooner or later they must combine; and once combined they would elect him.

[Sidenote: Democracy vs. tradition.]

There was practically but one issue in 1828,—a personal choice between John Quincy Adams and Jackson. Not one of the voters knew Jackson's opinions on the tariff or internal improvements,—the only questions on which a political issue could have been made. It was a strife between democracy and tradition. A change of twenty-six thousand votes would have given to John Quincy Adams the vote of Pennsylvania and the election; but it could only have delayed the triumph of the masses. Jackson swept every Southern and Western State, and received six hundred and fifty thousand popular votes, against five hundred thousand for Adams. It was evident that there had risen up "a new king over Egypt, which knew not Joseph."